SUN SIGN
SECRETS

Celestial
guidance with
the sun, moon
and stars

PATSY BENNETT

ROCKPOOL

A Rockpool book
PO Box 252
Summer Hill
NSW 2130
Australia

rockpoolpublishing.co
Follow us! f 🔘 rockpoolpublishing
Tag your images with #rockpoolpublishing

ISBN: 9781925946352

Published in 2021 by Rockpool Publishing

Design and typesetting by Sara Lindberg, Rockpool Publishing
Edited by Lisa Macken
Images from Shutterstock

A catalogue record for this
book is available from the
National Library of Australia

Printed and bound in China
10 9 8 7 6 5 4 3 2 1

CONTENTS

INTRODUCTION

Would you like to know in advance the best time to launch a new business or begin a fresh study course? The best time to move and, if you're single, to look for a partner? The best time to plan a holiday? If you're ready to start a family, the most likely times you'll conceive? If you tend to find that change just seems to happen to you out of the blue, you will discover in these pages that there is a force at work and that having advance knowledge of when significant changes will occur will allow you to work more proactively to create the life you want.

Astrology is an ancient practice that incorporates science, spirituality and interpretation, a practice that explains both the physical attributes of planets and their spiritual vibration on earth. Astrology embraces the essence of what and who you are, as you are made of the stuff of stars, planets and dark matter. You are an integral part of the universe you inhabit: you cannot be separate from it; you cannot be simply an observer of the outside world. The world is both outside you and a part of you.

Celestial events such as eclipses that may appear to be unrelated to you are in fact integral to your own being. For example, when you know that the moon governs the tides and that you as a human being are composed of up to 70 per cent water, you know that therefore the moon affects your body, moods, emotions, instincts and imagination. This book will teach you how to work with the planets that constantly revolve around the star in the centre of our solar system: the sun. The vibration of the sun, moon and stars is not only above but also below, and whatsoever occurs above is mirrored on earth.

It is important to be content and feel fulfilled in life, both of which can be achieved by working dynamically with your own unique gifts and talents in a proactive way. In this book you'll find out how to express your own inner power, how to generate a life filled with energy and purpose. Work with the movement of the sun and the moon, with full moons, eclipses and new moons and you'll find that new doors will open for you . . .

When you plan by the sun, moon and stars your life becomes an adventure. This book provides celestial guidance at your fingertips about key turning points in your life and the best way to plan ahead; use it as a guide to discovering the optimum times to make changes in your life.

New moons, full moons and eclipses tend to give you a gentle celestial nudge to embrace change, and you can find out here when these are likely: the tables at the end of the book will tell

1

you when eclipses and new and full moons will be and in which sign up to 2050. By using the table you can work with celestial energies rather than feeling life is haphazard and you are a leaf being blown about in the winds of change. Not only will you find ways to plan ahead, but you will also understand the phases and cycles of your life more deeply.

As an eternal soul you have limitless potential. You just need to tap into this potential through your deeper self and higher mind to release your best self and live to your optimum potential, to discover your higher calling and live this in your everyday life.

The ancient art of astrology holds the secrets to this transformational process. The more you learn about yourself and the universe you inhabit the more you are able to respond to your inner calling, to your soul. This process, which is often called spiritual enlightenment, has for thousands of years been privy only to seers, scribes, court counsel and mystic circles but now, in *Sun Sign Secrets*, you too can access the wisdom of the ages so you can live to your highest potential.

The sun, moon and stars are your guiding lights, and just as the sun is the centre of the solar system and generates energy and light, so also does your sun sign denote your true power and potential. Expressing your own inner calling through the knowledge you gain about your inner self will give you the opportunity to find the *right timing* to engage with the universe.

So how will this work in practice? First, follow the dictum 'Know thyself', which was inscribed on the Delphic Oracle at Mount Parnassus in central Greece: be aware of who you are and what your inner calling is. The first part of the chapter about your own particular sun sign will give you deeper insight into the spiritual calling of your sign. Next you will find out how your spiritual calling responds to the ever-changing rotation of the skies, of the sun, moon and planets.

Finally but most importantly, each person reacts and benefits in a different way to a celestial event such as a full moon depending on their own sun sign. You are an individual and your sun sign informs you how your own inner generator or engine in life can work with the phases of the moon, the planets and the sun to derive benefits in particular ways that are individual to you and your sun sign.

Information from the complex and multilayered field of astrology has never before been outlined in a format that everyone can understand; attempting to show each individual their own inner soul calling has been too colossal a task for one book . . . until now! The more you use *Sun Sign Secrets* to guide you through the ever-changing starry firmament you live in the more you will understand just how integral a part you are of cosmic developments.

HOW TO USE THIS BOOK

You already know your sun sign or, if you prefer, your zodiac sign, but do you know your spiritual calling? You will no doubt be familiar with the way your sun sign describes your attributes: your characteristics, behavioural patterns, compatibility with other sun signs, favourite colours, likely negative aspects and likely potential. However, your spiritual calling is often overlooked yet it is essential for an understanding of your purpose and potential: what your soul has brought you here to learn in this lifetime. And this is something you can gain from knowledge of your sun sign – if you know how!

The first part of the chapter for each individual sun sign outlines how your personal approach to life adds to your spiritual development. You'll discover how your values dictate your likely actions and the way you'll communicate to gain experience, and find information about your home and work lives, and your creativity. You'll read all about the way you relate to others and the big wide world: your partnerships, collaborations, studies, career, the types of groups and organisations you'll be attracted to and what your secret soul wishes are. Finally, you'll find out about your strengths and how to feel empowered and work out how to maximise your potential and avoid pitfalls.

The chapters contain a deep explanation of the benefits, talents, gifts and positive aspects of each sun sign, listed in separate chapters from Aries to Pisces. The section listed under each sun sign labelled 'Pitfalls' points out major potential stumbling blocks in your progress through life, enabling you to learn quickly and avoid obstacles. The 12 chapters have in-depth descriptions about how to feel fulfilled, listing the key areas of potential so you can exceed even your own expectations in life.

SOLAR AND LUNAR PHASES

Solar and lunar phases, especially new moons, full moons and eclipses, provide key direction in your progress through life. You may have a favourite celestial almanac you refer to or love your astrology diary, so you'll already know for example of an upcoming full moon in Libra. You can also refer to the tables at the end of this book that provide each new moon and full moon and solar and lunar eclipses until 2050.

Once you see that a significant celestial event is on the way you'll know it's time to take action: you must be proactive and participate in life for it to have meaning and bring success and fulfilment. For example, a full moon in Libra revolves around the importance of having symmetry and harmony in life and will signify it's time to make balanced decisions and avoid impulsiveness. You must work with celestial energies to make these changes occur for the better; then, as a result, your own endeavours will bring peace and tranquillity to your life.

But that's only half of the picture: the sun sign you were born under has an impact on how you experience each celestial event, from new moons to eclipses, full moons to the sun's passage through the zodiac sign. If, for example, you're a Scorpio you will react differently to celestial events than if you were a Leo.

In this book you can look up your own sun sign to find out how each full or new moon or eclipse will apply in your life, and how each event will affect the different aspects of your life from finances to home life to relationships to work. You can work with the celestial events to make life run more smoothly for you.

Some new and full moons will affect your life in similar ways as they mark the start or end of significant phases. Take note of the sign they are in; for example, a new moon in Aries may mark a new phase in your personal life just as a new moon in Libra could signal a new phase in a relationship. Note that these both could have the same effect, but the net result on your behaviour will arise in different ways. The new moon in Aries will spur you on to be more proactive in your personal life, while the new moon in Libra will ask you to exhibit more co-operative traits in your relationship.

You'll find out how these celestial events work for you and how to navigate through each solar and lunar phase in the best possible way. If for example your sun sign is Leo and you wish to know how best to work with an upcoming new moon – for example, the new moon in Taurus – you can look up 'New moon in Taurus' in your chapter.

SOLAR TRANSITS

The sun passes through the 12 signs of the zodiac and spends a month in each sign. Each of these four-week periods will produce fresh dynamics for you to work with and will create a myriad of different experiences. As a result you will experience a different aspect of your own qualities and abilities each month. The 'Solar transits' section of each chapter outlines the experiences that will be likely in your life and therefore the action you may take to be the best you can be as the sun traverses through the signs of the zodiac throughout the year.

For example, if you are a Taurus, when the sun is in your sign (from the end of April through May every year) you'll find you feel particularly energised and motivated and thus your projects are likely to succeed. On the other hand, if you are a Libran during the same four-week period you may experience this time as a phase where you indulge in sensual delights such as incredible food and romance.

Check out the areas of your life the sun enhances as it travels through each zodiac sign, and how to make the most of your strong points during each of the 12 months in which the sun travels through Aries to Pisces.

LUNAR TRANSITS

The moon travels through each of the 12 zodiac signs each month, changing zodiac sign approximately every two days. As it traverses through the signs the moon indicates the kind of focus you may experience in your emotional life and therefore the feelings you are likely to express. How will these lunar phases affect you?

Which zodiac sign the moon is in will engender different feelings and sensations. For example, if you are a Taurus, when the moon is in your sign for two days every month you may feel particularly in sync with your emotions, friends, partner and family and find you are therefore able to express yourself better. Your relationships may flow or your emotions may be heightened. It's a good time to express your feelings to those you love and must collaborate with.

Check out the 'Lunar transits' section of your sun sign chapter to find out how to make the most of your strong points during each phase. You may find you are particularly productive when the moon is in your sign so this will always be a good time to plan key events that spotlight your emotions, such as significant celebrations and get-togethers.

FULL MOONS

A full moon tends to signify the end of a chapter and, as you know, the end of something signals the start of something new. A new moon also signals the start of something new so, given that both new and full moons effectively start something new, what is the real difference? A full moon signals the culmination of a series of events or of a project or simply a situation where circumstances peak or come to a head, and in so doing provides you with a chance to move on. Conversely, a new moon signals the start of something entirely new and does not entail so much focus on the ending of a cycle.

Full moons can be intense as emotions run high and your imagination and spirituality become stronger. You may realise that you have had enough of certain circumstances as you get more in touch with your own emotions: a job or project may end or a relationship may come to its natural conclusion, and so a new phase begins. As full moons tend to engage fervent emotions it's important to stay grounded and to reconnect with your gut feelings. Strong emotions can lead you astray, whereas your intuition will always guide you to make the right decisions in the long term.

Each full moon will be in a consecutive zodiac sign each month, although on the rare occasion – once in a blue moon – you may find two full moons in the same month albeit in different signs. Each full moon will assume the characteristics of each zodiac sign it travels through and, what's more, each zodiac sign will experience a full moon very differently. To find out how best to work with a full moon, read the section in your sun sign chapter titled 'Full moons'.

NEW MOONS

New moons occur when the moon aligns with the sun from our perspective here in earth, so new moons in your own sign will arise when the sun is in your sign. Aries new moons, for example, will occur between the end of March and mid-end of April each year.

With a new moon something entirely fresh such as a novel project can begin through your own efforts, as a new moon represents a new shoot of growth as opposed to a culmination of events as at a full moon (which might be viewed as the flower stage of a plant). While a full moon means it's time to celebrate your achievements, a new moon is a good time to launch a project or bright idea through different actions and areas of your life such as at work or in your personal life.

New moons are ideal for setting intentions but, as the saying goes, 'Be careful what you wish for as it will surely come true.' Read the section in your own sun sign chapter under the heading 'New moons' to find out which new moons are most effective for launching your various plans.

LUNAR AND SOLAR ECLIPSES

Eclipses and supermoons are like super-charged new and full moons and represent turning points. Supermoons may make you feel particularly emotional, especially full moon supermoons. Eclipses in particular signal the beginning and the end of a certain phase in your life. They are the astrological equivalent of a new chapter in a book and on occasion, such as when they fall on or near your birthday, they signify a completely new book as you have completed the old one!

The effects of an eclipse can be felt on the exact day of the eclipse, as you may receive key news that day that signals major change. For some people the effects of an eclipse may be felt for several months before or after the eclipse. Eclipses generally fall in series of two and sometimes three eclipses, called an 'eclipse season', and the between-the-eclipses phase can be super intense, especially if one eclipse falls in your sign.

Lunar eclipses tend to affect moods and emotions more so than solar eclipses, which are a call to action, although this can depend on your emotional make-up. Do you react emotionally to events or intellectually? The more emotional signs such as the water signs may be particularly sensitive to lunations such as full moons and eclipses. However, those who are generally level-headed may be particularly bowled over by the heightened emotions around these events and feel them more severely or be nonplussed by developments as they are not generally equipped to deal with heightened emotions such as those that can arise during full moons and lunar eclipses.

Eclipse seasons can be very intense, but luckily there are usually only two per year (and sometimes three if each eclipse season begins at the start and at the end of the year). This book's entries often refer to the entire phase, which lasts two weeks but can last six weeks if there are three consecutive eclipses.

A **lunar eclipse** occurs when the moon aligns exactly opposite the sun and the earth in between and the earth's shadow is cast over the moon. Sometimes they are seen as partial eclipses and sometimes total eclipses, depending on where you are on the earth at the time of the alignment.

During lunar eclipses your deepest emotions will emerge, which can be overwhelming unless you channel the energy into something productive such as a work project you love or into physically and emotionally expressive activities such as sports, dance and the arts. During the weeks running up to and after lunar eclipses there are many activities you can undertake that will enable you to be strong during these peak times of change. Activities including yoga, meditation and spiritual development will all help you to feel resilient and calm during these major turning points in your life.

Lunar eclipses are mega-charged full moons that signify major junctures in your life. They not only represent the culmination of a chapter in your life, such as the end of a job or study course, but they also represent a fresh cycle in which you embark on a new emotional experience and learning curve such as parenthood, a significant move or a change of status from being single to married, from poor to comfortable and from unemployed to employed, for example.

Aim to harness heightened lunar energy at eclipses and set reasonable goals that magnify and enhance your sense of purpose and fulfilment in life. Find the delicate balance between understanding the ebb and flow of your destiny and your own power to propel yourself through your experiences in the most fulfilling ways.

Think about the kinds of experiences that are likely to add to the kaleidoscope of emotional experience and enable you to embrace all the more fully your own abilities to enjoy life, love and feel fulfilled. Find out how to work with lunar eclipses under the heading 'Lunar eclipses' in your chapter and you'll gain insight into how to manage emotional developments with the benefit of advanced knowledge.

Solar eclipses focus your attention on which actions you must take during major changes in your life. They are super-charged new moons, as the sun and moon align exactly with our planet from our perspective here on earth. The moon passes across the face of the sun, which results in partial and total solar eclipses depending on where you are on earth.

Each solar eclipse will have varying effects on you and on different areas of your life. A solar eclipse in your own sun sign, for example, will spotlight the need to bring about new circumstances in your personal life. And, even when developments at the solar eclipse occur in other areas of your life such as work, financially or health-wise, you will need to take action in your personal life so that all else flows easily from there.

Solar eclipses urge you to take action, especially if you have been reluctant to make changes in your life even if you know they're necessary! If you have avoided taking action in the past, life has a way at eclipses of nudging you on to the next chapter in any way it chooses, so ensure you are proactive, take bold choices and direct your life the way you wish it to go around solar eclipses.

Eclipses are excellent times to re-evaluate and take stock of where you are in life and where you wish to be in five years' time, to reconnect with your deeper, spiritual goals, aims and life purpose. As such the intentions you set at eclipses are super charged, so making changes during these times can catapult you on to new experiences over the ensuing months and years.

Find out how to work with upcoming eclipses under the heading 'Solar eclipses' in your chapter and you'll gain insight into how to make major changes in your life flawlessly and productively around the weeks before and after a solar eclipse.

BE YOUR OWN ASTROLOGER!

Once you get the hang of working with solar and lunar movements to plan major events or simply to understand your own self and loved ones better you'll see that you can work with celestial timeframes. For example, when the sun is in Sagittarius it's a good phase for learning for Aries, and a new moon in Sagittarius is a good time to plan a fresh initiative that involves study or is in some way a learning curve.

Pro tips: when your birthday falls on a new moon, full moon or solar or lunar eclipse you'll be beginning a radical new chapter that will be impossible to miss, so aim to be super proactive and positive at these times as they represent super-super-charged turning points!

If you know your rising sign (also known as your ascendant) you can also look up this sign under the chapter heading for each sun sign Aries to Pisces, effectively giving you double the information. So if your sun sign is Aries and your rising sign is Gemini, you can look up both the Aries chapter and the Gemini chapter to gain a deeper understanding of the astrological dynamics.

THE SUN
SIGNS

18 MARCH - 20 APRIL

SYMBOL
Ram

ELEMENT
Fire

CONSTELLATION

ARIES
SUN SIGN

INNER CALLING

Your inner calling is to be number one! You're competitive, a bright spark and you take no prisoners. You'll wish to develop your abilities to such an extent that you're an exceptional, independent individual able to show you are brave beyond your own reason, that your courage shines deep into the crevasses of darkness and that, ultimately, you feel you have conquered the world in some form: acting as a pioneer, bringing your inner hero to the surface by being proactive, taking action and not subscribing to your fears or anxieties.

To do this you'll experience the desire at various phases of your life to stand apart from others, to distinguish yourself from them and to even feel you must be a rebel or are alienated from other people. This process can be disheartening and may even feel counter-intuitive, as your dearest wish is to be admired and loved. And this is where the paradox lies: to be a hero, to be truly fulfilled and to feel accomplished you need to be needed; you need to be admired and wanted and yet to do so you need to remove yourself from the norm and from what people may expect you to do.

One solution to this conundrum is to find the sense of being number one through independent accomplishments and efforts rather than through validation or admiration from others, and then to ensure that in the process you have been inclusive of those who love you and wish the best for you. They will respond well to you if you remember to exercise an inclusive approach rather than taking a removed stance.

Adding to the complexities of attaining a sense of purpose in life is the fact that being number one will change depending on your circumstances. In other words, what you wish to achieve at age 18 may well be very different from your goals at age 50, so the more you can put in place an inner guidebook for basic fulfilment the more likely you will be happy regardless of your actual attainments. For example, you will feel fulfilled from being contented that you achieved your own best potential as opposed to trying to live up to someone else's perception of who you should be.

SELF-ESTEEM

To gain self-esteem you must feel you are productive and effective in life, that your presence has some form of positive influence and meaning. This is why you tend to attempt activities that others are less confident about; you are seen as being bold and courageous. You may also have a tendency to rush into activities or events without a backwards glance, let alone forethought.

You can be viewed as brave beyond all measure when in fact it's your need to be looked up to and for excitement and adventure that leads to impulsiveness – and it's often not courage at all! Effectively, your self-esteem blossoms when you take risks because then you're able to see yourself as a productive individual who is able to surmount obstacles, but impulsive and reckless can land you in hot water. You instead need to be brave when necessary and careful at other times.

The key to feeling that you are answering your inner calling is to accomplish tasks that boost your self-esteem. These tasks must resonate with your inner calling and a sense of purpose, otherwise you will not feel fulfilled. In addition, you must feel that you have conquered new territory and have excelled in some way or your self-esteem will plummet, because deep down you willknow that what you have done has little meaning either to yourself or anyone else.

HOME LIFE

You find comfort from looking around your home environment and admiring the achievements you have created for yourself. You may be super driven to create a true nurture cocoon at various phases of your life, although as a youngster you are more likely to be so busy with your career and work that your home life takes second place. You will nevertheless wish to be the leader and the go-to person at home. You're going to want to know everyone's secrets and be a part of every decision or, if not, to be the person who has the final say.

As your calling is to be admired and loved you need to take a compassionate approach: when you are kind and understanding towards others they will respond well, but when you are oppositional you will only be opposed. As you mature your home will become a relaxed haven with furniture that is both functional and comfortable. Family must have a nest, after all.

RELATIONSHIPS

It's your need for excitement, adventure and independence that can lead you to be seen as being bossy, arrogant and, worse, a bully, yet your intention is not to boss others around, feel superior to them or coerce them. Your intention is to be admired and loved; however,, you can appear overpowering because to feel fulfilled you must see yourself rising above your own abilities and excelling in some way. People therefore see your confidence as arrogance, your self-assuredness as bossiness and your impatience with the inability of others to be decisive as bullying. Unless, that is, you're the rare Aries who truly is unashamedly self-centred and arrogant, in which case it's time to take a long, hard look at yourself!

Your inner calling is to communicate and connect with others, not to distance yourself and isolate. Ultimately, you measure your success from excelling in some way against the herd or society. However, in working to excel you may be seen as separate because you wish to be the authority or the hero. There is nothing wrong with asserting yourself, but you must be wary not to overshadow others with your bright presence and influence as you may be viewed as being aggressive.

Take the time to integrate with others, because a leader must be understood and liked or else they become a tyrant.

CREATIVITY

Your creativity lies in your actions; in other words, you express your creativity by initiating and starting great ventures that may not in fact appear to be creative or even artistic. In essence, yours is the soul of a true creative because each action you take is the result of a creative process.

The essence of creativity is making something out of nothing, of initiating and forming matter, so in your actions you create something new; you are the archetypal creator. And being the first sign of the zodiac you are able to kick-start new projects easily, although you may tend to leave some of them unfinished as you're better at beginning projects than finishing them!

PITFALLS

Your pitfalls revolve very much around your own reactions to events. You are liable to succumb to the perils of your inherently impulsive nature: anger, oversight and impetuousness. Take the time to filter life events more serenely, to stay a while in the present and to savour life rather than constantly feeling you must conquer another mountain, begin another project or be a hero again. Rest assured you are the hero for so many, so rest and savour the sensation.

Aim to be the best version of yourself, not succumbing to someone else's or society's expectations of who you should be. In this way you can plan ahead, work with your own talents and abilities to be dynamic and the hero of your own story.

SOLAR TRANSITS:
harness the sun's power
every day of the year

The sun empowers you in different areas of your life as it travels through each zodiac sign from month to month. Find out here how to make the most of your strong points during each of the transits of the sun through the 12 signs.

Sun in Aries, March to April

TAKE ACTION!

Make hay while the sun shines! The sun in Aries phase begins with the equinox, which is always a great time to ask yourself where you could establish more balance and harmony in your personal life. This will be a proactive, upbeat four weeks, so aim to set in motion any plans you've had on the drawing board for a while and be ready for new opportunities.

Sun in Taurus, April to May

BE PRODUCTIVE TOBOOST FINANCES

The sun in Taurus will spotlight your values, principles and self-esteem and your ability to boost your own circumstances in material ways, so this phase can be a good time to boost your finances. It can also spotlight what is lacking in your life, and in this way will motivate you to boost self-esteem and provide better for yourself and those you love.

Sun in Gemini, May to June

IMPROVE COMMUNICATIONS AND TRAVEL

This is a good time for travel, communications and financial developments, so get busy and aim to negotiate if you are making decisions at work. Decisions you have made in the past should begin to bear fruit, and you will feel encouraged that you are on the right path. If handled carefully, a project, commerce or financial matter could become a success.

Sun in Cancer, June to July
IMPROVE YOUR HOME

While the sun is in Cancer it is an excellent time to feather your nest, both literally – by making your home more comfortable – and figuratively – by investing in your skills and abilities. This is a good time to start a family or to add to it. For some this phase is excellent for negotiations, especially if you demonstrate both your caring attributes and leadership skills.

Sun in Leo, July to August
ENJOY ROMANCE, FUN AND CREATIVITY

The sun will shine on your personal life during these four weeks, and you'll enjoy sprucing up your home décor and being more active about keeping your house in tip-top shape. You may enjoy receiving visitors or visiting someone else's home. Your focus could go towards family and children and also to friends and lovers, with you enjoying fun times with these key people.

Sun in Virgo, August to September
IMPROVE WORK AND HEALTH

The sun in Virgo will spotlight your work, health and daily routines. You are likely to be busy during these four weeks and may consider new work projects or find the time to boost your health. Your routine is likely to change; it's a good time to take a holiday. Some Aries may find this a particularly creative time.

Sun in Libra, September to October
RELATIONSHIPS

This phase will shine a light on your relationships: are they equal and balanced? If not, you'll get the chance to get them back on an even keel. This will be a romantic phase, so organise some treats! You may need to find more balance at work, too, but may initially feel a little frustrated by developments so you must avoid outbursts and bad tempers.

Sun in Scorpio, October to November
COLLABORATE

This is a good time to deepen relationships and develop your intuition. You may be drawn to dream work or an interest in psychology. You'll enjoy the chance to do something different, to collaborate and meet new people. You may feel super passionate about people, your principles and ideas, so avoid arguments that can be overcome with reason and patience.

Sun in Sagittarius, November to December
ENTER NEW TERRITORY

The sun in Sagittarius will provide incentive to be proactive and dynamic and to take the time to enjoy your favourite pastimes such as sport and spirituality and spending time with friends. Travel may appeal. Energy levels may improve but you must avoid being overly blunt or bossy during this time. Collaborations will benefit from tact and diplomacy.

Sun in Capricorn, December to January
BE PREPARED TO SHINE

With the sun in Capricorn you can shine in the workplace and your circumstances can improve. This is an excellent time to consider making changes at work and in your career, general direction and status. You are going to be more realistic, methodical and diligent than usual and prospective ventures are likely to be easier to implement, so take the initiative!

Sun in Aquarius, January to February
ENJOY THE COMPANY OF THOSE YOU LOVE

This phase will bring your outgoing, bubbly, pioneering self to the surface, and you'll enjoy entering fresh terrain by joining new clubs, socialising and networking. You may even discover an aspect of yourself you weren't aware of or develop a quirky new friendship or interest during these four weeks. If you're single you'll enjoy meeting people from a variety of backgrounds.

Sun in Pisces, February to March
FOCUS ON DEVELOPING A SENSE OF PURPOSE

You'll wish at this time to infuse your life with more purpose. The sun in Pisces will shine a light on inner abilities such as your intuition and unconscious self. You may be drawn to an interest in psychology, and to redefining who you are and boosting health. Spiritual interests can develop well.

LUNAR TRANSITS:
be calm and effective every day of the month

The moon spotlights different aspects of your emotional self as it travels each month through each zodiac sign, staying two days in each sign. When the moon is in each sign you gain the opportunity to express yourself more effectively in various areas of your life. Find out here how to make the most of your strong points during each of the two days each month.

Moon in Aries
FEEL COMFORTABLE IN YOURSELF

The Aries moon will feel motivating and will encourage you to be outgoing, sociable and adventurous, both at work and in your personal life. You must avoid overwork and maintain a steady health routine to avoid fatigue. Be ready to adapt to developments and avoid allowing your feisty inner warrior to call all the shots: be assertive, but avoid aggression.

Moon in Taurus
INDULGE YOUR SENSES

You'll feel emotionally motivated by your progressive values and principles. You will be driven to prove your skill sets during these two days, making them an ideal time to boost finances and self-esteem. You will be drawn to good food and luxury items, and will appreciate the opportunity to indulge your sensuality. Avoid overspending and impulse buys, as you may crave retail therapy.

Moon in Gemini
TRUST YOUR INTUITION

Your communications are likely to run more smoothly and you'll enjoy meetings and catch-ups with friends and neighbours. The Gemini moon will produce a chatty and varied time, so you're likely to be busy. If you're uncertain about various matters such as travel plans, the Gemini moon is ideal for research to overcome doubts and fears. Above all, trust your instincts.

Moon in Cancer

GET IN TOUCH WITH YOUR EMOTIONS

You may be feeling sensitive and intuitive and have clearer dreams. You'll focus more on domestic life and may feel super creative. You'll feel more in touch with your emotions and must maintain perspective with circumstances outside the home during a Cancer moon, as you may feel idealistic.

Moon in Leo

ENJOY ROMANCE, FAMILY FUN AND CREATIVITY

You'll enjoy the upbeat nature of the Leo moon but it may bring out your emotions, especially regarding domestic, property or love matters. Take your time to process the various fast-moving developments, seeking facts and avoiding making assumptions for the best results. You'll enjoy deepening your understanding of someone close.

Moon in Virgo

BE PRODUCTIVE

The Virgo moon will encourage you to be practical about your tasks. Some of your bigger-picture decisions will come down to nuts and bolts during this time, so you must be realistic. The Virgo moon will focus your mind on the importance of qualities such as job satisfaction and being helpful to others. Seek expert advice if you're unsure and avoid being critical.

Moon in Libra

FOCUS ON PEACE IN RELATIONSHIPS

The Libran moon will encourage you to look for balance and harmony in your life. If health or well-being have been issues the Libran moon phase is a good time to gain more serenity; meditation and yoga may be beneficial. You will also be drawn to improve your appearance.

Moon in Scorpio

INVEST IN COLLABORATIONS

The Scorpio moon will highlight strong feelings and impressions. You may feel particularly feisty, romantic and passionate during a Scorpio moon, which will guarantee a focus on what and who makes you happy so organise a treat for yourself and with someone special! Aim to collaborate during the four days when the moon is in Libra and Scorpio for top results.

Moon in Sagittarius

SATISFY YOUR CURIOSITY

You may feel chatty and inquisitive during the Sagittarian moon and drawn to projects in dynamic new territory and with exciting people. Travel, study and generally broadening your horizons will appeal. The moon in Sagittarius is particularly beneficial for study and learning new ideas.

Moon in Capricorn

DEVOTE TIME TO YOUR CAREER AND PROJECTS

You'll feel ready to negotiate amicably and to put your plans in place carefully and methodically. If you work hard during these two days it will be worthwhile. The Capricorn moon will spotlight those areas of your life you feel you could improve, especially your career, general projects and progress in life in general.

Moon in Aquarius

EXPRESS YOUR QUIRKY SIDE!

You may enjoy associating with a new social circle during the Aquarian moon, which will stimulate your inventiveness and ability to think outside the box – useful at work and with discussions and negotiations. You must avoid jumping to conclusions during this phase as you may be inclined to throw caution to the wind!

Moon in Pisces

TRUST YOUR INTUITION AND PSYCHIC ABILITY

The Pisces moon may produce a reflective mood, especially in connection with your work and the groups and individuals you meet. Be ready to go the extra mile but avoid overwork, as you may feel introspective or sensitive. It's a good time for art, creativity, meditation, spirituality and dream work. The Pisces moon will motivate you to deepen your spirituality.

FULL MOONS:
magnify your vibrant power

*Each full moon highlights different aspects of your power and vibrancy.
Find out here which full moons will be excellent times to turn a corner
in the various areas of your life to show just what you're made of.*

Full moon in Aries
GAIN A FRESH APPROACH TO LIFE

An Aries full moon will bring out strong emotions, and events may force you to adopt a more even-keeled approach to work and your personal life. You may feel motivated to finish a project in readiness for a new one or simply to be more positive, but if you feel restless or feisty you must avoid making impulsive changes. Analyse the facts first.

Full moon in Taurus
BE PRACTICAL WITH FINANCES AND BOOST SELF-ESTEEM

Expect a fresh agreement to develop that will involve finances or take you in a new direction. Check that agreements you make serve your higher purpose; that is, that they resonate deeply with bigger-picture goals that include those you love and your long-term plans. Look for ways to ground your projects.

Full moon in Gemini
BOOST COMMUNICATION SKILLS

You'll develop an understanding with someone that could kick-start a considerable new phase in your life. For some this will involve travel; for others spiritual matters, study, a relationship or legal matters. Base your plans on realities, practicalities and feasibility. Developments in your status or career may require adjustment, but you will adapt.

Full moon in Cancer
RE-INVENT YOUR HOME LIFE

A fresh chapter in a domestic, family or property matter is waiting in the wings, and some Aries will be busy with communications, meetings and talks during this phase. A trip or a visit could be more relevant than meets the eye, so ensure you prepare well for travel and/or a change of environment.

Full moon in Leo
REFRESH YOUR PERSONAL LIFE AND PROJECTS

The Leo full moon will fall in your creative, family and fun zone; you are likely to experience developments in one or all of these areas. You'll feel motivated to meet upbeat characters, and there may be a sparkle of romance and excitement in the air. A new chapter regarding family or a creative project is likely.

Full moon in Virgo
EMBRACE A FRESH DAILY SCHEDULE

The Virgo full moon signals the end of a particular routine, for some at work and for others concerning health and fitness. Check all the facts if you are making commitments to avoid mistakes being made during this full moon. Be prepared to put in hard work to see a new chapter flourish, and it will. Family and friends may also be a focus.

Full moon in Libra
REBALANCE YOUR LOVE LIFE AND RELATIONSHIPS

You'll appreciate the opportunity to consider your work/life balance and to enjoy more time for yourself and those you love around the Libra full moon. Focus on finding ways to avoid arguments with partners, friends and groups and to establish mutual territory and common ground. You may experience a key change in a business or personal collaboration.

Full moon in Scorpio
CONSIDER AGREEMENTS IN A NEW LIGHT

Your circumstances are undergoing change for the better even if in the process you must negotiate fairly chaotic or even dramatic circumstances. The Scorpio full moon means you must look at a shared area of your life such as finances including taxes, for example, and duties in a new light. You may enjoy an ego boost or a financial improvement such as receiving an inheritance.

Full moon in Sagittarius

RESPOND TO THE WINDS OF CHANGE

You'll respond to the call of the wild – that is, unless you've recently ended an adventurous phase or a trip, in which case now it'll be back to work! A financial matter or shared duty will require careful thought as several adjustments may be necessary.

Full moon in Capricorn

EMBRACE A TURNING POINT IN YOUR CAREER OR STATUS

As a project or circumstance ends a fresh phase in your general direction, career or status will come about. You may welcome changes in your career, activities or status. Pace yourself as it could be an intense time that makes you feel warrior-like; sometimes your bluster can let you down so you must temper emotions with practicalities.

Full moon in Aquarius

ADAPT TO THE STATUS QUO

Be prepared to alter the way you see your life and loyalties. Your involvement with a group or organisation may come full circle or change tack. This is an excellent time to think laterally, as new ideas and opportunities are likely to arise as if from out of the blue – if they haven't already.

Full moon in Pisces

DEVELOP YOUR SKILL SETS AND SENSE OF SELF

A fairly lengthy chapter is about to end that will encourage you to tie up loose ends, especially to do with work and health. You'll appreciate the chance to indulge in your favourite activities and to socialise and network. You may enjoy a particularly inspired or spiritual phase and be ready to improve your skill sets.

NEW MOONS:
start something fresh

Each new moon points to the start of something fresh for you in different areas of your life. Find out here which new moon to work with and how to make lasting change by starting something new, especially if you have been putting off change for some time.

New moon in Aries
REVEAL THE NEW YOU!

You are likely to feel motivated in your personal life and at work. You may already be aware that fresh projects could point you in a new direction, which will feel invigorating. Key news may encourage you to see the world through fresh eyes or to adopt a fresh, dynamic approach to life. A new look may also appeal.

New moon in Taurus
A FRESH FINANCIAL CHAPTER

This is a positive time to make new investments and financial decisions and boost self-esteem and organise ways to more firmly express your values in your daily life through the actions you take. Aim to transform your thoughts and plans into actions.

New moon in Gemini
PUT FRESH AGREEMENTS AND PLANS INTO ACTION

Developments will signal options that could improve your communication skills, self-esteem and relationships. A new chapter concerning a trip, finances or the start of a fresh agreement or relationship can arise so be proactive and upbeat and seek ways to implement new ideas. Check vehicles and communication devices and update if necessary.

New moon in Cancer

INVEST IN A HAPPIER HOME

The Cancer new moon suggests that a more inclusive and nurturing approach to domestic and property matters will work well as a fresh phase is set to begin in your family or domestic life. The secret to this success lies in honing your communication skills: employ less fire and more dynamism and caring, entrepreneurial and leadership skills. This is a good time for a move or renovation.

New moon in Leo

LET YOUR INNER ARTIST OUT!

Musical, inventive, romantic Aries will enjoy adding more colour and vibrancy to your life. Your relationships could blossom and be greater fun. If you wish to start a family or add to your existing family this could be a good time to start. You could begin a refreshing cycle in your domestic life, signalling changes property-wise too.

New moon in Virgo

INVESTIGATE FRESH WORK AND HEALTH INCENTIVES

A fresh incentive may catch your eye at work or involving a favourite project, interest or study course. If you work in a therapeutic or sporty field a new project could be appealing. Keep an eye on your energy levels to avoid fatigue, as you are likely to be busy at this time. Assist your health with energy-boosting modalities such as walking, running, a fresh diet, meditation and yoga.

New moon in Libra

REVITALISE YOUR LOVE LIFE AND RELATIONSHIPS

You'll be in a position to negotiate the terms of an agreement that affects your personal or business relationships. It's important you do your research, as your tendency to act first and think later could get you in hot water. Look for peace if stress has been a factor in a relationship.

New moon in Scorpio

BEGIN A NEW ARRANGEMENT

This will be a perfect time to gain a deeper understanding of a circumstance, someone else or even yourself. You may experience the strength of your own intuition and will be guided by this to make changes in your life through a collaboration, contract or financial agreement. Your thirst for knowledge will kick-start a creative and productive 12-month cycle of collaborations.

New moon in Sagittarius
EMBRACE NEW EXPERIENCES

An adventurous phase is about to begin in which you'll feel more optimistic about your projects, interests and relationships. A new legal, travel, study, sporting or written venture could open doors. This is a good time to improve your relationships by bringing more upbeat energy into them.

New moon in Capricorn
EMBRACE A FRESH DIRECTION

Prepare to make key changes in your career, status and general direction. Ensure your decisions resonate on a fundamental level, as commitments may be long term. Be realistic and consider financial circumstances in a practical light. Avoid limiting your progress in the name of stability and security – after all, you are a fiery, dynamic and effective Aries.

New moon in Aquarius
CONSIDER PROGRESSIVE NEW IDEAS

A new arrangement with a friend or organisation may be progressive or will open doors. Avoid seeing only black and white in a circumstance and aim to get on with someone whose ideas are different from yours, as there may be many advantages to being flexible. Humanitarian projects could draw your attention.

New moon in Pisces
RESEARCH A HOLISTIC APPROACH TO YOUR DAILY LIFE

You may feel more in tune with your intuition and instincts. This is a good time to kick-start a fitness regime that includes gentle exercise such as yoga and meditation. Spiritual Aries will be drawn to philosophical and devotional groups. This is a good time to do the background research on a fresh work initiative or project.

LUNAR ECLIPSES:
be strong during peak emotional changes

Each lunar eclipse signals a major turning point in your life and may bring about intense emotions. Eclipses point to circumstances that seem to disempower you and subsequently motivate you to address any imbalances, so keep an eye on those areas in which you lack control as that is where you can make the most changes and become strong. Find out here which lunar eclipse will bring change in which area of your life, and how to make the most of these changes.

Aries lunar eclipse
CULTIVATE PERSONAL GROWTH

Take the initiative, as you could boost your circumstances; however, you must be discerning about what and who you focus on. This will be a major turning point in your personal life so you are likely to feel emotional, but it is a good time to tackle complex tasks despite feeling compromised or under the weather or pressured.

Taurus lunar eclipse
STRENGTHEN YOUR RESOLVE

You must find a way to co-operate so you can accommodate someone else's priorities and values while also standing up for yourself. Your own principles may change as a result. Be assertive but non-confrontational, as key financial developments will depend on it.

Gemini lunar eclipse
CONSIDER A FRESH PATH

Be prepared for research and to develop your communication skills. A trip or news will take you into new territory, and you will gain insight into how you feel about a long-term decision. For some events will revolve around work and money and for others travel, spirituality, study or legal matters. A sibling or a key relationship may take a new path around this time.

Cancer lunar eclipse

INVEST IN YOURSELF AND THOSE YOU LOVE

You need stability, yet change is inevitable. This may be due to developments in your career or home and activities, and for some due to a new relationship, trip or venture that broadens your horizons. Be honest about what and who really mean the most to you, as this realisation will propel you into fresh horizons.

Leo lunar eclipse

BE CREATIVE IN YOUR PERSONAL LIFE

The Leo lunar eclipse will shine a light on creative matters, romance and the chance to get ahead with your projects, even if you feel that your projects are overshadowed by other concerns or that you're not up to the challenges that lie ahead. Your inner strength will prevail and you'll make progress. Boost your health for the best results.

Virgo lunar eclipse

STABILISE YOUR EVERYDAY LIFE

As you let go of a past expectation or circumstance that no longer resonates with your bigger-picture aims, this is an excellent time to focus more on your daily work and health concerns to build a strong situation that will prove nurturing and stabilising as you move forward.

Libra lunar eclipse

REGAIN EMOTIONAL BALANCE

The Libra eclipse will spotlight your feelings about collaborations and romantic partnerships. It's a good time to look at your long-term commitments in a calm, practical light as you may feel super emotional. You may need to find more equity in your relationships or better harmony in your work/life balance.

Scorpio lunar eclipse

ALTER PERSONAL ARRANGEMENTS

Intense feelings will arise about a change in a shared situation such as a financial arrangement or communal space at home. A fresh approach to a relationship may appeal if you find emotions spinning out of control. Negotiations will be necessary and research will benefit you. Psychological help may also be of benefit if your emotions are super intense.

Sagittarius lunar eclipse

A LEARNING CURVE

You'll feel motivated to learn new things and so may be inclined to change many aspects of your life, from starting a family to broadening your interests through study, for example. For some Aries, a legal matter will put you in a strong position to gain experience and knowledge. You'll obtain a deeper understanding of life.

Capricorn lunar eclipse

RE-ORIENT YOUR COMPASS

The Capricorn lunar eclipse will spotlight your feelings about a turning point in your general direction in life. Some Aries may be drawn to making career changes, while others may alter their activities or status (for example, from single to married or vice versa). You will be looking for more stability and security, but in order to find it you may need to first go through a little disruption.

Aquarius lunar eclipse

ENTERTAIN NEW PEOPLE AND IDEAS

Trying something new will truly appeal to you, such as travel, esoteric studies, humanitarian or spiritual endeavours and even quirky new hobbies. You may wish to socialise with a new circle.

Pisces lunar eclipse

INVEST IN PRIORITIES AND HEALTH

Follow your dreams but avoid being overly idealistic and easily distracted by the concerns of others. You may feel inspired to join humanitarian or spiritual groups. You could be sociable or will be deeply affected by an idealistic if impractical person. For some there will be fresh work developments or the need to focus on health.

SOLAR ECLIPSES:
making major changes run smoothly

Each solar eclipse signals a major turning point in your life that points to ongoing change for years to come. Find out here which solar eclipses will bring change in which areas of your life, and how to make the most of those changes.

Aries solar eclipse
LET YOUR INNER HERO OUT

Change is daunting, so you must let your inner hero out: bring your courage, gusto and chutzpah into full force! This eclipse signals the start of a new chapter in connection with your bigger-picture goals and sense of purpose. You may begin a fresh health or work schedule, or will find that aspects of your relationships undergo a change that draws on your reserves.

Taurus solar eclipse
RAISE SELF-ESTEEM

Be practical above all else, whether you experience change in your personal life or financially. You will feel a sense of increased security as a result of gaining more certainty about your circumstances, even if you must first undergo a degree of change or turmoil. Avoid limiting your options too much if you are making long-term plans.

Gemini solar eclipse
TAKE ACTION WITH PAPERWORK AND TALKS

Meetings and travel will provide you with food for thought as the prospect of beginning a fresh chapter will be enticing regarding your agreements, the way you travel, study and how you broaden your horizons and key relationships. Developments could boost your self-esteem and finances.

Cancer solar eclipse

LOOK AFTER YOURSELF AND DEEPEN SPIRITUALITY

Considerable change will require you to nurture yourself in the face of developments that are beyond your control. This eclipse will put focus on property and family, and spiritually minded Aries will find ways to rely more on your intuition and develop empathy or psychic abilities.

Leo solar eclipse

RETHINK YOUR PRECONCEPTIONS

Look for inspiration: it's everywhere! This eclipse offers the chance to rethink your preconceived ideas, not only those of others but also your own. You may be surprised by what you can accomplish: if you are disappointed by events see them as a chance to get back on track and to excel in inspired ways.

Virgo solar eclipse

IMPROVE YOUR LIFE

If you're looking for a fresh way ahead that can broaden your horizons, this is it! Circulate your resume and network and socialise during this phase, as you could take steps into a new everyday routine. For some Aries this solar eclipse will spotlight the need for changes in your family or love life.

Libra solar eclipse

BE FAIR, DIPLOMATIC AND TACTFUL

A close business or personal relationship will transform. It's an excellent time to embrace a fairer outlook and to find ways to have a calmer frame of mind, such as via meditation. You may be required to mediate or be a peacemaker. Show respect and ask for it in return. There may be hard work involved in a new daily routine, but also the chance to boost well-being.

Scorpio solar eclipse

ADAPT TO CIRCUMSTANCES OUTSIDE YOUR CONTROL

You'll be required to take action regarding a shared circumstance such as at home or at work. You may need to alter financial arrangements by making a key investment, repaying a debt or receiving an inheritance. For some this eclipse can signify the need to adapt to the transience of life.

Sagittarius solar eclipse

BREAK NEW GROUND

Prepare to immerse yourself in a new venture: schedule in the time to adapt to any developments and to deal with a change of circumstance that will take you outside your comfort zone. Travel, study or fresh dynamics in relationships will be a part of the developments.

Capricorn solar eclipse

PREPARE TO SUCCEED

Great changes at work and in your career or general direction will require hard work. If you feel your power is eclipsed by someone, be practical and avoid entering into battle. You may need to secede power in the short term but will win the war, knowing that success is the best revenge. Apply yourself well to changes and you will gain a sense of accomplishment.

Aquarius solar eclipse

LOOK FOR FRESH OPPORTUNITIES

This is an excellent time to consider fresh avenues. Avoid limiting your options; the world is your oyster if you embrace diversity, opportunity and change. The Aquarian solar eclipse will kick-start a fresh phase in your relationship with a group, friend or organisation. For some, a quirky chapter in your career or direction will begin.

Pisces solar eclipse

DEEPEN SPIRITUAL UNDERSTANDING

Be courageous and look beyond appearances. As one door closes another will open, which will become apparent in the context of work and, for some, in the context of your social circle or an organisation. By embracing spiritual growth you will improve health, vitality and happiness.

20 APRIL - 21 MAY

SYMBOL
Bull

CONSTELLATION

ELEMENT
Earth

TAURUS
SUN SIGN

INNER CALLING

Your inner calling is to experience deeply that you are earthed, that you have a place in the world, that you are needed and that, in turn, you love with all your heart. You need to feel your soul rising to the challenge of earthy love – love that is never perfect but is, nevertheless, passionate and without end, love that needs to be fulfilled and will in turn feel fulfilling.

Your inner calling is also to provide: to those who themselves are responding to the need to be loved and to feel they belong and have an integral purpose in life. Above all your inner calling is to experience the sensuality of the human experience, to experience the divine within the mundane and to experience earthly pleasures while knowing that within these rests the seed of the divine and the spiritual.

SELF-ESTEEM

To gain self-esteem you must feel there is value in what you do. You cannot simply exist and enjoy life as there must be a correlation between what you do, who you are, what you value and how you express yourself. For this reason you will never stray off the path unless you do not rise to your inner calling experiencing earthly love in all its many guises.

Your self-esteem grows to a large extent through your caring and sensuous nature. You love to provide for others and bask in the gratitude you receive. As your self-esteem rests ostensibly in the hands of others one pitfall for you is that you risk giving your power to be happy to other people. Luckily your self-esteem, which is generally high, kicks in when there is inequality in a give-and-take relationship and your love turns to stone, cutting off ties with those who do not respect and honour your giving nature.

You'll feel rewarded in life by your giving and loving nature and you will experience the exponential curve of giving and receiving: making you one very happy Bull!

HOME LIFE

Your home is your castle, and you'll appreciate the many luxuries of soft furnishings, sensual fabrics and mood lighting. You will prefer to stay in one place for many years, as moving too often will be unsettling; and there's nothing a Taurus likes more than feeling settled, stable, sumptuous and that your home is your cradle, your place of true relaxation and luxury. It's your nest where you can cocoon and refuel energy levels.

You like to be the king or queen of your castle, too, and may need to work on creating peace and harmony at home to provide a foundation for the happy family you crave.

RELATIONSHIPS

Being such a people person, you love to be with other people. You surround yourself with those who love life, who wish to celebrate being alive just as you do. You are not a fair-weather friend: once you have made your choice about who to be close to you will be loyal and faithful, as you prefer stability and security to the thrill of the chase.

As your many friends will confirm you can be stubborn, although you might contest that you simply uphold your beliefs. Being an earth sign makes you slow to budge once you have formed an opinion, so maintaining a keen eye on common ground in relationships rather than sticking merely with one established thought will serve you well.

You're well known for your obstinacy when you're opposed; aim to establish a sense of inner calm rather than feeling stuck in a particular mindset. Cultivate your own sense of peace. Only you will know that your calm exterior hides the much tougher Bull beneath that has tenacity, strength and loyalty at its core.

CREATIVITY

The arts, design, crafts, beauty, music and beautiful objects will fuel your spirit. As a creative character you enjoy surrounding yourself with art and beauty, and although you love to express yourself creatively it needn't always be through an art form. You may love fashion, make-up, design and a beautiful wardrobe. Your creativity may extend to being inventive with cooking, gardening and home interiors, and you also love to express your creativity at work. Many Taureans are very good with finances and with planning and design.

PITFALLS

You risk resting on your laurels and your lust for life can cause you to overindulge in the good things in life: anything from rich food and drink to relationships that are sensual but ultimately unfulfilling. Your sentimentality can cause you to linger too long out of habit or nostalgia in relationships that have outgrown their loving purpose.

Your stubbornness can predispose you to missing out on new opportunities. A good technique to avoid too many pitfalls is to annually review your life, asking if you are hanging on to circumstances that are actually making you unhappy.

SOLAR TRANSITS:
harness the sun's power
every day of the year

The sun empowers you in different areas of your life as it travels through each zodiac sign from month to month. Find out here how to make the most of your strong points during each of the transits of the sun through the 12 signs.

Sun in Taurus, April to May
INVEST IN YOURSELF

This is an excellent time to do a mini review and decide if you are living your life according to your own values and principles. It will be a productive time that is excellent for boosting work, health and well-being. You'll feel more expressive and demonstrative in your love life, so it is an ideal time for a romantic break.

Sun in Gemini, May to June
BOOST FINANCES AND SELF-ESTEEM

Focus on improving your circumstances and ensure they still align with your beliefs and desires. This is a good time to consider a new look or to improve fitness. You may feel inclined to enjoy life's luxuries and comforts but also to speculate, so seek expert advice to avoid financial errors.

Sun in Cancer, June to July
IMPROVE COMMUNICATIONS AND TRAVEL

You can make great progress with your projects, negotiations and agreements. You may be inclined to travel to see family members and those you care deeply for and to improve your relationships. You may be drawn to invest more in yourself and those you love and potentially to make considerable financial and emotional investments.

Sun in Leo, July to August

IMPROVE YOUR HOME LIFE

You'll appreciate your role at home and will enjoy focusing on improving domestic dynamics. You may not tolerate self-centred people at this time so could need to self-censor your adverse response to big egos so you can avoid conflict and enjoy your own downtime. This aside, you'll enjoy being more outgoing, and travel and communications may be busy.

Sun in Virgo, August to September

BOOST ROMANCE, FUN AND CREATIVITY

This is a good time for creative projects, both at home and at work. Be practical about how you manage your personal life, fun and hobbies. The best way to feel sexier, have more fun and be more creative will lie in harmonious domestic circumstances and boosting your own well-being.

Sun in Libra, September to October

IMPROVE WORK AND HEALTH

Your work life will improve with a balanced approach to your regular routine. You'll embrace creativity, dance, music and romance as ways to enjoy life more on a daily basis. Your focus may be on family and children. If you're considering starting a family, this could be a fertile time.

Sun in Scorpio, October to November

BOOST YOUR LOVE LIFE AND RELATIONSHIPS

You'll feel more passionate in your relationships. If you're looking for a partner this is a good time to do it, but they may be super intense! You could also feel passionate about what you do in your daily life and at work. It's a good time to motivate yourself to embrace exciting ventures, which could also boost relationships.

Sun in Sagittarius, November to December

COLLABORATE ON JOINT DECISIONS

This is a good time to alter some of your arrangements, so be super honest about where your loyalties lie both at work and in your personal life. The sun will shine a light on how you share your finances, various commitments and agreements. If you're single you may feel more adventurous and positive about meeting a match.

Sun in Capricorn, December to January

PLAN AHEAD

This phase will bring your inner strategist out: you'll enjoy planning events, travel, get-togethers and long-term projects. You will be more practical than at other times of the year, making this an excellent time to get your feet on the ground with your long-term aims and goals, including work and your status in general.

Sun in Aquarius, January to February

ADD TEXTURE TO YOUR CAREER

You tend to be fairly focused once you have set your mind on certain projects, aims and goals. However, during these four weeks, you are likely to try fresh activities and may even develop an interest in a new field at work. It's a good time to broaden horizons and to inject life with more fun and variety.

Sun in Pisces, February to March

ENJOY THE COMPANY OF THOSE YOU LOVE

You'll enjoy being inspired by the people around you, both at work and in a social group over the next four weeks, but you must be practical and realistic with your planning or you risk being easily influenced and falling down a merry rabbit hole.

Sun in Aries, March to April

FOCUS ON PRIORITIES AND HEALTH

This can be a busy, successful time, especially at work and health-wise. You'll find this phase is an upbeat time socially so take time out for fun get-togethers, but if you find you are a little more introspective or even frustrated that some chores are more difficult to accomplish ensure you aim for success albeit with careful planning behind the scenes.

LUNAR TRANSITS:
be calm and effective every day of the month

The moon spotlights different aspects of your emotional self as it travels each month through each zodiac sign, staying two days in each sign. When the moon is in each sign you gain the opportunity to express yourself more effectively in various areas of your life. Find out here how to make the most of your strong points during each of the two days each month.

Moon in Taurus
INDULGE IN YOUR PERSONAL LIFE

Plan romance: these two days each month will motivate you to indulge in favourite activities, good food and great company! You'll feel more inclined to treat yourself and will crave romance, music and candlelight as you are in touch with your own emotions and sensuality. You'll wish to express your practical side, too, so this is an ideal time for getting work done.

Moon in Gemini
ASSESS FINANCES AND SELF-ESTEEM

You will feel motivated to improve the way you express yourself and are seen by others in order to boost your self-esteem. This is a good time to assess both your finances and work commitments, especially if you feel changeable. You must check you are adhering to your values; if you find you are not you must get back on track!

Moon in Cancer
ORGANISE COMMUNICATIONS AND TRAVEL

You may be sensitive to other people's moods during this phase, so take things one step at a time. As you are so good at organising engage a little logistical strategy, especially at home and with travel and communications, as the moon in Cancer could bring your inner vulnerabilities out and contribute to you feeling more emotional than usual.

Moon in Leo
ENJOY A CHANGE OF PACE

Take things slowly as this could be a busy time, but be prepared to also be spontaneous. You'll be glad you were, as you'll enjoy a fun time! You'll appreciate a change of pace such as a trip somewhere beautiful or a meeting with an upbeat friend. All these scenarios take you outside your home, so you will appreciate the comfort when you return home all the more. It's a good time for DIY projects.

Moon in Virgo
INVEST IN ROMANCE, FUN AND CREATIVITY

You'll appreciate the opportunity to spend more time on various projects and people. You may find you are a little perfectionistic about your projects or people's behaviour, so monitor this tendency as it could detract from the fun. You'll enjoy get-togethers and favourite pastimes, and a financial matter may deserve careful appraisal to avoid overspending.

Moon in Libra
ENHANCE WORK AND HEALTH

Try to incorporate art, music and ways of enhancing your well-being into your daily life; focusing on your own appearance and fitness will have a wonderful effect. Art and family may feel super nurturing at this time, so focus on these aspects of your life to boost satisfaction.

Moon in Scorpio
ENJOY YOUR LOVE LIFE AND RELATIONSHIPS

When the moon travels through your seventh house it has an intense effect on a partner's emotions – and also on your own. Take things one step at a time, as passions could run high. Romance could soar but people may seem moodier than usual, so while this may be a passionate time it could be volatile. Be calm.

Moon in Sagittarius

CONSIDER JOINT DECISIONS

This is a good time for negotiations and being optimistic about your relationships. If you are under pressure to co-operate more but feel reluctant to make changes in some of your agreements or beliefs, consider the real positives and advantages of making long-term change as this is a good time to do so.

Moon in Capricorn

ENTER NEW TERRITORY

Promote a hands-on, methodical and capable outlook, as this is a good time to get ahead with your projects and venture into new territory if required. You'll appreciate the opportunity to advance both at work and with your favourite activities.

Moon in Aquarius

THINK LATERALLY AT WORK

Think laterally: let your imagination free. A group, friend or organisation may be helpful or inspiring during this phase. You'll feel encouraged to try something new either at work or in your field of interest, so think outside the square for the best results.

Moon in Pisces

BE INSPIRED BY THOSE YOU LOVE

Trust your instincts and seek inspiration from friends, groups and experts, especially if key choices must be made. You may feel you're ready to dream big and may also feel super romantic but that you have loyalties and projects underway that must be catered to first. Be practical and schedule socialising into a busy schedule to keep on track.

Moon in Aries

FOCUS ON PRIORITIES AND WELL-BEING

You may feel edgier and a little restless during this time, so find calming modalities such as meditation to soothe your nerves. This is likely to be a super-busy time, especially at work or with someone special. Take the time to indulge in your favourite activities and duties, but avoid clashes with argumentative people.

FULL MOONS:
magnify your vibrant power

*Each full moon highlights different aspects of your power and vibrancy.
Find out here which full moons will be excellent times to turn a corner
in the various areas of your life to show just what you're made of.*

Full moon in Taurus

ADD MEANING AND PURPOSE TO YOUR LIFE

Decide on your long-term plans as they could add value to your life. This phase represents a fresh chapter that will include a new situation at work or with your health. For some, a change in your personal life such as your status from single to married, for example, may arise as an opportunity to gain fulfilment.

Full moon in Gemini

RESEARCH FINANCES AND BOOST SELF-ESTEEM

Research facts at the Gemini full moon as otherwise you will be indecisive. A different financial circumstance due to a new agreement at work or in your personal life will mean the chance to earn more – but also to spend more. Lively discussions point to a fresh agreement. Aim to boost self-esteem through positive self-talk and adhering to values.

Full moon in Cancer

EXPRESS YOURSELF

Your caring side will come out. Be assertive and avoid being oversensitive through boosting a positive self-image. A trip or negotiation or simply the chance to catch up with loved ones will feel nurturing, bringing you closer to family and friends. Attention to finances will stimulate your need to express your values and the desire to be adequately paid for your hard work.

Full moon in Leo
BE CREATIVE AT HOME

Make upbeat changes such as engaging in DIY projects or welcoming a family member to stay. Changes regarding children may be in the spotlight, so this is a great time to be positive and admit a heart-centred chapter. You may be drawn to visit beautiful places that boost your self-esteem.

Full moon in Virgo
BOOST CREATIVITY WITH A LITTLE FUN

Be practical, realistic and ready to plan ahead, but avoid feeling pressured to get everything in life absolutely perfect. Retain a sense of fun. You may gain more insight into your true priorities, especially regarding work, career or status. For some this full moon will spotlight new circumstances in your personal life such as at home or with family.

Full moon in Libra
MAKE PEACE AT WORK AND WITH YOURSELF

This is a good time to make peace with yourself and the rest will follow; avoid taking events personally. A fresh chapter could include more love, romance, art and enjoyment, but you must consciously focus on creating optimum circumstances for health and creativity so that your work and personal lives flourish.

Full moon in Scorpio
DISCUSS NEW IDEAS IN YOUR RELATIONSHIPS

News may represent considerable change at this full moon. Take the time to navigate through potentially intense feelings as you consider a fresh routine or circumstance or a change in your love life. This full moon signals the chance to negotiate or discuss a fresh chapter in a business or personal agreement.

Full moon in Sagittarius
MAKE BOLD DECISIONS AND COLLABORATE

You are ready to renegotiate the terms and conditions in an agreement. Meetings or a trip will be a catalyst. There is a general draw towards the new and better and you can't help but get swept up in events, but you must decide if what you already have is enough.

Full moon in Capricorn

EARTH YOUR VENTURES

Turn a corner with ventures in your inimitably practical, realistic and dedicated way. Luckily, this full moon will effectively earth your projects and provide more stability even if, in the process, you need to overcome some hurdles, especially financially or regarding shared duties and goals.

Full moon in Aquarius

BE INNOVATIVE WITH YOUR CAREER AND STATUS

Adopt an open mind to work, your status or general direction as new possibilities will arise and trying something new could appeal to you, especially as a tired chapter at work or regarding your general status in life comes to an end. This may come about in surprising ways, so be prepared.

Full moon in Pisces

ENJOY THE COMPANY OF THOSE YOU LOVE

This will be a family-oriented, sociable or romantic time, so enjoy being inspired but maintain a sense of reality as your judgement may not be at its best. You may see life through rose-coloured glasses so be practical, especially with a group, organisation or friend.

Full moon in Aries

TAKE THE INITIATIVE WITH PLANS AND BOOST HEALTH

You could turn a corner with a work or health matter and gain more balance in life. You must put all your cards on the table and avoid mix-ups. You may be ready for a change of routine or environment, but if you're negotiating a key agreement work towards your goals methodically and avoid being put off by intense feelings.

NEW MOONS:
start something fresh

Each new moon points to the start of something fresh for you in different areas of your life. Find out here which new moon to work with and how to make lasting change by starting something new, especially if you have been putting off change for some time.

New moon in Taurus

RECONNECT WITH YOURSELF

Re-energise your life by investing in yourself more emotionally, spiritually and financially. For some the new moon points to a fresh chapter at work or health-wise. For others a new chapter is coming in a relationship, so it's a good time for singles to look for a partner and for couples to revive your relationship if it's in a rut.

New moon in Gemini

MAKE CLEAR FINANCIAL DECISIONS AND BOOST CONFIDENCE

Your values and principles will come into sharp focus, so this new moon can provide clarity from practical and financial points of view. For some the Gemini new moon will kick-start a more fun and upbeat chapter in a close relationship. Aim to boost confidence and organise fun events.

New moon in Cancer

BELIEVE IN YOUR COMMUNICATION ABILITIES

Take the time to strengthen your convictions and your belief in your own ability to succeed and you could make a dream trip or relationship a reality. Find ways to boost your communication skills. There may be matters to do with nurturing – especially self-nurturing – that arise during this time.

New moon in Leo
BOOST YOUR SENSE OF SECURITY

Your home is your true cocoon, and you will find ways to boost your sense of security at this time as changes are likely. It's a good time to move and also to travel to the homes of other people. You'll gain the opportunity to be proactive and hands-on to bring out the best in circumstances.

New moon in Virgo
START A NEW PROJECT AND REVIVE ROMANCE

Put your ideas to good use in practical ways. This is a good time to start a creative project, romantic involvement and family, but if you've been unrealistic with some of your planning you may discover flaws. Find out the variables that affect your plans and be methodical to create an upbeat and fun environment.

New moon in Libra
KICK-START A NEW WORK OR HEALTH ROUTINE

Consider a fresh horizon and potentially something completely counter-intuitive, as you could attain more peace and balance in your daily schedule and health by beginning something that resonates more deeply with you. If events put a spanner in the works, be realistic and practical to regain a sense of work/life balance.

New moon in Scorpio
INFUSE YOUR RELATIONSHIPS WITH MORE PASSION

Take the initiative as you could see your love life blossom, which will motivate you to be more adventurous and outspoken. But look out: you must find the middle ground between tact and honesty with a partner or sparks will fly.

New moon in Sagittarius
BEGIN JOINT PROJECTS

Be optimistic with bold and new ideas and you'll see positive outcomes with a shared initiative, relationship or partnership. Be more outspoken and proactive, as a fresh approach could be beneficial. However, if a challenge arises avoid conflict, as arguments may escalate quickly.

New moon in Capricorn

BE PRACTICAL WITH NEW PLANS

Start a new venture, take an exciting trip or begin a fresh project, as these activities could provide stability down the line. Make sure you factor in your need for security and self-nurturance into your plans. A helpful friend, business or personal partner or organisation may prove particularly supportive.

New moon in Aquarius

TAKE A NEW TURN IN YOUR CAREER

A brand new chapter is about to begin, and the more you can look outside the square at the benefits in your circumstances the better it will be for you. A change in your status, career or general direction may involve a surprise or simply the chance to do something different. Not everyone will agree with you now, so ensure you get your facts right and avoid conflict.

New moon in Pisces

SPEND MORE TIME WITH LIKE-MINDED PEOPLE

Embrace your social and networking skills and boost the talents you have as yet not developed. A friend or organisation may inspire you to develop your interests and activities. Romantic Taureans may find this a particularly inspiring, creative and eye-opening time.

New moon in Aries

BEGIN A NEW WORK OR HEALTH SCHEDULE

Start a different health and fitness regime, and begin a new work routine that feels more motivating for you. Invest in what truly makes you happy; dig deep to find that spark of enthusiasm. You may revitalise a friendship or work relationship or renew your membership to a group or an organisation.

LUNAR ECLIPSES:
be strong during peak emotional changes

Each lunar eclipse signals a major turning point in your life and may bring about intense emotions. Eclipses point to circumstances that seem to disempower you and subsequently motivate you to address any imbalances, so keep an eye on those areas in which you lack control as that is where you can make the most changes and become strong. Find out here which lunar eclipse will bring change in which area of your life, and how to make the most of these changes.

Taurus lunar eclipse
GAIN AN UNDERSTANDING OF YOUR DESIRES

This eclipse will mean considerable changes in your personal life; the more realistic you are the less disruptive the eclipse will be. If you're single you may meet someone or form a commitment. Couples may alter some aspects of your agreements and relationship. Some Taureans will begin a fresh daily schedule. Take the opportunity to align your activities with a sense of purpose.

Gemini lunar eclipse
RE-EVALUATE YOUR PRIORITIES

Be prepared to look at your finances, values and principles in a new light. Ask who and what is most important to you. You must be more outgoing or adaptable with your relationships. Obtain all the facts and figures before making decisions, as events can highlight areas you have not researched adequately and can predispose you to glossing over details.

Cancer lunar eclipse
FOCUS ON COMMUNICATIONS AND TRAVEL

Your deepest feelings will be stirred through travel or key talks. You will need to be careful with communications. This eclipse will spotlight how you truly feel about an investment, finances, relationship and your values. Look after yourself and those you love in a more transparently nurturing way.

Leo lunar eclipse

BE GUIDED BY YOUR HEART AT HOME

Choose your decisions and options compassionately. You may need to put family matters ahead of your own or, conversely, rid yourself of the shackles of other people's concerns. A fresh phase will enable you to move ahead with your domestic, family or property matters.

Virgo lunar eclipse

A TURNING POINT WITH ROMANCE, FUN AND CREATIVITY

You will gain insight into how you truly feel about someone close or a project. You'll get a stronger sense of who matters the most to you and insight into how best to move ahead slowly and in practical terms. Avoid feeling sentimental; look to the new.

Libra lunar eclipse

BALANCE WORK AND HEALTH

Establish more work/life balance and de-stress, especially if your emotions are strong right now. Consider how you could make your work schedules more efficient. A more pleasing situation is on the horizon, but you must look for it. You may begin a fresh work cycle, so if one job comes to an end rest assured there will be another.

Scorpio lunar eclipse

TRANSFORM YOUR LOVE LIFE AND RELATIONSHIPS

A fresh understanding is in the making with someone close in your personal life or at work. Avoid viewing life from a purely emotional stance; be practical and realistic. Make financial and work decisions from a long-term point of view. A new activity, job or interest could take off, especially if an old chapter ends.

Sagittarius lunar eclipse
EMBRACE NEW HORIZONS

As you are a creature of habit, the Sagittarius lunar eclipse will feel disruptive but also exciting! A fresh chapter in your shared resources, such as finances or space at home, will begin due to a change of status: for example, from single to married. An inheritance may be indicated. Be bold.

Capricorn lunar eclipse
EARTH YOUR PROJECTS

Be positive about making changes in your activities and relationships; take responsibility for your own happiness. Be grounded and realistic about your projects and the people with whom you share duties and responsibilities. Avoid clinging to the past purely because it is familiar.

Aquarius lunar eclipse
BE CONFIDENT IN YOUR CAREER AND CHOICES

You'll want more stability yet also more freedom. If this sounds like a paradox it's because it sums up various aspects of your life around this time: paradoxical! Luckily, a plan at work, activity, trip or belief will gain traction the more you focus on good communications and collaboration.

Pisces lunar eclipse
ENTERTAIN NEW IDEAS, SOCIAL NETWORKS AND WORK PLANS

You may feel particularly drawn to being idealistic at this time, so remember to keep your feet on the ground. Get set for developments at work, in your status or in your general direction. For some these will revolve around groups and organisations of like-minded people.

Pisces lunar eclipse
ADOPT A HEALTHY OUTLOOK TO WORK, WELL-BEING AND SPIRITUALITY

Take the time to boost your interests and ventures by being proactive and positive about new directions and taking your plans further. Gain perspective, as you may feel emotional or even that your ideas and principles are being challenged or ignored. You are ready to step into something new at work or to embrace a fresh diet, look or spiritual understanding.

SOLAR ECLIPSES:
making major changes run smoothly

*Each solar eclipse signals a major turning point in your life
that points to ongoing change for years to come. Find out
here which solar eclipses will bring change in which areas of
your life, and how to make the most of those changes.*

Taurus solar eclipse

RECONNECT WITH YOUR VALUES AND PURPOSE

Reprioritise your activities and loyalties as it's time for a fresh cycle in your personal life (this
applies mostly to Taureans with birthdays exactly at the eclipse or just before or after), and at
work or health-wise for most other Taureans. It's important now to reconnect with what and who
means most to you. If someone opposes your will, stand firm and be kind.

Gemini solar eclipse

LOOK FOR SOLUTIONS TO FINANCIAL CONUNDRUMS

Be careful with decisions, especially regarding finances, a project or a joint investment. You may
be pleasantly surprised by the outcome of events but you must avoid snap decisions and impulsive
choices. Take the time to hone your negotiation skills.

Cancer solar eclipse

FIND SUPPORT AND PROVIDE NURTURANCE

You can plan now for a more secure future, so act to make things more stable in your life. This
may involve, for example, a better budget or cultivating a more nurturing atmosphere at home.
You may feel the need to upgrade a vehicle or digital device.

Leo solar eclipse
CO-OPERATE AND COLLABORATE

The Leo solar eclipse suggests you're ready to turn a new leaf in a particular relationship or domestic circumstance. Maintain dignity while also coming to an agreement that will be the catalyst for personal growth in your life. Avoid being at loggerheads; find solutions.

Virgo solar eclipse
ADOPT NEW STRATEGIES, SCHEDULES AND IDEAS

This eclipse will highlight your creativity and ability to get things done constructively. You may be inclined to step into new territory with your interests and ventures, and your family, domestic and personal lives will undergo positive changes as a result of good planning.

Libra solar eclipse
DEVISE A MORE WORKABLE AND EXCITING DAILY LIFE

You can improve your work and health by scheduling more of what you love in your life. You may need to help more people, such as family members, or create more time for a creative project. Let your inner artist out, as you'll find inspiration from within.

Scorpio solar eclipse
CHOOSE YOUR COMMITMENTS CAREFULLY

The Scorpio solar eclipse shines a light on a relationship. You will be ready to make a firm commitment or will, contrarily, realise a relationship has run its course. Some Taureans may receive a work boost and realise you must be more proactive and engaged at work. Be inspired.

Sagittarius solar eclipse
LOOK FOR FAIRNESS IN COLLABORATIONS

Embrace adventure! You will be drawn to a fresh course in your life, such as study or a new pastime. For some a close relationship or a change in your family and those close to you will mean you must share duties or finances differently. Be ready to step into the new and to make bold decisions with fair play in mind.

Capricorn solar eclipse

BEGIN BOLD PROJECTS, RELATIONSHIPS OR PLANS

Be prepared to begin a fresh plan, project, trip or agreement. The eclipse will illuminate various terms and conditions in a particular business or personal relationship. You may be ready to make a commitment or to vary the terms of your existing arrangement. A legal matter may be settled.

Aquarius solar eclipse

BOOST YOUR STATUS AND DIRECTION

A new career direction or status, for example from single to married, will begin. And while you prefer life on an even keel it's in your interest to enter fresh territory. Avoid clinging to something or someone you have outgrown. Developments now may come out of the blue. Try something quirky over the coming weeks and months.

Pisces solar eclipse

LEARN LIFE'S MYSTERIES

You will gain a deeper understanding of life and the role you play in it even if you feel that living life on the surface is just fine for now. A new chapter won't evolve overnight, although events will spur you on to make long-overdue changes. You'll thrive by mixing curiosity about the hidden depths of existence with being realistic.

Aries solar eclipse

REVITALISE YOUR SOCIAL AND COMMUNITY LIFE

You'll appreciate the chance to join a new group or organisation. A stronger sense of commitment to a humanitarian venture may begin. You are likely to feel more outgoing and dynamic during this time, even if it is due to pressure to be more adventurous at work or boost your health.

21 MAY - 21 JUNE

SYMBOL
Twins

ELEMENT
Air

CONSTELLATION

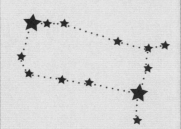

GEMINI
SUN SIGN

INNER CALLING

You are a social butterfly but you can be misunderstood as someone who is superficial and – even worse – two-faced. It is a myth that Geminis are insincere and duplicitous. You are in fact answering your inner calling to understand as much of life and of people as possible so you tend to flit from one circumstance and activity to another, seeming to rest still for just a short while before flitting to the next venture. If you occasionally change your mind it will be in response to new information that comes your way, not from duplicity.

To gain traction it's vital you slow down, resting for a longer time between flights here and there and developing your wonderful ability to see the humour in life and contribute your own typical Zen approach. You never take yourself or anyone else too seriously, and a little light-heartedness never hurt anyone.

SELF-ESTEEM

Your mercurial nature means that you tend to flit from person to person in relationships and from job to job, never allowing yourself to gain a sense of fulfilment and completeness nor strong self-esteem. Your tendency to not give yourself enough time to savour life, let alone your own abilities, can lead to low self-esteem.

As you are so fast moving you may experience a shallowness of understanding about life and relationships, especially when young, which can add to low self-esteem. The good news is that once you mature and are more inclined to commit to stable relationships and work that is enduring and fulfilling your self-esteem will grow, and because you will have experienced so many different activities your skill set will be way beyond that of other people.

HOME LIFE

As you are constantly on the move, physically fidgety and a traveller your home life will be low in your priority. Your mind is active and you're likely to spend more time outside your home than in it. Your home may even have an unsettled, impermanent vibe to it and be filled with furniture that has been hastily put together to suit your current phase in life.

As you mature you'll see how important your home life is as a place to unwind and settle your mind. You may also have more than one home or divide your time between two. Twins may run in the family or you may have more than one family; that is, a blended family or a stepmother or stepfather.

As you are such an adaptable character you should find a busy home life easy to manage. However, you may tend to feel unsettled and will enjoy updating and renovating décor so your environment changes with your needs.

RELATIONSHIPS

You are a natural-born communicator who finds initiating relationships much easier than do other sun signs. You are adept at socialising, and business negotiations are second nature to you. Commitment may only come later in life because you're likely to enjoy being free and unattached while relatively young, but once you commit to someone special you are a truly loyal partner who will demand a similar commitment. If you feel this is lacking you tend to become aloof and hard to pin down.

You may prefer to be single or free from commitments, choosing loving but freedom-based relationships especially when young. You may choose to live apart or travel frequently and may be absent from family units from time to time. However, you are fun loving and family and children are sources of great joy to you and great incentives to make commitments and create stability in your life.

CREATIVITY

Being short on spare time to develop your creativity could predispose you to not being artistic until later in life. As you are constantly on the move you may initially find the stillness and inspiration necessary to facilitate the creative process foreign to your restless temperament. However, you are an inspired communicator and may find working with images and words extremely satisfying, as your mind pours itself into frameworks that contain your vivid imagination.

PITFALLS

The sound of your own wheels constantly turning could become too loud even for you to bear. It's vital you take the time to rest and breathe or you risk burning the candle at both ends and fraying your nerves. As you are such a live wire you risk being easily distracted in all areas of your life and subsequently spreading yourself too thin. At work you will be multitalented and multiskilled but may become the classic Jack of all trades and master of none unless you focus on developing a particular skill and calling. Similarly in your personal life it's important you consciously commit to those you love, or you risk flitting from person to person.

Indecision can be a true pitfall for you, so the earlier in life you find that still centre within that provides inner guidance the better off you'll be.

SOLAR TRANSITS:
harness the sun's power
every day of the year

The sun empowers you in different areas of your life as it travels through each zodiac sign from month to month. Find out here how to make the most of your strong points during each of the transits of the sun through the 12 signs.

Sun in Gemini, May to June

GET BUSY!

Aim to bring your efforts to fruition, especially at work and health-wise. Take your time with key talks and forge fresh agreements. You're going to be busy, so schedule in 'me' time to avoid fatigue. If Mercury is retrograde you may be drawn to update your wardrobe and looks.

Sun in Cancer, June to July

SELF-NURTURE

Aim to boost your self-esteem through self-nurture by investing in a better and more nutritious diet and fitness regime, for example. You may also be inclined to nurture someone else. You may be drawn to invest in financial schemes, but you must ensure these schemes line your pockets and not someone else's.

Sun in Leo, July to August

ENJOY COMMUNICATIONS AND TRAVEL

You will be communicating well and will attract like-minded people during this phase. You may enjoy travel, and could appreciate the morale boost of feeling vibrant no matter where you are or who you are with.

Sun in Virgo, August to September

FEATHER YOUR NEST AND BOOST YOUR SKILL SET

Communications will be busy, so look for ways to boost your communication skills. A trip, community involvement and study may be a drawcard. You'll appreciate the time to improve your home environment. If Mercury is retrograde you may need to update a device or work on a vehicle, such as replacing your car's tyres.

Sun in Libra, September to October

ENJOY ROMANCE, FUN AND CREATIVITY

This phase is like a celestial season pass to activities you love, and you'll enjoy being sociable. Singles will appreciate being footloose and fancy free, and couples will enjoy adding a spritz of fun to your relationship. A holiday may appeal. Just avoid appearing frivolous, which is a real pitfall during this time.

Sun in Scorpio, October to November

IMPROVE VITALITY AT WORK, CREATIVITY AND HEALTH

Be prepared to shine at work and in your love life and family by expressing what motivates you creatively. You may feel especially drawn to art, romance and family time. This may also be a super-sexy time, so singles should mingle!

Sun in Sagittarius, November to December

BOOST YOUR LOVE LIFE AND RELATIONSHIPS

Gregarious and outgoing people will enter your environment. If you're single you may feel more outgoing yourself, enjoying the company of a diverse crowd. Couples will find this an upbeat time to add adventure to your relationship, such as a holiday or time away from the mundane. Some Twins will find this a busy time at work.

Sun in Capricorn, December to January

FOCUS ON SERIOUS JOINT DECISIONS

A focus on shared areas of your life, such as joint finances and duties, will take some of the lustre off your usual light-hearted attitude but you will manage to forge strong bonds. Some restrictions in life may be tedious but your practical side will find expression, so this is a good time for financial planning and investments and to make rational and realistic arrangements.

Sun in Aquarius, January to February
ENTER NEW TERRITORY

Your fun-loving, light-hearted qualities will come out, and pressures will slip from your shoulders as your inner maverick rises to solve problems. You may alter your perception of life and relationships. A pitfall will be that you skim over problems, allowing them to grow deeper. This is a good time to take a break, learn new skills and consider fresh perspectives.

Sun in Pisces, February to March
BOOST YOUR CAREER

Your clever projects and ventures could take shape in inspiring ways. If you work in the esoteric, healing or spiritual fields it may be a busy time. All Geminis will enjoy feeling inspired about your ventures and you could make progress; just be sure to remain practical at the same time to avoid unrealistic expectations.

Sun in Aries, March to April
SOCIALISE AND NETWORK

This is a good time to boost your friendships and love life. You may be drawn to enjoy good food and upbeat company. You will give expression to your more outgoing self, and groups and organisations that can help you to relish life such as self-development classes will appeal.

Sun in Taurus, April to May
BOOST SELF-WORTH

Be practical at work and with your health; you may experience a busy time. Some Twins may be inclined to overwork, so you must look after your nerves. Boost your health through self-care. You may be inclined to indulge in comfort food, so choose more nutritious options.

LUNAR TRANSITS:
be calm and effective every day of the month

The moon spotlights different aspects of your emotional self as it travels each month through each zodiac sign, staying two days in each sign. When the moon is in each sign you gain the opportunity to express yourself more effectively in various areas of your life. Find out here how to make the most of your strong points during each of the two days each month.

Moon in Gemini

FEEL COMFORTABLE IN YOURSELF

The moon in Gemini will bring your best attributes out: you're resourceful and able to negotiate and plan ahead. You will gain a sense of stability and security as the days go by, so trust in the positive outcome of negotiations, talks and meetings.

Moon in Cancer

BOOST INSIGHT, FINANCES AND SELF-ESTEEM

You are super sensitive and intuitive with strong instincts, which you'll do well to trust, but you may tend to overshare or even misunderstand key discussions. If you're uncertain of how to proceed or in doubt about facts during this phase do your research, especially concerning financial matters.

Moon in Leo

KICK UP YOUR HEELS!

You'll enjoy an upbeat, energising time and travel and socialising will appeal. However, you must avoid overspending as the Leo moon could bring your generosity out to a fault! This is a good time to improve relationships and to contemplate travel or take a trip.

Moon in Virgo
INCREASE DOMESTIC BLISS

You can move forward with DIY projects and communications at home, and a patient and understanding approach to circumstances will be best as you may feel a little more pedantic and meticulous. If you work from home it's a good time to steam ahead with paperwork, meetings and written projects.

Moon in Libra
INVEST IN ROMANCE, FAMILY FUN AND CREATIVITY

This is a good phase for planning as you'll be thinking in a balanced and philosophical way about your home life and love life and your family. You may be drawn to improve your décor and to invest in family dynamics. Spiritually minded Twins will enjoy deepening your beliefs.

Moon in Scorpio
IMPROVE WORK AND HEALTH

You will be super productive now and motivated to succeed. Look for balance in your work life and boost health and well-being. You'll make the most of a change of environment even if developments involve frustrating logistics.

Moon in Sagittarius
CONNECT MORE DEEPLY IN YOUR RELATIONSHIPS

This is a good time to discuss matters with someone in a progressive frame of mind with the aim of finding solutions to problems either collaboratively or yourself. Financial and personal matters will deserve careful attention to detail to avoid a gung-ho approach.

Moon in Capricorn
COLLABORATE

It's a good time to get down to the nitty-gritty with shared agreements and relationships and to go over your finances with a fine-toothed comb, putting in place a realistic budget. You may be asked to offer practical and wise support and, if you need it, it will be available from an expert.

Moon in Aquarius

THINK LATERALLY ABOUT NEW TERRITORY

You can make great progress at work and with your general plans, and may even experience the chance to move forward from circumstances that have grown stale. Be prepared to think laterally about your pastimes, activities and investments so you can enjoy life more.

Moon in Pisces

BE INSPIRED BY YOUR CAREER

Let inspiration influence your work and dreams. The Pisces moon contributes to a philosophical outlook but you must be careful with key decisions that could alter the course of your activities and direction. Seek expert help if necessary as you may see life through rose-coloured glasses during this time.

Moon in Aries

CHANNEL ENERGY INTO PRODUCTIVE ACTIVITIES

You'll feel energised and can excel socially and at work, especially through your great communication skills. However, you must avoid presupposing that everyone is on the same page as you as otherwise your energy and vitality may seem threatening.

Moon in Taurus

FOCUS ON INNER HAPPINESS

You'll appreciate the opportunity to devote a little time to your friends, groups and organisations. If interpersonal dynamics are a little strained, take the time to smooth these out. This is a good time to gain deeper appreciation of the divine nature of life, which will boost spiritual and mental health.

FULL MOONS:
magnify your vibrant power

Each full moon highlights different aspects of your power and vibrancy. Find out here which full moons will be excellent times to turn a corner in the various areas of your life to show just what you're made of.

Full moon in Gemini
SHOW JUST HOW MULTIFACETED AND SKILLED YOU ARE

Draw on your best traits, especially if an old chapter comes to an end at work, health-wise or in your personal life. Develop a fresh understanding or commitment with someone but ensure you have done your research if you are making long-term financial commitments.

Full moon in Cancer
GAIN PERSPECTIVE WITH FINANCES AND VALUES

You may feel that you are more emotional about expressing your values. Draw on your nurturing side and reconsider a personal agreement. This full moon will spotlight financial agreements for some Twins and romance for others. Singles may meet someone new, and couples could revitalise love as long as your values still align.

Full moon in Leo
SPOTLIGHT COMMUNICATION AND NEGOTIATION SKILLS

A fresh understanding with someone special is possible, for some involving paperwork and for others travel, financial, spiritual or legal matters. The Leo full moon signals an exciting if restless chapter, and breaking new ground will appeal.

Full moon in Virgo

BOOST YOUR PROSPECTS

Your analytical brain will be in full flight, so you will rise to challenges. Just avoid allowing your head to do all the talking; consult your heart and also your intuition. Bring your inner strategist out to make decisions regarding domestic matters, travel or work.

Full moon in Libra

REMEMBER ROMANCE, FUN AND CREATIVITY

Remember to boost fun and creativity in your life and you'll turn a corner relating to your home life or property. Bring more comfort and sumptuousness into your home life or love life, enjoying sensuality, perfumes, music, romance and dance.

Full moon in Scorpio

TRANSFORM WORK AND WELL-BEING

This can be an introspective time and may involve a review of your deeper needs and sense of purpose and the way you express this in your everyday life. You'll appreciate investing time in yourself and your well-being, so be prepared to embrace a fresh daily schedule at work.

Full moon in Sagittarius

TURN A CORNER IN YOUR RELATIONSHIPS

A fresh understanding in a key relationship is signalled by this full moon. You are in a position to renegotiate arrangements that could provide an upbeat way ahead, but you must be super clear about the terms. A new way to share your resources, finances or even work duties will be a catalyst.

Full moon in Capricorn

SEE SHARED RESPONSIBILITIES IN A NEW LIGHT

You may alter financial agreements and personal arrangements. This may be an intense but enjoyable time of change, so aim to overcome speed bumps. You could avert a difficult financial circumstance by using your excellent communication skills.

Full moon in Aquarius

TAKE THE INITIATIVE AND WELCOME ADVENTURE

This full moon will spotlight a turning point with a favourite activity, project, trip or simply your own interests. You may feel more independent and be drawn to spiritual ideas and belief systems that are a little unorthodox, or will enjoy expressing a quirky aspect of yourself.

Full moon in Pisces

BOOST ASPECTS OF YOUR CAREER THAT YOU LOVE

The Pisces full moon will spotlight an enjoyable area of your work or general interests and activities. If your career is lacklustre, prepare to be more inspired by stepping into new territory. You may, however, be forgetful or idealistic, so ensure you focus that little bit extra on the details.

Full moon in Aries

REVITALISE YOUR SOCIAL LIFE

You may enjoy joining a new club or circle. Meetings or a turn of events signal a fresh direction or an opportunity. If you're single, you may meet an upbeat and sociable character; couples will enjoy infusing your relationship with vitality and new interests.

Full moon in Taurus

CREATE A STRONG FOUNDATION

Take things in your stride, but be prepared to make key decisions that could create more stability in your life. You can build strong foundations at work, health-wise and with a beloved project. Ensure you're happy with the general terms, as these could be in place for a long time.

NEW MOONS:
start something fresh

Each new moon points to the start of something fresh for you in different areas of your life. Find out here which new moon to work with and how to make lasting change by starting something new, especially if you have been putting off change for some time.

New moon in Gemini

UPDATE YOUR LIFE

A fresh chapter is beginning. To be true to yourself means sometimes taking calculated risks, so ask yourself this: has risk-taking worked for you in the past? If so you may surge ahead now with clever decisions, but if not you must research circumstances. You're a maverick and only you know if new ideas will work.

New moon in Cancer

PROMOTE YOUR TALENTS

The Cancer new moon is a good time for self-promotion, so be bold and step up! Confidence holds the key to success, especially with someone special and financially. You'll find your work and relationships will feel more rewarding.

New moon in Leo

BEGIN NEW PROJECTS AND NEGOTIATIONS

Dust off your networking skills, as opportunities could open doors and broaden your mind. Key news, a trip or a visit will bring changes to your environment. A new undertaking concerning a work contract, agreement or romantic commitment may be on the way.

New moon in Virgo

EMBRACE CLEVER IDEAS

You'll gain perspective at this new moon, finding out where you could do better and where you already excel. This will be at home for some Twins, and with certain relationships or a trip for others. It's a good time to instigate domestic, transport and digital repairs and updates.

New moon in Libra

TURN A NEW LEAF IN YOUR PERSONAL LIFE

This is a good time to aim to improve happiness, and specifically dynamics in your domestic life and romantically. Some issues may revolve around making duties fairer and more equal. Creative Twins may experience a productive time. It's a good time to plan a family and for more romance.

New moon in Scorpio

RE-IMAGINE WORK AND HEALTH

Meetings in your personal life will naturally incline towards activities that involve creativity, family and romance, which you'll love. This is an excellent time to channel excess energy or frustrations into a new fitness regime, which will increase your energy reserves so you can take on an extra workload that may keep you busy for several months.

New moon in Sagittarius

REVITALISE YOUR LOVE LIFE AND RELATIONSHIPS

You'll feel more audacious and adventurous in life in general, but must avoid rushing into decisions. The Sagittarius new moon will feel refreshing relationship-wise for Twins born at the new moon or before, and at work or health-wise for Twins born after the new moon.

New moon in Capricorn

MAKE A FRESH COMMITMENT OR AGREEMENT

You could gain more stability in a collaborative or co-operative venture. Do your research and you could make steady progress in a fair-minded and even-tempered negotiation. A work contract or agreement could prove to be stabilising in the long term.

New moon in Aquarius

INITIATE FRESH VENTURES

Maintain an open mind. This is an ideal new moon for finding direction, especially if you are looking for new opportunities through travel or study, for example. You may discover renewed interest in a favourite activity. This is a good time to begin new sporting or spiritual endeavours, and also for legal enquiries.

New moon in Pisces

CHASE DREAMS

Be inspired and chase a dream, but ensure you're also practical or your imagination could run away with you. You'll gain the opportunity to learn more about life and to deepen your understanding of yourself. For some, opportunities will be via a new work project while for others it will be via a change in relationship status, study, a trip or a legal matter.

New moon in Aries

SOCIALISE AND NETWORK

You'll feel more outgoing, positive and sociable and will appreciate the chance to begin fresh projects with upbeat people. It's a good time to start a new job or initiate a new venture, so ensure you take the initiative with your various projects and ideas.

New moon in Taurus

GAIN MORE STABILITY

Take the initiative if you're looking for more security in life. If you're looking for job security, start discussions that could bring this about. This may also be a sociable time, especially if you've been a hermit recently, but if you've been super sociable you're likely to feel more inclined to enjoy the comforts of home. It's a good time to begin a stable health routine.

LUNAR ECLIPSES:
be strong during peak emotional changes

Each lunar eclipse signals a major turning point in your life and may bring about intense emotions. Eclipses point to circumstances that seem to disempower you and subsequently motivate you to address any imbalances, so keep an eye on those areas in which you lack control as that is where you can make the most changes and become strong. Find out here which lunar eclipse will bring change in which area of your life, and how to make the most of these changes.

Gemini lunar eclipse
MANAGE FREEDOM OF MOVEMENT

You'll manage a change in your personal life well, as you're the most adaptable sign of the zodiac. If you're single you may meet someone new; if a couple you may look for more autonomy or wish to find ways to be more light-hearted and to bring a fun element into your partnership. For some Twins this lunar eclipse signals a new health or work routine.

Cancer lunar eclipse
REVIEW FINANCIAL AND EMOTIONAL INVESTMENTS

You may be ready to change the way you share responsibilities and communal space, finances or duties. For some this will be in connection with developments at home or with someone special. Be prepared to review how much you invest in activities, people and values. Above all, nurture yourself.

Leo lunar eclipse

BE DECISIVE

Conversations and agreements will need attention. Some people will be particularly supportive; others may prove their loyalty lies elsewhere. Be decisive about where you want key relationships to go, otherwise your indecision could put you at a disadvantage. A key trip may be a catalyst for a decision.

Virgo lunar eclipse

BE CONSTRUCTIVE WITH TALKS AND NEGOTIATIONS

You'll proceed with more certainty in an area that has been sketchy, even if events draw on your inner resources. Positive talks and negotiations will be the key to your success. Events will include the chance to promote yourself, to improve your communications and to gain direction in a key venture.

Libra lunar eclipse

FEATHER YOUR NEST

As the most adaptable sign of the zodiac, you are best equipped to bend with developments now. Plan to feather your nest so you have a soft landing after the inevitable changes this lunar eclipse will bring that will affect your daily life and home and/or family situation.

Scorpio lunar eclipse

CHOOSE YOUR ACTIVITIES AND LOYALTIES

This could be a passionate, emotional time and you must make valid, informed choices despite strong emotions. Adopt a fresh approach to work, family and your own abilities. You must invest more completely in your endeavours, especially as you may be under pressure either from others or via inner tension.

Sagittarius lunar eclipse

DISCOVER NEW ASPECTS OF YOUR RELATIONSHIPS

A relationship development will involve either your personal partner or family members or your work circumstances. This eclipse will bring your independent streak to the surface, and you will discover new aspects of your work and relationship skills. Be bold and strong but maintain loyalty to those you love.

Capricorn lunar eclipse

TURN A CORNER WITH SHARED INCENTIVES

Use your excellent communication skills to avert a difficult financial circumstance. The Capricorn lunar eclipse points to a fresh phase, especially with shared responsibilities. You may alter financial agreements and personal arrangements. This may be an intense but enjoyable time, so aim to overcome speed bumps.

Aquarius lunar eclipse

FIND NEW WAYS TO COLLABORATE

A fresh agreement in shared areas such as duties or finances will arise. A new contract may be on the table. Your involvement with organisations and friends will be in the spotlight, as you'll appreciate the opportunity to co-operate in new ways.

Pisces lunar eclipse

BE INSPIRED BY YOUR INTERESTS

You'll feel inspired to turn a leaf with a new venture, study, travel or someone special. It's important to take the initiative with new ventures but also to be discerning, as your imagination may easily run away with you and leave practicalities a poor second place to your impulses.

Aries lunar eclipse

EMBRACE A NEW DIRECTION

Show what you're made of as a new chapter opens that affects your status, direction and, for some, career. If you are bold and courageous you could accomplish a great deal. Avoid being daunted by the doubts of others or being put under unnecessary pressure.

Taurus lunar eclipse

AIM TO REVITALISE ON ALL LEVELS

This eclipse marks the end of a long phase. Some Twins will wave goodbye to the past, whether a job, past friendship or affiliation with a group or organisation. You may also let go of a bad habit. Health may require focus, and you'll get the chance to adopt a self-care schedule or a care package for someone else.

SOLAR ECLIPSES:
making major changes run smoothly

Each solar eclipse signals a major turning point in your life that points to ongoing change for years to come. Find out here which solar eclipses will bring change in which areas of your life, and how to make the most of those changes.

Gemini solar eclipse
TIME FOR 2.0

Get ready to reveal a new you, especially if the eclipse falls on your birthday. For some change will arise in your personal life, while for others it will be at work. Use your considerable communication skills for careful negotiations to avoid dramas. You may feel eclipsed by someone else's power but will find clever ways to be true to yourself – and to develop an even better version of you!

Cancer solar eclipse
MONITOR FINANCES AND PERSONAL TIES

Be careful with transactions and interactions. You may be easily affected by someone's opinions and influence. You may be drawn to cut ties suddenly or to assume responsibility for someone else's actions. Maintain focus on your values and self-esteem.

Leo solar eclipse
ALTER RELATIONSHIP DYNAMICS

You may be ready to change the context of a relationship, investment or collaboration that involves logistical conundrums, but it will be worthwhile. Weigh up the level of upheaval versus the outcome: if the upheaval is worth it, take action. A fresh financial agreement may arise.

Virgo solar eclipse

EMBRACE BETTER RELATIONSHIP DYNAMICS

If you work in communications you are most likely to see great change at work. For others developments will occur at home, and you may be particularly invested in the details of the changes you undertake now such as DIY projects, gardening or building. Some Twins will deepen spiritual development as a way to understand others better.

Libra solar eclipse

BE CREATIVE ABOUT DOMESTIC CHANGE

Infuse your life with a sense of healing and well-being. Creative Twins could be particularly busy as a project grabs your attention. A family matter may require a balanced decision. A new opportunity may come out of nowhere, or you will be ready to initiate change yourself at home or with family or property.

Scorpio solar eclipse

BOOST WORK FULFILMENT

This eclipse will spotlight ways you could be more proactive about pursuing your purpose through your daily activities and work. A fresh health, work or daily routine will enable you to alter some of your usual schedule, so aim to be adaptable now to gain more time for yourself and a sense of fulfilment.

Sagittarius solar eclipse

CONSIDER A FRESH COMMITMENT

This eclipse will alter your commitments, be these at work or in your personal life. You may even experience a change with a creative or personal venture. If you're single you may decide you're ready to commit; partners may look for more adventure in your relationship, which could be expressed via a desire to travel or have more independence.

Capricorn solar eclipse

NEGOTIATE AN AGREEMENT

A fresh chapter will begin in a shared venture or partnership. Be ready to discuss the terms and to arrange a new understanding. Avoid underselling yourself, aiming instead to provide stronger foundations for yourself. You may need to interact with key authoritarian figures or undergo a legal battle, so take the time to consider your priorities.

Aquarius solar eclipse

EMBRACE FRESH INTERESTS

You may already have an inkling of events that signal a turning point in your life. News from a friend, group or organisation will mean changes and at the least will engage your curiosity. You are likely to be busy or highly mentally stimulated, so avoid being easily distracted and take time to research your true options.

Pisces solar eclipse

ADD SPARKLE AND INTEREST TO YOUR LIFE

A high-impact phase will be kick-started around this solar eclipse that will add mystery to your life and highlight where you could bring more synchronicity and magic into being. Be prepared to adapt to new circumstances or for a change of plans. You could move mountains, but in the process you may make waves when you'd be better off taking things one step at a time.

Aries solar eclipse

LOOK FOR A POSITIVE AND NON-DISRUPTIVE PATH

You are ready to kick-start a fresh project or venture. Maintain focus on your goals, sense of purpose and meaning in life. Avoid snap decisions during this phase as transits through Aries have a tendency to bring sudden and impromptu events your way. Avoid making changes simply out of restlessness.

Taurus solar eclipse

KICK-START A SUPPORTIVE DAILY ROUTINE

Find ways to be practical and grounded, and avoid actions that could limit your long-term growth. A new chapter with a group, friend or organisation could be supportive. Be methodical and realistic, especially financially and with work and health.

21 JUNE - 22 JULY

SYMBOL
Crab

ELEMENT
Water

CONSTELLATION

CANCER
SUN SIGN

INNER CALLING

Your inner calling is to masterfully and yet delicately combine your abilities to stand tall and be assertive with your softer, inner sensitivities. In this way you are able to use your considerable intuitive skills in productive ways. You are an extremely caring individual, and the more you use your nurturing abilities in creative, productive ways the more this nurturing and caring energy will flow through your life, bringing nurturance not only to yourself but also to those you love. In this way you'll feel buoyed in life as the cycle of love comes full circle back to you one hundredfold.

To be assertive it's important that you develop your intuition and instincts, otherwise you risk being uncertain about so many important choices that will come your way. You may also find yourself in a constant state of frustration as your most assertive side wishes to steam ahead and be counted in life yet your uncertainty holds you back.

Your sign's ruler, the moon, is your backbone. It is the most intuitive and instinctive of influences astrologically, so the more you learn to trust these aspects of yourself the more they will empower you to be the best version of yourself.

Psychic development, even if you do not wish to be a professional psychic, will benefit you, as will assertiveness training.

SELF-ESTEEM

You can tend to feel daunted by other people's egos, especially when young, as you are such a gentle, sensitive character at heart, so it's important to find ways to boost your sense of self from an early age. As you are essentially a strong character yourself and naturally have high self-esteem, this tendency to feel inferior can lead to frustration and aggression unless you find ways to lovingly assert yourself.

You will gain solid self-esteem by focusing on your independent ability to be strong and a leader. You may even surprise yourself by your inner strength. You are one of the four cardinal signs (the others being Aries, Libra and Capricorn) and, as such, you are a born leader and have a strong backbone. Believe in yourself and you will find ways to overcome the aspect of sensitivity that can lead to insecurity.

By strengthening your self-esteem, your sensitivity can then become a source of great value, as your intuition and instincts will find a conduit to help you in life rather than make you feel vulnerable or inferior. You know how to fight for your rights and make a worthy opponent, but it's better for you to not have to enter into battle.

HOME LIFE

Your home is important to you, far more than it is for any other sun sign. Your family is also supremely important and, even if during various phases of your life you do not like your home or family, they will nevertheless have deep influences over you. It is thus important to find ways to provide the comfort and nurturance you need from your home life and family, which you can do by focusing on maintaining a sense of belonging and security.

When things go awry at home it can affect your entire demeanour and even the way you approach your work and relationships. This is all the more reason to find ways to provide the comfort and sumptuousness you need in life so you have a place to retreat from all the chaos outside.

RELATIONSHIPS

Maintaining positive relationships feeds your soul, so if you feel discordant within key relationships, especially at home, you can feel truly put out. Romance in particular feeds your soul, and you will love providing the ideal atmosphere in which to indulge in sensuality and love.

Family relationships are vital to your self-development and you are formed by these as a youngster. You are truly sensitive, even if you build a tough outer shell to maintain a sense of optimism and strength when you feel the undercurrents of the moods of others. Be aware that you are empathic, and your moods may stem as much from your own sensitivity as they do from picking up on other people's moods. Find ways to be certain of what are your own emotions and what are those of other people or you may find yourself on an emotional roller coaster.

When you first meet a prospective partner, use your excellent instincts to assess whether they are truly suitable. Your intuition will not let you down.

CREATIVITY

Writing, singing, art, music and dance will all appeal to your romantic soul. Your sign's ruler, the moon, controls words, both spoken and written, so you will love to talk, write and read. Your creativity in the bigger picture stretches to your enjoyment of family, literally to your ability to create another life and then to care for it.

You will enjoy using your creative abilities in relation to family, property and, broadly speaking, your domestic life. You may enjoy working with property, in property and for property, in sales, development, building and décor. The more you express your creativity the more abundant and assertive you feel, so clicking into your creativity is a sure-fire recipe for success.

PITFALLS

Being so sensitive means you can be easily influenced by other people, then liable to be resentful if you discover you have been persuaded into actions that do not resonate with you on a deep level. It is therefore important to self-monitor that you are not being influenced in areas that are meaningless to you.

You may fall in love easily as you are such a romantic soul, so before you do so double check that your prospective lover or partner has similar values to yours or you will easily be misled by their ideas, feeling ultimately that you are living your life to their principles and values rather than according to your own.

SOLAR TRANSITS:
harness the sun's power
every day of the year

The sun empowers you in different areas of your life as it travels through each zodiac sign from month to month. Find out here how to make the most of your strong points during each of the transits of the sun through the 12 signs.

Sun in Cancer, June to July
POWER UP!

The sun in your own sign for four weeks will feel empowering. You will feel quite proactive and likely to be more daring and bold. A heads-up, though: people may find you a little bossy unless you are careful to express your caring side. You will be more self-confident, making this a good time to step up your plans, aims and dreams.

Sun in Leo, July to August
BOOST YOUR LUST FOR LIFE

You'll enjoy breathing fresh air into your activities and will enjoy the company of those you love, such as family and friends. You may improve your finances, but will as a result tend to spend time and money on treats. If you're in debt avoid deepening it, and if you're trying to lose weight be careful now as the reverse may occur!

Sun in Virgo, August to September
UPDATE IDEAS AND PLANS

This is a good time to touch base with your principles and values and check you are up to date with circumstances such as world events and the situation of people close to you. Could you update your ideas so they sit better with current times? It's also a good time to put in place a solid budget. You may be drawn to travel.

Sun in Libra, September to October

BRING PEACE INTO YOUR HOME LIFE

You'll appreciate the opportunity to establish more balance and harmony in your home and relationships, but avoid passing a sentence on those who are disruptive in your life as they may not appreciate being told how to behave! Aim to bring peaceful vibes into your home and relationships by setting a good example through being gentle, sensitive and loving.

Sun in Scorpio, October to November

FOCUS ON FUN AND CREATIVITY

Are you putting enough energy into your domestic life, family and property? If not, now's the time to flood these areas with attention. You can rely on your intuition, and it's a good time to boost spiritual, meditative and psychic abilities. Rest assured you will overcome a hurdle should one arise, but you must avoid having a combative approach.

Sun in Sagittarius, November to December

BE ADVENTUROUS WITH WORK AND HEALTH

A sense of discovery and optimism will grow in your activities. You may be busier at work, or will enjoy socialising and spending more time with friends and family. Creative Crabs may be super inventive and could see progress with artistic efforts. You may be drawn to improve health and fitness and travel will appeal.

Sun in Capricorn, December to January

CREATE STABILITY IN YOUR RELATIONSHIPS

It's a good time to work towards a solid commitment in your love life. Take practical steps to get ahead with collaborations via teamwork and realistic step-by-step planning at work. Be realistic about commitments and plan work and health schedules so they work better for you in logistical terms.

Sun in Aquarius, January to February

COLLABORATE ON JOINT DECISIONS

Invest time and energy into business or personal collaborations; you'll enjoy breathing fresh air into your relationships. This is a good phase to trust in your wisdom and experience but also to be open to the ideas of others. You may be drawn to a different kind of social circle and will gain experience as a result.

Sun in Pisces, February to March

SEEK INSPIRATION

The sun in Pisces will bring your inner romantic out. You will enjoy the arts, candlelight, indulging in your creative side and connecting with people on an intuitive level. Artistic, healing or spiritual work can move ahead in leaps and bounds; however, if you're considering an investment it's important to check the details to avoid mistakes.

Sun in Aries, March to April

BOOST YOUR CAREER

You'll rise to challenges when the sun is in Aries, especially in the field of work and exciting ventures. If obstacles arise, avoid feeling that it's down to you alone to overcome these; seek collaboration and support. You may feel a little feisty, so aim to relax when you can.

Sun in Taurus, April to May

ENJOY ACTIVITIES YOU LOVE

When the sun is at the zenith of your chart you feel at your most optimistic. You will savour expressing yourself through music and dance and enjoy the company of like-minded people. Your values may be uppermost in your mind, so embrace and express your principles now both at work and at play.

Sun in Gemini, May to June

DEVELOP A STRONG WORK ETHIC AND GOOD HEALTH

You'll enjoy diversifying your interests and friendship circles. You may find a group, organisation or friend helpful. Be prepared to communicate with a new circle, at work or socially. Meetings with mentors, teachers and advisers will be fruitful. This is a good time to alter and improve work and health practices.

LUNAR TRANSITS:
be calm and effective every day of the month

The moon spotlights different aspects of your emotional self as it travels each month through each zodiac sign, staying two days in each sign. When the moon is in each sign you gain the opportunity to express yourself more effectively in various areas of your life. Find out here how to make the most of your strong points during each of the two days each month.

Moon in Cancer

WHEN YOU FEEL MOST COMFORTABLE IN YOURSELF

You'll feel more in sync with events and your intuition may be spot on over these two days. The Cancer moon makes for a romantic outlook; however, if you feel overwhelmed by events you must move one step at a time. Avoid being easily influenced, as this will be a true pitfall during this two-day phase.

Moon in Leo

BOOST YOUR CONFIDENCE

You'll appreciate a change of pace but may also find the Leo moon creates a restless feeling. This will be a good time to channel restlessness into positive self-talk and believing your productive pursuits can catapult your projects into a more dynamic circumstance, especially financially and at work.

Moon in Virgo

IMPROVE COMMUNICATIONS AND TRAVEL

Rely on your common sense and self-confidence as you can make great progress both at work and in your agreements and relationships. Just avoid pushing for results and impulsive decisions for the best measure. Financial and travel matters could progress with due planning.

Moon in Libra

INCREASE DOMESTIC BLISS

During this time you will gain a matter-of-fact yet sensitive outlook towards others. You may get insight into someone close at home, either a partner or family member, which could help you gain more balance and harmony in life. It's a good time for psychic development.

Moon in Scorpio

INVEST IN ROMANCE, FAMILY FUN AND CREATIVITY

Your emotions or those of someone close are likely to be strong, and when all is going well this can point to a fabulously passionate time. But if conflict is brewing, keep things in perspective. You will reconnect with your intuition. Art, music and romance will all inspire you.

Moon in Sagittarius

RE-ENERGISE WORK AND HEALTH

The key to success during the Sagittarius moon? Good communication skills and a positive outlook. You'll appreciate the opportunity to be a little more outgoing in your daily schedule and to approach work and health with renewed vitality and sparkle.

Moon in Capricorn

BOOST YOUR LOVE LIFE AND RELATIONSHIPS

Give practicalities your full attention, especially in negotiations and partnerships. You'll appreciate the opportunity to put in place solid commitments but must avoid limiting your self-expression and options too much. This is a good time for a health check or to invest more in health.

Moon in Aquarius

BE OPEN TO COLLABORATING

You'll enjoy being creative and thinking laterally, especially about investments, finances and shared responsibilities. Romance could blossom, so take the initiative. You'll enjoy the company of upbeat and inventive or even unorthodox characters who may illuminate positive ways to collaborate better.

Moon in Pisces
FOLLOW YOUR INSPIRATION

You'll feel inspired to follow your creative ideas and let your inner artist out when the moon is in Pisces; just be aware that you may be forgetful or super idealistic. Romance could flourish, as will your interest in the arts, spirituality, study and, for some, travel.

Moon in Aries
TAKE THE INITIATIVE WITH YOUR CAREER

You will feel productive and motivated. Good results at work due to better productivity will be just what you want to keep your mood positive. An Aries moon can bring other people's feistiness out – and your own! If someone behaves out of character, look for solutions rather than problems and avoid being intimidated by aggressive people.

Moon in Taurus
SOCIALISE AND NETWORK

What makes your heart sing? You have permission to indulge in life's delights, to socialise and be with those you love, and you're likely to enjoy doing just that! You'll enjoy showing off your work skills, but if finances are short live to your budget as you may be inclined to splurge.

Moon in Gemini
FOCUS ON PRIORITIES AND INNER HEALTH

You will gain insight into a health, personal or work matter, but you must focus or you may be forgetful or even appear flippant during this time. To remain practical and effective, find ways to earth yourself. You are intuitive, but you can also be easily distracted by emotions and undercurrents.

FULL MOONS:
magnify your vibrant power

*Each full moon highlights different aspects of your power and vibrancy.
Find out here which full moons will be excellent times to turn a corner
in the various areas of your life to show just what you're made of.*

Full moon in Cancer
EMBRACE YOUR POTENTIAL

It's time to turn a corner. You may be drawn to reveal a deeper, more caring you. You may feel particularly emotional, intuitive or instinctive, so remember you can self-empower and choose the life you want to live. A new look and health routine may appeal.

Full moon in Leo
FIRE UP SELF-ESTEEM

The Leo full moon will empower you to be more adventurous and confident. In the process you may encounter a strong character who has influence over you, so be bold but avoid snap decisions you may regret, especially financially.

Full moon in Virgo
IMPROVE SELF-EXPRESSION

You may be drawn to express two different aspects of yourself: the romantic, sensitive you, and the practical, realistic you who is keen to avoid making mistakes. An approach that combines the two qualities will work wonders, especially with meetings, travel plans and finances. When you express your values clearly and concisely major decisions will become clear.

Full moon in Libra

BRING BALANCE TO YOUR ENVIRONMENT AND HOME

You will be drawn to establishing a more calming and uplifting environment and to finding ways to soothe your nerves. If arguments are brewing avoid a Mexican stand-off; be ready to make agreements and to establish your common aims.

Full moon in Scorpio

RE-INVEST IN ROMANCE, FUN AND CREATIVITY

You may feel intense emotions regarding someone close, so take time out if necessary. Changes regarding your personal life, property or a creative project may signify the end of a cycle. Rest assured new plans will revitalise close relationships and interests.

Full moon in Sagittarius

BEGIN A FRESH DAILY ROUTINE

Developments will provide you with more direction, both in your personal life and at work. Consider how you feel most adventurous and motivated, as this is a good time to instigate a revitalising, dynamic work and health routine. A new understanding with someone important could be ideal, but this will depend on establishing the correct facts and figures.

Full moon in Capricorn

TURN A CORNER IN YOUR RELATIONSHIPS

This can be a decisive time that brings a great deal more security into a relationship, even if certain commitments must be made first to make the changes take. Romance could blossom. Avoid conflict and show just how level-headed you are. For some, though, this full moon could mark the time is ripe to go your separate ways.

Full moon in Aquarius

TAKE THE INITIATIVE WITH COLLABORATIONS

A fresh, unorthodox or unexpected chapter is about to begin in the way you share resources such as communal finances, space at home or everyday duties. This may involve a new agreement with a business or personal partner, and news that arrives will mean you must look outside the box at your options and carve out new agreements.

Full moon in Pisces

DEEPEN YOUR UNDERSTANDING OF LIFE

The Pisces full moon will bring increased romance and spirituality into your life. If you're single you may meet an alluring character. If you're making long-term financial decisions, avoid being idealistic and deal only with the facts. You may be drawn to study, to alter key arrangements and to travel.

Full moon in Aries

BOOST YOUR KUDOS AND IMPACT

Take the initiative; be bold and practical and your interests, key connections and rewarding events will soon materialise. A new project or a considerable change of activity and pastimes will appeal.

Full moon in Taurus

INVEST IN YOUR STATUS AND INTERESTS

Consider how to gain more security and stability. You may begin a fresh career phase, or a change in direction will provide you with the stability and security you need. This is a good time to focus on changing some of your activities, travel, spiritual endeavours or legal agreements.

Full moon in Gemini

CHOOSE PRIORITIES AND GOOD HEALTH

The choices you make can really change the outcome of your life, so if you're unsure of a decision seek expert advice and also trust your instincts. Your affiliation with a group or organisation may come to an end at this time, and you'll look for new friendships and allegiances. Romance could blossom, so be open to love.

NEW MOONS:
start something fresh

Each new moon points to the start of something fresh for you in different areas of your life. Find out here which new moon to work with and how to make lasting change by starting something new, especially if you have been putting off change for some time.

New moon in Cancer
PUT YOURSELF FIRST

The Cancer new moon really is the best time to start a fresh chapter in your life. This will involve an appreciation of your brilliance: your work and/or daily routine and your helpfulness and kindness. For some it's the chance to deepen your commitment to your self-healing and independence. A partnership or joint venture could flourish, as could romance.

New moon in Leo
BELIEVE IN YOURSELF

You will wish to succeed at a particular job or to boost your finances or status and hard work will certainly bring results, especially when you collaborate with people you know are on your side. Keep an eye on your values and principles to avoid making mistakes. Believe in yourself and don't make snap judgements or be overly generous financially.

New moon in Virgo
TURN A CORNER WITH RELATIONSHIPS AND PROJECTS

This is a good time to make new commitments and to put in place a solid structure for projects and finances. If you tend to look at your projects idealistically you'll gain perspective about the basics and the realities of your circumstances, enabling you to fix a mistake if this should arise (especially financially). You may step up the career ladder and gain better self-esteem as a result.

New moon in Libra
CREATE A HAPPIER ENVIRONMENT

You may be drawn to update décor or carry out DIY projects or even move. This is a good time to update contracts, paperwork and communications so you are more comfortable about your agreements. You may initiate a trip and be ready to set things straight that have been hard work. A new communications device or vehicle may appeal as it will make life easier.

New moon in Scorpio
CREATE DEEPER CONNECTIONS

This is a good time to start a fresh, exciting chapter in your personal life such as a change with family or a partner or a new friendship or lover. For some, though, developments will revolve around your deepening spirituality. Some people will understand the deeper you, and these are the relationships that will flourish now.

New moon in Sagittarius
INNOVATE AND BROADEN YOUR HORIZONS

Success will flourish with an outgoing approach, because where previous ventures have failed this new moon suggests it's time for something fresh. Be bold and approach your work and personal investments from a long-term viewpoint. New opportunities to broaden your knowledge and experience will arise.

New moon in Capricorn
LOOK FOR COMMITMENT IN A RELATIONSHIP

This is a good time to begin a fresh agreement. For some Crabs it will be in your personal life, such as a fresh commitment to a partner, while for others a fresh work contract may be agreed upon. Aim to put into action new agreements that bring more stability into your life, but avoid compromising on your beliefs.

New moon in Aquarius
START A NEW COLLABORATION

If you want to share your resources, space or duties in a fresh way, this is it! It's a good time to share your time and energy together in more inspired and innovative ways and to kick-start a fresh financial arrangement. If making long-term decisions, ensure you have all the facts before committing to plans.

New moon in Pisces

BE INSPIRED BY YOUR DREAMS

Aim to revitalise your status, general direction and career. It's a good time to fully express your spiritual ideas and compassionate sense of caring and understanding. You may be particularly intuitive, so this is a good time to follow your instincts if you wish to begin a fresh project or revitalise or end a key relationship such as a marriage. However, you must avoid being misled.

New moon in Aries

BE MORE ADVENTUROUS AND OUTGOING

Be proactive and upbeat about your projects, especially at work. Plant seeds for a more empowered future. Re-align yourself with your various priorities, and put your attention where it is most needed to kick-start a new venture or make the most of an opportunity.

New moon in Taurus

CREATE SOLID FOUNDATIONS

This is a great time to plant seeds for long-term plans, projects and your career. You'll appreciate the chance to improve your circumstances and create solid foundations, but if things seem stuck find ways to gently budge them rather than staying stalled or starting conflict. A group, organisation or friend may prove helpful.

New moon in Gemini

DIVERSIFY AT WORK AND SOCIALISE AND NETWORK

This is a good time to be more adaptable at work and with your daily schedule but you must make decisions based on facts, not supposition. Your social life may be more upbeat and you will meet people from diverse backgrounds. You may meet a fun crowd or feel more light-hearted.

LUNAR ECLIPSES:
be strong during peak emotional changes

Each lunar eclipse signals a major turning point in your life and may bring about intense emotions. Eclipses point to circumstances that seem to disempower you and subsequently motivate you to address any imbalances, so keep an eye on those areas in which you lack control as that is where you can make the most changes and become strong. Find out here which lunar eclipse will bring change in which area of your life, and how to make the most of these changes.

Cancer lunar eclipse
DEEPEN YOUR INTUITION

Trust your instincts. You are likely to be super emotional, which will cloud your judgement. Focus on positive, constructive ways to leave someone or something behind in your personal life or at work. Your interest in spirituality may deepen.

Leo lunar eclipse
BE MORE ASSERTIVE ABOUT MONEY AND PRINCIPLES

Find ways to be assertive without appearing domineering or bossy when expressing your values. Aim to clarify financial matters so you can work on other matters that require more focus such as relationships, love and the activities you adore.

Virgo lunar eclipse
REPURPOSE TIME AND ENERGY

The amount of focus you place on areas you cherish, such as your space at home, money and time, will begin to change as you align your ideas with practicalities and who and what means the most to you. You'll enjoy moving forward with an assertive rather than aggressive approach.

Libra lunar eclipse

DEVELOP A CALM ATTITUDE

Communications could be complex or feisty during this phase, so the most productive approach will be to establish a calm attitude to smooth the way forward. A turning point concerning your decisions, travel or key relationships may be reached during this time.

Scorpio lunar eclipse

CREATE ORDER OUT OF CHAOS

During a Scorpio lunar eclipse phase you may be particularly emotional and sensitive. If you have developed your psychic abilities you may be super intuitive during this time, which will bring order to chaos. Make time to fact find your circumstances, and maintain perspective through meditation, yoga and fitness.

Sagittarius lunar eclipse

RE-INVENT YOUR DAILY LIFE

Your daily schedule will change considerably due to developments either at work or with your family. You may need to go out on a limb, so be bold. If you're health conscious you will find this a key time to invest more in your health and fitness.

Capricorn lunar eclipse

BE LEVEL HEADED IN A KEY RELATIONSHIP

This will be a decisive time, and you could bring a great deal more stability into a relationship even if certain commitments must first be made. Romance could blossom, but if a difference of opinion or a battle of wills derails your romantic plans, avoid conflict and show how level-headed you are. Consider perhaps if the relationship is no longer viable.

Aquarius lunar eclipse

COLLABORATE INNOVATIVELY

The more constructive and practical yet also imaginative you are with new and exciting projects and collaborations the more these will flourish. You could gain the upper hand in a business sense. Ensure you are in the right place financially and take the time to review agreements.

Pisces lunar eclipse
SHARE IN AN INSPIRED WAY

How do you share resourcessuch as finances, space at home and responsibilities? A new agreement with a business or personal partner may bring out your quirkier side, and you may wish to find more inspired ways to share assets and duties. Trust that spiritual and psychic research will add insight and be guided by your instincts.

Aries lunar eclipse
BE PROACTIVE ABOUT CHANGE

This eclipse will spotlight your feelings about projects, interests and pastimes. Take decisive action, even if not everyone agrees with you. If a disagreement arises view it philosophically, and try to establish common ground with loved ones so you can move forward. But if certain relationships are irreparable this lunar eclipse could signal it is time for a fresh, independent chapter.

Taurus lunar eclipse
EMBRACE A NEW DIRECTION

The Taurus lunar eclipse signals a change of status, peer group or career. For some it can mean a move as you accommodate a new domestic chapter in your life. This is a good time to focus on practicalities and take a reasonable, realistic approach to changes, especially if you feel emotional or if life is chaotic.

Gemini lunar eclipse
ADAPT TO A FRESH DAILY LIFE

For some Cancerians new arrangements will be at work, while for others they will be within a relationship. You may be ready to make a commitment to a new path or will need to negotiate new terms. Avoid snap decisions but be flexible. For some there will be a focus on the need to be better informed about health circumstances.

SOLAR ECLIPSES:
making major changes run smoothly

Each solar eclipse signals a major turning point in your life that points to ongoing change for years to come. Find out here which solar eclipses will bring change in which areas of your life, and how to make the most of those changes.

Cancer solar eclipse

SELF-TRANSFORMATION

Considerable transformation will arise, either personally or in your status and especially if it's your birthday at the eclipse. You will feel strongly about certain matters and your intense and warrior-like personality traits will seek expression, even if your first inclination is to sidestep conflict. Be strong but also willing to see another's point of view.

Leo solar eclipse

REBALANCE RELATIONSHIPS AND SELF-EXPRESSION

Relationships cannot thrive without a balance of power, and at this time you'll discover which relationships need rebalancing. You may need to rethink a personal commitment. Consider where your personal power sits, and also how your finances express your power. Will you go next level and become more communicative and outgoing? This is your chance.

Virgo solar eclipse

EXPRESS YOUR VALUES BETTER

The Virgo solar eclipse will spotlight your values and the way you express them in your life. If you feel your ideas are generally disrespected, find ways to be heard and stand up for your principles and morals. Finances will deserve focus but you must avoid obsessing with the details and being hypercritical.

Libra solar eclipse

GAIN A NEW UNDERSTANDING WITH LOVED ONES

This is a good time to research how to bring more of what you love into your life, especially with those you love. Restlessness will motivate you to make changes. Approach discussions and negotiations in a relaxed way to avoid misunderstandings and words spoken in haste. You could make changes at home or with family.

Scorpio solar eclipse

EMBRACE DEEP CHANGE

This solar eclipse could spell drama for some Cancerians, especially if you have been reluctant to make changes in your life due to fear of change or obstinacy. Trust your instincts, which will guide you to a better situation. You'll find a way to alter the way you share domestic space or work duties.

Sagittarius solar eclipse

DEVELOP A MORE UPBEAT DAILY LIFE

Take the opportunity to boost the feel-good factor in your life, despite or because of feeling you are under a dark cloud. Take the initiative to boost health, as you may need to focus more on this important aspect. Working Crabs may be super busy but will relish the chance to step up in your chosen field.

Capricorn solar eclipse

GAIN STABILITY VIA A PARTNERSHIP OR AGREEMENT

Make arrangements to gain more security in life but avoid limiting your movements as you progress. If you experience a loss, rest assured you will gain stability as a result in the long term. You may be ready to make a key financial or personal commitment to be happier, whether alone or in a relationship.

Aquarius solar eclipse

VENTURE INTO NEW TURF

Be prepared to venture outside your comfort zone to negotiate or find the best new territory for you and those you love. Your duties, finances or commitments will be shared in new ways in the coming weeks and months, so be prepared to negotiate the terms.

Pisces solar eclipse

BOOST YOUR CIRCUMSTANCES AND STATUS

The outcome of your projects and concerns could be ideal in many ways, especially if you're ready to act intuitively on imaginative ideas that will boost your circumstances, relationships and activities. But to succeed you must avoid being easily led.

Aries solar eclipse

KICK-START EXCITING PROJECTS

Display your independence and dynamism as an exciting project will bring your skill set into play. You may wish to feel more appreciated, but if you feel let down by someone avoid taking the disappointment personally. Embrace a fresh interest such as study or travel, which will open new horizons for you.

Taurus solar eclipse

EMBRACE A FRESH OPTION IN YOUR CAREER OR STATUS

If one door closes another will open during this eclipse phase, so it's important to view developments as opportunities to prove yourself rather than as a closed book. Take a moment to consider the most reasonable path to take forward while avoiding limiting your options. Be practical and avoid being caught up in other people's dramas.

Gemini solar eclipse

STRENGTHEN YOUR CONSTITUTION

During the Gemini solar eclipse phase a new daily routine due to a fresh health, personal or work schedule may arise. This will be your chance for revitalisation. An old chapter may end, but you'll appreciate the opportunity to socialise and network and romance could blossom. You may be drawn to travel, which you'll enjoy.

22 JULY - 23 AUGUST

SYMBOL
Lion

ELEMENT
Fire

CONSTELLATION

LEO
SUN SIGN

※

INNER CALLING

As you are ruled by the sun you are the sun sign that shines the brightest . . . At least, that's how you see it! You will understand why you feel the world revolves around you sometimes because, in the same way that the planets revolve around the sun, you prefer people to revolve around you. So if you're ever called egotistic, just remind people of that fact!

On a more serious note, your calling is to express yourself fully in the most generous, abundant and positive way. You embody positivity yourself, and can feel truly downcast when you feel eclipsed by someone else's will, demands and domineering behaviour.

You are a kind, helpful person, and when you are judged harshly simply for being an outgoing, optimistic and on occasion larger than life character you'll dismiss criticism on the surface. But it can cut deeply.

Your courage and generosity are unparalleled and you do tend to expect the same of others, yet they are simply not wired that way so you must avoid feeling downhearted if you feel your good deeds are not reciprocated.

SELF-ESTEEM

You may be surprised to know that people believe you have high self-esteem as you can truly doubt your own abilities from time to time. You know that you are responsible for all the light and laughter in your life, and you are aware that you generate your own happiness and this is what propels your actions – but not necessarily your self-esteem. Others see merely the net result: that you take action confidently and have a purposeful outlook. You know that deep down you have as much self-doubt as anyone else. You may be confident-looking and dynamic, but the expectation put on you by the belief of others that you're super sure of yourself can add more pressure on you to be a runaway success.

So how will you shine? By continuing what you do best: being proactive and optimistic and generating your own happiness in life. In these straightforward ways you'll gradually boost your self-esteem, as you'll see how the actions you take from an optimistic standpoint invariably open doors for you.

HOME LIFE

Your home is the area where you feel you can express yourself fully. You are unlikely to feel at home if you need to watch your words, be quiet or toe the line in some other way. You are a passionate character in your home and like to feel it is an area where you are truly free, and your décor and relationships will be a full expression of who you are: bright, dynamic and uncluttered. Enter a Leo's home and you'll see their character in the choice of furniture; there will be no beige or muted colours unless these are the backdrop to bright or expressive art and to loud or distinctive musical notes.

You will enjoy being the lion to your lioness and vice versa, the lion or lioness to your cubs and the power and passion behind a thriving family as you mature. As a young Leo you are likely to surround yourself with music, friends, art, parties and fun at home. As a mature Leo you will enjoy being the cat that purrs in front of the fireplace with family all around.

RELATIONSHIPS

You like to be the centre of attention and feel you are in control. That doesn't mean you're controlling or egotistical, it's simply in your make-up to shine: you can't help it! Just be aware that others may see you as being attention seeking or a bit of a drama queen on occasion. If you feel this is the case, certainly don't dim your light but ensure you are equally attentive to the needs of others as well as your own.

You will feel passionately about your ideas and will fuel projects you undertake with friends, family and partners with intensity. As such you make an attentive partner both in your personal life and at work. However, you may seem overbearing on occasion, and if you feel your outgoing personality is eclipsing a partner's don't forget to ask them how they see shared ventures and concerns. Demonstrate your caring side more often.

CREATIVITY

Yours is a truly creative sign, although you're not generally known as the most creative sign of the zodiac. This accolade is generally reserved for the water signs of Pisces, Cancer and Scorpio, whose inspiration and imagination contributes to artistry. Your creations and projects are on a much larger scale than art: you create families, jobs and opportunities for others, and you also provide space and platforms for yourself and other people to be creative.

You gain high self-esteem from feeling you have produced wonderful work or brilliant children, and the more you connect with the inner spark that wishes to bring your creative spirit into manifestation the happier you are.

PITFALLS

A true pitfall for you in your spiritual path through life is feeling undervalued and therefore unfulfilled. Despite being such a dynamic, generous and outgoing character you can feel that your well-meaning actions are not reciprocated and, as a result, you can feel depleted.

You tend to mirror other people's high expectations of you, which they set very high because they mistake your dynamism and outgoing approach for high self-esteem.

You can consequently feel under pressure to succeed and excel at impossibly high benchmarks. The key to avoiding this is to understand that the benchmarks set by others are done so as a result of your abilities and not despite them. Trust in the fact that others see you as being successful and start believing in your own abilities.

SOLAR TRANSITS:
harness the sun's power
every day of the year

The sun empowers you in different areas of your life as it travels through each zodiac sign from month to month. Find out here how to make the most of your strong points during each of the transits of the sun through the 12 signs.

Sun in Leo, July to August
TIME TO SHINE

You'll feel at your best, and will appreciate the opportunity to boost your vitality, well-being and charm and will attract similarly optimistic people. You may, however, tend to be a little prone to seeing things only your way, so spare a thought for the perspectives of others as well or you'll be accused of being self-centred.

Sun in Virgo, August to September
BE PRACTICAL WITH MONEY

You'll appreciate the opportunity to get down to brass tacks with important areas of your personal life and especially your finances. Be realistic and methodical during this time and you could improve both your self-esteem and productivity.

Sun in Libra, September to October
IMPROVE COMMUNICATIONS AND TRAVEL

The sun in Libra is a good time to redress any imbalances in your relationships but also to show your softer, more kittenish side. You may be more indecisive at this time, so rely on loyal friends and advisers if you're unsure of what choices to make.

Sun in Scorpio, October to November

BOOST DOMESTIC RELATIONSHIPS AND CREATIVITY

This is a good time to deepen relationships with those you love, especially at home. You may feel passionate about your beliefs so aim to gain perspective, and when you have you'll steam ahead all the more assuredly with both relationships and passion projects.

Sun in Sagittarius, November to December

BE BOLD

You'll be drawn to enter new territory and feel more daring about making changes at home via updated décor or a little DIY. Travel may appeal, and you may be drawn to explore other environments or welcome visitors to your home. Singles will feel more outgoing and enjoy socialising.

Sun in Capricorn, December to January

BOOST WORK AND HEALTH

This is an excellent time to get ahead at work; you may be particularly busy. If life has been adventurous but a little chaotic, this is a good phase to get back down to earth and feel more grounded, both at work and with health and well-being. Some Leos may experience an earthier, more sensual phase in your personal life.

Sun in Aquarius, January to February

BOOST ROMANCE AND RELATIONSHIPS

This is a good time to find new ways to co-operate with business and personal partners. You may need to step into new parameters at work or consider fresh ways to boost healthy relationship dynamics. Adopt a varied approach to those you love. Singles may meet an original and eccentric character.

Sun in Pisces, February to March

BE INSPIRED

The sun in Pisces is inspiring but may also bring your inner idealist out, so if you keep your feet on the ground and find the middle ground between optimism and reality you'll experience a truly romantic time ideal for a break or slowing down in the evenings. As you may be forgetful or have your head in the clouds, obtain financial advice if you are making large investments.

Sun in Aries, March to April

IMPROVE NEGOTIATION SKILLS

The sun in fellow fire sign Aries will fire you up. You may feel more animated, motivated and dynamic during this month but you must avoid appearing super feisty as people may not respond too kindly to your outlook, possibly even seeing you as being bossy.

Sun in Taurus, April to May

MAKE CONCRETE PROGRESS

You may wish to express your principles and sense of fair play through work, study and general activities, which will help you set up strong foundations. You will also be drawn to indulging in the sensuous side of life and may wish to express your romantic, soft self more. Travel and treating yourself will appeal.

Sun in Gemini, May to June

BOOST SOCIAL LIFE AND STATUS

You'll feel more fun loving and likely to socialise and network, and may embrace new projects and meet upbeat people during this time. You could be drawn to learning new skill sets. Just choose your activities carefully or you may end up frittering away your energy and being distracted.

Sun in Cancer, June to July

IMPROVE SELF-CARE

This is a good time to put in place a work and daily routine that is more supportive of your ideas and skills, health and well-being. If you work in a caring industry you may be super busy. Working with humanitarian groups and organisations will appeal more than usual.

LUNAR TRANSITS:
be calm and effective every day of the month

The moon spotlights different aspects of your emotional self as it travels each month through each zodiac sign, staying two days in each sign. When the moon is in each sign you gain the opportunity to express yourself more effectively in various areas of your life. Find out here how to make the most of your strong points during each of the two days each month.

Moon in Leo

FEELING ENERGETIC AND OUTGOING

The Leo moon will add a spring to your step, and you'll enjoy the chance to socialise and meet friends and family and be creative and upbeat. If you've felt a bit introspective recently you'll relish the chance to be more outgoing.

Moon in Virgo

BE METICULOUS

Plan ahead and be diligent and focused to make great headway both at work and with your various interests and pastimes. You may enjoy a change of routine during the Virgo moon that breathes fresh air into your days. Avoid perfectionism.

Moon in Libra

BE DECISIVE WITH COMMUNICATIONS AND TRAVEL

This phase may bring deeper emotions out, so ensure you focus on the best-case scenario and outcome and adopt a constructive approach to communications and travel. Luckily, the Libran moon will also promote a philosophical outlook.

Moon in Scorpio

INVEST IN DOMESTIC BLISS

This is an ideal time for romance and creativity, so plan cosy nights in and work around the house and garden. This could be a productive time but equally may produce intense talks that risk escalating into conflict. Strong emotions are best approached carefully; avoid taking someone's mood swings personally.

Moon in Sagittarius

EXPRESS FUN AND CREATIVITY

You'll feel confident during the Sagittarius moon and your upbeat, outgoing side will seek expression. Creative Leos may be particularly drawn to art. Romantic and family-minded Leos will enjoy upbeat time with those you love, so plan treats and get-togethers.

Moon in Capricorn

BE PRACTICAL WORK- AND HEALTH-WISE

This is a good time for planning, scheduling and taking realistic steps forward at work and with health schedules. You will feel more practical and realistic with your various ventures and will enjoy immersing yourself in work and being productive.

Moon in Aquarius

BE INNOVATIVE WITH YOUR RELATIONSHIPS

Keep an open mind, as you may learn something new and incorporate this newfound wisdom into your love life. You'll be attracted to quirky, independent people at work and will feel the need for more freedom of expression. This is a good time to reach out to people you would not usually associate with.

Moon in Pisces

BE BOTH INSPIRED AND PRACTICAL

A romantic frame of mind during the Pisces moon will certainly encourage you to express your love and devotion to someone close. You may, however, tend to see people idealistically at this time so it's important to be realistic and practical, especially with key decisions at work.

Moon in Aries

BE ACTIVE AND EMBRACE NEW VENTURES

You may feel restless and ready for new activities. Seize opportunities but avoid being impulsive, especially at work. You may feel spontaneous but must avoid risk-taking activities. A partnership or collaboration should prove positive, but you must avoid snap decisions if starting new collaborations.

Moon in Taurus

BOOST YOUR CAREER AND FAVOURITE INTERESTS

A slower change of pace will help you get your feet on the ground with important projects and at work. You'll feel more inclined to follow your heart and true interests. Romance could blossom as you take the time to indulge in your favourite activities, interests and friendships.

Moon in Gemini

DIVERSIFY

The Gemini moon will offer the chance to revitalise both your social and work lives. If you are unclear about your choices to do with various duties or concerns at work, take the time to gain direction by getting in touch with experts and those who can help. This is a good time for research and networking.

Moon in Cancer

TRUST YOUR INSTINCTS

Your intuition will not lead you astray with important decisions at work and around health-related activities and your love life, but you must avoid rushing into decisions. Trust your intuition during this time, as it is uncharacteristically strong and will guide you to make the correct choices.

FULL MOONS:
magnify your vibrant power

*Each full moon highlights different aspects of your power and vibrancy.
Find out here which full moons will be excellent times to turn a corner
in the various areas of your life to show just what you're made of.*

Full moon in Leo
START A COURAGEOUS CHAPTER

You are ready to turn a corner in your personal life if you were born before or on the date of the full moon and for a new daily work or health routine if you were born after it. For some this full moon will point to a relationship that has run its course, while for others it means a fresh relationship.

Full moon in Virgo
BE REALISTIC WITH FINANCES AND RELATIONSHIPS

Be practical as you will turn a corner financially or in a key relationship and, at the very least, get on top of your budget and spending habits, especially if you've been careless with spending. You will feel more secure as a result.

Full moon in Libra
FIND BALANCE IN YOUR LIFE

This is a time to make peace. A fresh financial chapter may involve making fair agreements that require considerable focus. For some this full moon will signal the chance to collaborate better with a partner or to accept your differences and work with them rather than fighting against them, unless you realise you have gone beyond this option.

Full moon in Scorpio

MAKE CONSTRUCTIVE CHANGES AT HOME

This full moon will highlight your real emotions regarding your domestic life, family or a creative project. A trip or significant news may be a catalyst to bringing out strong emotions, so find ways to channel these into a positive outcome such as DIY projects or creativity.

Full moon in Sagittarius

FORGE STRONG TIES

You'll enjoy favourite activities and connecting with like-minded people to forge strong relationships. The Sagittarius full moon will kick-start a fresh chapter in your personal life, home or creative projects. If you make new agreements ensure they are clear and avoid unrealistic expectations, otherwise you may set yourself up for later disappointments.

Full moon in Capricorn

GAIN STABILITY WITH WORK AND HEALTH

Be practical and methodical with agreements at work and put in place long-term health schedules. A fresh daily work or health routine should provide you with increasing stability and progress, although there may be a tough call or important developments to consider first.

Full moon in Aquarius

STEP RELATIONSHIPS UP TO A NEW LEVEL

Key developments in a business or personal partnership may come unexpectedly or will spotlight the quirky nature of your relationship. You could see romance truly blossom, so aim to deepen existing relationships. For some this full moon can signal the end of a growth phase in a relationship and even a parting of ways.

Full moon in Pisces

BE PATIENT TO IMPROVE COLLABORATIONS

As a fire sign you like to gallop through life, yet the Pisces full moon sets a much slower pace. Patience will be a true virtue, as will tuning in to your intuition. Be inspired by those you admire and love. Romance and creativity could blossom, but if you are disappointed avoid taking it personally. Take practical steps to boost your circumstances.

Full moon in Aries

A CALL TO TAKE ACTION

You'll feel motivated to engage in your favourite interests such as study and travel, and may feel particularly strongly about a beloved project. A particular interest may come to completion, and you'll get the chance to catapult yourself into a new agreement or venture as a result.

Full moon in Taurus

SEE YOURSELF IN A NEW LIGHT

This is the time to invest in yourself and shine as your most authentic self. If you experience deep feelings or the sense that you're inundated by other people's demands, ensure you strategise and plan ahead to avoid being distracted from your goals.

Full moon in Gemini

LEVEL UP YOUR CAREER AND STATUS

If you have been planning something new or considering a fresh direction for some time there's no time like the present to research your circumstances and begin laying plans for success. A fresh work contract or interest could take off, and you may see the end of a job or relationship in the process.

Full moon in Cancer

MAKE TIME FOR YOURSELF AND OTHERS

This is a sentimental and nostalgic full moon for you, and you may wish to help someone who is less able than you are. Help yourself too by devising a healthy routine, as this full moon will mark the end of a cycle at work and for some Leos regarding your health.

NEW MOONS:
start something fresh

Each new moon points to the start of something fresh for you in different areas of your life. Find out here which new moon to work with and how to make lasting change by starting something new, especially if you have been putting off change for some time.

New moon in Leo
UPDATE YOUR APPEARANCE AND WARDROBE

You may feel more self-confident during this time and will surprise yourself with your newfound optimism. The Leo new moon will feel empowering and you can expect new opportunities to arise to boost your work, health and personal life. It's a good time to start a new collaboration.

New moon in Virgo
DEVISE A STABLE BUDGET

Research circumstances around your financial plans and areas of interest. You may find that you are ahead financially or the reverse. Boost your fortunes via support from others. Aim for your goals with full confidence and avoid being super self-critical or critical of others.

New moon in Libra
ESTABLISH EQUALITY IN RELATIONSHIPS

A fresh chapter in your relationships will begin. It's a good time to seek fair play and more balance in your relationships and also in shared finances. It is certainly a good time to re-establish the status quo, and you may need to review an agreement to re-establish the balance.

New moon in Scorpio

BOOST COMMUNICATIONS AND ENJOY A HAPPIER HOME

There is always room for improvement, and this is a good time to find better ways to be clearer to avoid mix-ups. A fresh device may boost communications, but even better is that you'll feel more outgoing and will enjoy the opportunity to meet new people. Feeling more upbeat, passionate and communicative will translate as more contentment at home.

New moon in Sagittarius

KICK-START ROMANCE, FUN AND CREATIVITY

It's a good time to be more outgoing. DIY projects, renovation or even a move may appeal. A fresh chapter is about to begin in your domestic zone with family, property or your home. If you've been introspective you'll enjoy being more outgoing and outspoken, enjoying music, art and dance.

New moon in Capricorn

CREATE MORE STABILITY WITH A FRESH SCHEDULE

This is a good time to make a new commitment, at home or at work or to a project or person. You may need to prioritise certain values and people to improve your daily routine. A helpful colleague or friend may prove their weight in gold.

New moon in Aquarius

REVITALISE YOUR LOVE LIFE

Whether you're single or married this new moon could revitalise your love life, so plan a break, celebration or fun event! The key to success will be to be super clear, not only in your own actions but also in understanding your partner. A heads-up: this new moon could bring out unpredictable behaviour, both in you and in someone close, so make solid plans ahead of time but also be flexible.

New moon in Pisces

CLARIFY AGREEMENTS

You're likely to be entering fresh and inspiring territory during the Pisces new moon, which could be in association with someone close or a partnership. Don't be afraid to ask for clarity where there is uncertainty: a mystery may be in the making, so ensure you gain the facts.

New moon in Aries

START A FRESH PROJECT

Be bold and enjoy life! This is a good time to organise your activities so you can be more efficient and take time out to enjoy life and relationships. A holiday or study course may appeal. It's a good time to commit to a fresh relationship or agreement. Romance could blossom.

New moon in Taurus

EMBRACE NEW EXPERIENCES

Embrace exciting new ventures that give a sense of purpose, stability and security in your life in the long term. If a difficult circumstance has been lingering, find ways to move ahead constructively in your life so you feel more fulfilled.

New moon in Gemini

ENJOY A FRESH SOCIABLE PHASE

You'll begin to see communications and relationships, networking and teamwork in a fresh light. Information and developments that create new perspective on your endeavours will encourage you to take action in new directions.

New moon in Cancer

INCUBATE AND BIRTH CHANGES

Find ways to infuse your life with more of what and who you want in it. It's time to nurture yourself a little with all the luxuries and favourite activities life has to offer. Aim to boost health. A refreshing relationship with a group or organisation could signal stimulating times ahead.

LUNAR ECLIPSES:
be strong during peak emotional changes

> *Each lunar eclipse signals a major turning point in your life and may bring about intense emotions. Eclipses point to circumstances that seem to disempower you and subsequently motivate you to address any imbalances, so keep an eye on those areas in which you lack control as that is where you can make the most changes and become strong. Find out here which lunar eclipse will bring change in which area of your life, and how to make the most of these changes.*

Leo lunar eclipse
BOOST SELF-ESTEEM IN RELATIONSHIPS

A fresh approach to your well-being and how you attain a sense of fulfilment may be needed in your relationship dynamics. Avoid allowing someone to steal your thunder, but also avoid being domineering yourself. Expect changes in a key relationship at work or in your daily routine, especially if the eclipse is on your birthday.

Virgo lunar eclipse
GAIN A FRESH PERSPECTIVE

Consider a fresh approach to someone at work or in your personal life. You may see your finances and commitments in a new light, and where there are uncertainties discuss the practicalities and details of your various ideas and plans. Developments should ultimately boost your circumstances even if you feel emotional.

Libra lunar eclipse
RE-ESTABLISH PEACE IN AGREEMENTS

Your interests can progress but you must re-establish a sense of balance first, either within an arrangement or financially. Approach talks with the aim of finding common ground rather than highlighting your differences and you will reach a compromise and find a solution.

Scorpio lunar eclipse

BOOST NEGOTIATION SKILLS

While your communication skills may already be good, developments will spotlight the need for a new approach or arrangement with someone so negotiation and relationship skills must be developed to a higher standard. You may feel more emotionally invested in circumstances and must focus hard on keeping emotions on an even keel.

Sagittarius lunar eclipse

BRING YOUR INNER ADVENTURER OUT

Family-minded Leos will enjoy travel and will love investing your time and energy in those close to you. You may travel with your family or someone special or wish to be super creative in your domestic or creative lives. Singles will enjoy being more sociable and may meet someone from overseas or a far distance away.

Capricorn lunar eclipse

RELY ON FACTS

A fresh daily work or health routine will provide you with an increasing sense of stability and progress, although there may be a tough call or important developments you must first undergo. You may discover that some communications or relationships are based on assumptions and you will need to seek out the facts.

Aquarius lunar eclipse

CREATE WORK/LIFE BALANCE

Take the time to build stability even amid change. Key partnerships, arrangements and agreements are likely to change unexpectedly; a new partnership or business agreement could begin. For some Leos a new work or health schedule may start soon if it hasn't already, and you'll appreciate the chance to create more work/life balance once the dust has settled.

Pisces lunar eclipse

BE INSPIRED BUT REALISTIC ABOUT PARTNERSHIPS

Someone close may be more forgetful or distant during this phase, so be practical. Romance may take a fresh turn as someone either enters or leaves your life. You could experience key developments in a business partnership. You'll feel particularly idealistic about how arrangements should be so you must ensure you maintain perspective.

Aries lunar eclipse
TREAD CAREFULLY WITH COLLABORATIONS

Establish common ground with colleagues and employers as you could kick-start a promising collaboration. You are likely to be busy as projects and ideas grab your attention. If you need someone's co-operation be careful, as they may have their own ideas about how things should be. Avoid unnecessary arguments.

Taurus lunar eclipse
ANCHOR YOUR DREAMS

Consider which activities and people are your priority and take the time to anchor these interests, as you could make real progress with a particular course of action or relationship. Changes may transpire through a dramatic process that feels intense or highly emotional, so aim to ground yourself.

Gemini lunar eclipse
BE APPROACHABLE AND ADAPTABLE

A fresh approach to a friend or organisation could provide opportunities to make things happen for you, but you may need to first overcome a hurdle. You may feel inclined to be fancy free but must be practical about a key choice regarding a friend, organisation, career or status. Choose your path carefully; avoid gambling.

Cancer lunar eclipse
BREAK INTO A NEW FIELD

You will feel emotionally drawn to find deeper meaning and purpose in your work and daily routine. You may choose to alter some of your allegiances and commitments and re-order priorities so you derive an increased sense of nurturance. A fresh health routine may appeal.

SOLAR ECLIPSES:
making major changes run smoothly

Each solar eclipse signals a major turning point in your life that points to ongoing change for years to come. Find out here which solar eclipses will bring change in which areas of your life, and how to make the most of those changes.

Leo solar eclipse
REBOOT YOUR LIFE

This eclipse is the ultimate chance to make changes in your life that you know are long overdue. Be positive and take action that will boost your sense of fulfilment and self-worth. Find out what you want from life and make tracks to attain your personal goals.

Virgo solar eclipse
RESEARCH FINANCIAL AND PERSONAL CIRCUMSTANCES

You may feel uncharacteristically calm and determined during this phase and could accomplish a great deal as a result. The more robust you are in your health routine the better. A discerning, respectful, enquiring and pragmatic approach will work best during this time. Avoid obsession and succumbing to victim/martyr roles.

Libra solar eclipse
REVITALISE YOUR RELATIONSHIPS AND ENVIRONMENT

It's a great time to update communication devices or travel options. A lovely opportunity for a trip or a visit will excite the senses. You may be drawn to travel and to welcome visitors. If you work in the communications industry you may experience changes at work as a new chapter begins. Be decisive.

Scorpio solar eclipse
EMPOWER YOURSELF

Avoid feeling you must agree with everyone; you may need to make an agreement that is a tough call but is also empowering. You'll feel ready to usher in a new phase via a venture or project. Travel and commerce and your community and neighbourhood will be in the spotlight as you gain the chance to alter one or all of these areas.

Sagittarius solar eclipse
MAKE POSITIVE PERSONAL CHANGES

You'll gain insight during the eclipse phase into how to make positive changes in your financial and personal circumstances but must be prepared for some soul searching. You may be ready to renovate: a fresh décor may appeal. It's a good time to spruce up your interpersonal dynamics.

Capricorn solar eclipse
REVITALISE INTERPERSONAL DYNAMICS

A fresh chapter concerning your family, a loved one or a creative project will bring new understanding into being. You are ready to make a commitment to a fresh personal or professional arrangement. Consider a solid and steady well-being plan to better manage your health.

Aquarius solar eclipse
ADOPT A FRESH PERSPECTIVE TO RELATIONSHIPS

You may find that people seem erratic or even unreliable, which may be due to their own pressures rather than the relationship. Instead of mirroring their oddball behaviour, adopt a fresh approach to them in order to resolve any issues. If a business or personal partner wants to go it alone, consider the benefits as opposed to the negatives.

Pisces solar eclipse
SHARE DUTIES AND FINANCES IN A NEW WAY

Several developments can be brought to a successful conclusion as long as you steer your life cleverly onto a more satisfying course that suits you better on a gut, soul level. Developments may entail a catalytic event that will draw on your reserves and may even reveal hidden mysteries.

Aries solar eclipse
BE ASSERTIVE

Consider how to collaborate in an assertive rather than aggressive way, as this will improve your relationships. A new arrangement, fun activity or contract may be appealing but you must check it aligns with your big-picture values. Consider if there is a fairer way to share duties and to delegate work within collaborations.

Taurus solar eclipse
BOOST YOUR INTERESTS

Be prepared to invest more heavily in a favourite interest or study. If progress with a work or personal option seems blocked, consider a new option. Be innovative and adventurous but also practical during this time for the best results.

Gemini solar eclipse
REINVIGORATE WORK

This eclipse will open new doors, especially if a shabby old chapter is ending or you're simply tired of your existing routine. A fresh activity or project is in the air. Making plans will be exciting, but you must consider details and logistics carefully.

Cancer solar eclipse
BOOST WELL-BEING

An authority figure may impose limitations but you'll find a way to triumph regardless. A more self-nurturing phase will be productive. A new chapter may involve changes in your health and work schedule. You may decide to cocoon for a while or to look after someone else.

23 AUGUST - 23 SEPTEMBER

SYMBOL
Virgin

ELEMENT
Earth

CONSTELLATION

VIRGO
SUN SIGN

INNER CALLING

Your calling is to help others and be of service to them. Sound boring or tedious? It needn't be, especially as karma will reward your actions and helpfulness and your good deeds will come full circle to you. You gain a sense of fulfilment, completion and accomplishment from your calling and may find that helping others comes in all shapes and sizes: from building, to art, to medicine and to care giving.

You are more in line to feel fulfilled than any of the sun signs based solely on the karmic chain reaction of helping others, and you can't help but help yourself because you know how to help others. It's not a chore to do the same for yourself; on the contrary, to be of help to others you must first know how to help yourself! You like to feel useful and being busy drives your sense of fulfilment.

SELF-ESTEEM

You are a perfectionist and, as such you can tend to beat yourself up when things don't run as well as you might hope or even demand of yourself. This can lead to low self-esteem.

You are sensitive but most of all realistic and practical, so people can tend to overlook your sensitivity. And because you are so practical people also tend not to offer you help yet they will expect your help. This may seem unfair on the surface, but don't forget the law of karma! Your good intentions will not go unnoticed in the big-picture karmic cycle, but in the everyday you must avoid being caught in a vicious cycle of feeling inferior because people seem not to help you when you need support. If you are able to, then view people's lack of help as a compliment because they see you as being strong and self-sufficient.

HOME LIFE

You express your individuality at home and are unlikely to stand on ceremony in the privacy of your home or insist on certain traditions or customs. You may travel a fair amount and are not afraid of living in another country and experimenting with different types of dwellings or living arrangements. You do appreciate comfort and enjoy expressing your sensuality in home décor with plush pillows and calming, earthy, natural tones. You will appreciate feeling stable in your home life even though you are not afraid of change.

RELATIONSHIPS

As an earth sign you enjoy the sensuality of intimate relationships and the deep connection that comes from intimacy. In family relationships you may be pragmatic about how certain karmic connections are formed. Being so practical means you are able to understand in philosophical terms that while some people will always get along, others will not. And while at first you may take relationship disappointments personally, you are able to rise above your disappointments and move on in realistic ways.

You are extremely sensitive, and it's vital you avoid the victim-martyr role in relationships. You'll do so by being philosophical and avoiding blame, especially when you see relationships as a great learning ground for spiritual growth rather than a battlefield of emotions.

CREATIVITY

You express your creativity through your actions. You are earthy, practical and accomplished, and enjoy being hands-on at work and employing your ability to create solid results on a daily basis.

Creativity is a great source of self-expression for you, especially if you find your mind becomes over-analytical and your perfectionism becomes too exacting. You may express yourself through art, crafts, building or any activity in life that engages your sense of earthiness and the need to see tangible results for your hard work. You will enjoy the creativity of family life, of looking after children and the joys and concomitant highs and lows of parenthood.

PITFALLS

A common pitfall for Virgos is to run yourself so far into the ground in the effort to be liked and helpful that you exhaust yourself and are then no longer able to help anyone – least of all yourself! Perfectionism is a true pitfall for you as you can tend to push yourself so hard and be so hyper self-critical that you become negative.

You can tend to be critical of others all in the name of perfectionism, and can let go of many a good relationship as a result. A compassionate approach to the fact that no one is perfect will serve you much better in the long term.

You have a tendency to take on other people's problems as your own even if they do not directly concern you, and as a result feel the weight of the world on your shoulders. Learn to be less self-critical and celebrate, instead, your many gifts and talents, not least being kind.

SOLAR TRANSITS:
harness the sun's power
every day of the year

The sun empowers you in different areas of your life as it travels through each zodiac sign from month to month. Find out here how to make the most of your strong points during each of the transits of the sun through the 12 signs.

Sun in Virgo, August to September

EMBRACE YOUR SKILLS

The sun in Virgo will shine a light on your skills and abilities. You may achieve a goal or will make progress in a valuable way. If, however, you sense opposition to some of your ideas and plans, align your actions with your priorities and focus on being inspired and bright in your daily life, work and health and your abilities will shine through and lead to success.

Sun in Libra, September to October

BOOST HAPPINESS

You could boost your situation by taking the initiative during this phase in all areas, especially financially and in your love life. You may find agreements are easier to make and that you can gain a deeper understanding of people and money, all of which will bring sense and reason to your life.

Sun in Scorpio, October to November

CULTIVATE YOUR LUST FOR LIFE

You'll feel impassioned to get things right both at home and at work. You must avoid allowing your perfectionism to deter you from being spontaneous. You may feel adamant about principles, so ensure you have done your research before staking money on ideas. You could improve your finances but must avoid overspending as a result in your quest for happiness.

Sun in Sagittarius, November to December

LET YOUR INNER EXPLORER OUT

This is a good time to get in touch with friends and siblings, to get involved with your community and to travel, learn new skills and broaden your horizons. Your inner chatterbox will seek expression. You may feel drawn to update your technological devices, home or a vehicle to facilitate exciting plans.

Sun in Capricorn, December to January

ENJOY LIFE'S DELIGHTS

The Capricorn sun will shine a light on people and activities that make you feel appreciated, fulfilled and happy. You will be drawn to good food, dance and music. Some Virgos will appreciate the chance to feather your nest, it being a good phase to invest in your home life and in those you love.

Sun in Aquarius, January to February

IMPLEMENT NEW IDEAS AND VENTURES

Take note of your bright-spark ideas: although they may seem left field they will be insightful. You'll embrace new work schedules and will be prepared to try new skills and upscale your responsibilities. It's a good time to improve health, and complementary or alternative treatments for health niggles may appeal.

Sun in Pisces, February to March

BOOST YOUR LOVE LIFE AND RELATIONSHIPS

This is a romantic time, so plan treats for yourself and your loved one. You may also feel increasingly inspired at work, but if you feel you are in a rut you'll be motivated to create a schedule that suits you better over the coming weeks and to work with people who inspire you. Practicalities will lead you to make the right decisions; avoid idealism and change for the sake of it.

Sun in Aries, March to April
BE POSITIVE ABOUT COLLABORATIONS

You'll feel motivated to get things done and could move mountains; however, people may seem feistier than usual. Avoid allowing a personal matter or a difference of opinion to turn into a war zone. Keep proceedings calm and you will avoid allowing feisty people to become opponents.

Sun in Taurus, April to May
BE MORE EXPRESSIVE

You will feel more expressive in your various activities and may wish to collaborate more, and you will maintain a view to fairness within the sharing of duties and finances. You will feel drawn to express your sensuality more during this phase, both romantically and in your choice of preferred environment and favourite activity.

Sun in Gemini, May to June
MULTITASK AND DIVERSIFY

You can make progress at work and with your special projects and may even receive good news at work or financially because of your hard work. Your multitasking skills will peak and may be in demand. You'll enjoy spicing up your usual activities and trying something new in your spare time or at work.

Sun in Cancer, June to July
ENGAGE IN HUMANITARIANISM

You will be drawn to express your compassionate qualities, enabling you to carry out work and activities that better express your humanitarian interests. Your considerable skills and abilities can put you in a stronger position at work and within key ventures and interests, so take the initiative now.

Sun in Leo, July to August
FOCUS ON PRIORITIES AND HEALTH

You may feel more energetic than usual and could be busy at work, but if health has been a worry this is the right time to address niggling ailments. You may feel more motivated to excel at work yet this is also an upbeat time for a fun holiday or change of routine.

LUNAR TRANSITS:
be calm and effective every day of the month

The moon spotlights different aspects of your emotional self as it travels each month through each zodiac sign, staying two days in each sign. When the moon is in each sign you gain the opportunity to express yourself more effectively in various areas of your life. Find out here how to make the most of your strong points during each of the two days each month.

Moon in Virgo
BE MOTIVATED

You will feel particularly productive and co-operative and could excel, but not everyone will feel the same way! Avoid pressuring others into actions they are not ready for and also avoid perfectionism during this phase, as you may be particularly inclined to lay down the law.

Moon in Libra
ADJUST EXPECTATIONS

Take a mini progress check: Are you happy with the way things are? If not, it's a good time to make changes. You may be emotionally invested in a particular outcome so will find benefit in reviewing your circumstances, including your finances and loyalties.

Moon in Scorpio
ENJOY LIFE MORE

This phase can bring out strong feelings, so if you have unresolved or negative feelings about business with someone then channel bubbling resentment or a desire to engage in conflict into constructive plans to make things work for you. You may be inspired to indulge in the good things in life, which you'll enjoy, but you must avoid overspending and overindulging; you'll regret it!

Moon in Sagittarius
BOOST DOMESTIC BLISS

Focus on improving domestic dynamics. You may feel more outspoken, so if conflict has been brewing at home be tactful, as diplomacy will work far better than arguments. A little home improvement and the opportunity to put your feet up and relax a little will help you unwind.

Moon in Capricorn
MAKE PLANS AND ENJOY GOOD COMPANY

This is an excellent time for planning and organising your itineraries. You'll feel motivated to be busy with creative projects and spend time with those you love. Avoid over-analysing issues; a practical and realistic stance will work well for you during this time.

Moon in Aquarius
BE OPEN TO NEW IDEAS

A varied daily routine means you'll need to be flexible, but don't forget your own plans and desires or you'll resent those who demand your attention, especially at work. A friendly or unorthodox approach to a relationship could blossom in unusual circumstances.

Moon in Pisces
INVEST IN YOUR LOVE LIFE AND RELATIONSHIPS

You will feel inspired and romantic but may also be easily distracted, so focus a little more during this moon phase as your characteristic earthiness may be swamped by forgetfulness and daydreaming. You may find out if you have over- or under-estimated someone; if so, you will gain clarity as a result.

Moon in Aries
MAKE TIME FOR SOMEONE SPECIAL

The people you admire for their energy and sass will make for lively company and romantic inspiration. But if someone is being disruptive in your life now you must find ways to smooth troubled waters and avoid conflict and argumentative people.

Moon in Taurus
INVEST IN FAVOURITE ACTIVITIES

You'll enjoy making solid plans for holidays and making more time for yourself and those you love. You'll also relish planning ahead for study, research and doing more of what you love. You'll deepen romantic ties and share your innermost thoughts with someone special.

Moon in Gemini
BOOST YOUR CAREER

This is a favourable moon for you as you'll feel flexible and adaptable, communicative and engaged and therefore more prepared to take on challenges, new projects and upbeat ideas. However, you may also tend to overwork, so ensure you focus on priorities first up and avoid dispersing your energy.

Moon in Cancer
SOCIALISE AND MINGLE

You'll enjoy being with friends, family and colleagues but you may also be more sensitive to undercurrents and people's mood swings, so ensure you maintain a rational outlook. You will be more romantically inclined and more responsive to the needs of others.

Moon in Leo
FOCUS ON PRIORITIES AND SPIRITUALITY

You may experience a slightly introspective time even if other people seem more upbeat. It is nevertheless a good time to get work and chores done and for improving health, fitness and your appearance. You may enjoy meditation and yoga, as these modalities will provide you with the chance to earth yourself if you get caught up in dramas.

FULL MOONS:
magnify your vibrant power

Each full moon highlights different aspects of your power and vibrancy. Find out here which full moons will be excellent times to turn a corner in the various areas of your life to show just what you're made of.

Full moon in Virgo

INVEST IN YOUR WELL-BEING

This is a great time to establish strategies that work for you, creating a healthy and sustainable daily life. A fresh look such as a new outfit or hairstyle may appeal. You may receive key news from a personal or business partner if your birthday is on or before the full moon. Virgos born after the date of the full moon will begin a fresh cycle at work or with health.

Full moon in Libra

RESTORE BALANCE

Get set to turn a corner in your personal life and financially, as events will spotlight where you could find more balance. You may draw up a fresh beauty or health regime. If you have overspent in the past you may need to configure a new budget. You will restore balance in a close relationship by boosting your self-esteem.

Full moon in Scorpio

EMBRACE INSPIRING IDEAS

Get set to embrace new ideas and activities as events could broaden your horizons. Consider a fresh agreement or deepening a romantic relationship. A trip may be transformational. You will be drawn to update digital devices or even a vehicle. Creative Virgos will be productive.

Full moon in Sagittarius

BE ADVENTUROUS

The end of a chapter regarding family, home or property will arise. Special connections will be significant, and a lovely tie with someone will last. But if you feel it's time to let an old friendship, circumstance, house or relationship lapse it may be time to go your separate ways. An adventure or holiday will clear your mind.

Full moon in Capricorn

FORGE A NEW AGREEMENT

A new understanding with someone close will involve the need to work hard and make decisions based on practicalities, long-term strategy and a sense of realism. This is an earthy full moon that may bring your sensuous nature out, so romance could blossom. Plan a date!

Full moon in Aquarius

DIVERSIFY YOUR INTERESTS

Be prepared to seek fresh frontiers even if you are not yet prepared to actually stride out into something new. You may be surprised by developments at work. You'll appreciate the chance to create more work/life balance, which may come about in unusual ways. Someone close may wish for more freedom of movement.

Full moon in Pisces

TURN A CORNER IN YOUR PERSONAL LIFE

You will enjoy the chance to bring more romance and mystery into your life via music, creativity or through your interest in art, beauty or spirituality. For some this full moon could signify the end of a relationship or arrangement at work. Rest assured that a new beginning is just around the corner.

Full moon in Aries

BE BOLD WITH COLLABORATIONS

Ask yourself where in life you are fed up with compromise and of thinking of others first, potentially even putting yourself last. This full moon will motivate you to think afresh about how to collaborate better with people and also how to express your individuality.

Full moon in Taurus
A CALL TO ADVENTURE

An endeavour such as a trip or study could be exciting, so plan ahead! You may feel romantic and sensual and could make a long-term commitment. This full moon will resonate deeply, especially regarding decisions about shared resources such as space at home, duties or finances. If a relationship ends at this time the call to adventure will act as a panacea.

Full moon in Gemini
BE FLEXIBLE WITH YOUR CAREER AND INTERESTS

Key talks could produce a refreshing new chapter, especially if you're flexible with the people in your environment. A trip could signal a turning point in your life, and socialising and networking could open doors to new ventures. It's a good time to improve communication skills, and if a relationship ends you'll relish freedom for a while.

Full moon in Cancer
SHOW JUST HOW CARING YOU ARE

You're known as a perfectionist and a hard worker but less so for your caring attributes, yet you are super helpful and supportive. You'll wish to increasingly demonstrate your caring attributes through your affiliation with humanitarian or benevolent groups and friendships. Consider joining a new group.

Full moon in Leo
LET GO OF THE PAST

As a chapter ends at work or with a health situation you'll be ready to step into new territory. This may come in surprising ways through a change of routine or circumstances and you may need to help someone out. It's a good time to ditch a bad habit.

NEW MOONS:
start something fresh

Each new moon points to the start of something fresh for you in different areas of your life. Find out here which new moon to work with and how to make lasting change by starting something new, especially if you have been putting off change for some time.

New moon in Virgo
BEGIN A NEW RELATIONSHIP OR JOB

You'll feel in your element and be clearer about how you'd like to see your life progress under this new moon, so it's a good time for a makeover, boosting health or beginning a fresh romance or job. If it's your birthday at the new moon you'll turn a corner in your personal life, while Virgos born afterwards may begin a fresh daily or health routine. This is the ideal time for research, as your efforts to move ahead will be rewarded.

New moon in Libra
LET YOUR DECISIONS REFLECT YOUR VALUES

Be practical with financial matters and consider whether all your hard work is paying off or whether there is a case for working smarter rather than harder. You'll turn a corner by establishing more balance in your life, which may involve smoothing out inconsistent or erratic circumstances. Let your finances and choices reflect your values and stand up for your principles.

New moon in Scorpio
INITIATE TALKS AND REVITALISE RELATIONSHIPS

Be prepared to step into new territory both at work and in your personal life. You may already see signs of financial growth or better relationship dynamics, so initiate talks and negotiations. This is a good time to update a digital or technological device but you must avoid impulse buys.

New moon in Sagittarius

KICK-START FRESH DYNAMICS AT HOME

Be prepared to be more outgoing and people will respond in kind. Consider approaching family and those at home with a more upbeat attitude. Plans for travel and domestic developments such as DIY projects or improved décor will point to a breakthrough.

New moon in Capricorn

ASK FOR A COMMITMENT

If you want more stability in your personal life then ask for a commitment at this new moon, and if you're undecided about a personal partnership your wish for more clarity will be answered. If you're single you may meet someone attractive who provides you with a sense of security. If things have been a little unpredictable, prepare to establish more calm.

New moon in Aquarius

DIVERSIFY WORK AND HEALTH SCHEDULES

You may be ready for something quirky or different that involves your imagination or a new daily routine. Place intentions at this new moon to create a better health schedule, more time to enjoy life and a fresh diet that brings something exciting to the table.

New moon in Pisces

REVITALISE YOUR LOVE LIFE AND RELATIONSHIPS

You'll appreciate the chance to revitalise a relationship, to improve work conditions or to boost health. You may feel particularly romantic or creative during the Pisces new moon phase. If you feel uncertain or even disoriented, wait for the moon in Aries to gain clarity before you take action.

New moon in Aries

BE PROACTIVE ABOUT JOINT DECISIONS

Aim to turn a corner with a business or personal partnership. Take the initiative and draw a line in the sand if you feel you're being taken for granted, or make a new agreement so you know where you stand. New relationships begun now and arrangements made may be exciting and refreshing if a little tempestuous.

New moon in Taurus

BROADEN YOUR INTERESTS AND MAKE AGREEMENTS

Initiate talks and make agreements. Avoid obstinacy; aim to collaborate. Consider re-organising a shared circumstance such as duties or communal space. You may contemplate fresh activities and financial arrangements. If you're unsure of your next step, consider practicalities first up. This new moon could revitalise your relationships in the long term, and romance could blossom.

New moon in Gemini

LAUNCH NEW VENTURES

A fresh chapter in your status, general direction or career promises to be more in line with your upbeat, capable and sociable personality, so if you're looking for a career change or to launch new projects take the initiative now. This may be a busy time, and your chatty and inquisitive nature will find full expression.

New moon in Cancer

PRESENT NEW IDEAS

A nurturing celestial aspect will support your plans, be these in your career or in life in general. What's more, you should find that people you must agree with will be more open to your ideas but you must avoid pushing for results.

New moon in Leo

DRAW UP EXCITING PLANS

While this new moon is good for many zodiac signs to begin new projects, for you it is better for drawing up plans behind the scenes and for networking with friends and organisations. A new project may begin with an organisation, but this is more a time for you and those you love. A focus on well-being will put you in a strong position moving forward.

LUNAR ECLIPSES:
be strong during peak emotional changes

Each lunar eclipse signals a major turning point in your life and may bring about intense emotions. Eclipses point to circumstances that seem to disempower you and subsequently motivate you to address any imbalances, so keep an eye on those areas in which you lack control as that is where you can make the most changes and become strong. Find out here which lunar eclipse will bring change in which area of your life, and how to make the most of these changes.

Virgo lunar eclipse
A FRESH ATTITUDE

You will benefit from adjusting your expectations so they match circumstances a little better. This can be empowering, as you will face the people in your life in a more practical and less idealistic way. Key discussions could bring a fresh dynamic to both domestic and work matters, so take the initiative.

Libra lunar eclipse
UPDATE YOUR FINANCES AND PERSONAL VALUES

Consider which areas of your life are unbalanced or simply don't add up, as this will provide you with the chance to create new growth and potential. Avoid pushing for results and conflict; find gentle ways to move ahead during this phase.

Scorpio lunar eclipse
EXPRESS YOUR VALUES

You may feel emotionally motivated to have things your way at work, financially, with a project or in a relationship. This eclipse will spotlight the way you express your values, self-esteem and principles through your finances and relationships, and you may wish to adjust one or all of these areas. The best way is to be calm and collected and maintain perspective.

Sagittarius lunar eclipse
TRAVEL AND EXPLORE

This eclipse will bring out your inner bohemian and your need to travel and communicate with many different people. If you have family commitments you may travel as a family, or welcome visitors to your home. Communications, study and relationships may assume a fresh role in your life, as you will be ready to explore new horizons both domestically and away.

Capricorn lunar eclipse
MAKE AGREEMENTS TO GAIN STABILITY

A new understanding with someone will involve the need to dig deep into your inner resources and achieve an agreement based on compassion and potentially to offer more than you may initially be willing to do. Strong emotions will be a major part of proceedings, but if you manage circumstances well you could provide future security.

Aquarius lunar eclipse
MANAGE YOUR PERSONAL LIFE

A family or personal matter could undergo a great deal of change, so organise special events to maintain the status quo. This eclipse could also bring key changes at home or within a creative project, so take extra time to manage projects and personal or family plans.

Pisces lunar eclipse
GET IN TOUCH WITH YOURSELF

If your life has become mechanical and predictable it's time to get back in touch with your deeper spiritual self. A fresh health and fitness schedule may appeal. For some this eclipse signals a fresh chapter within a business or personal relationship such as a new work interest and the chance to create more work/life balance.

Aries lunar eclipse

MANAGE YOUR RESPONSES

During this phase people can appear more emotional, impulsive or impatient, and so can you! Be mindful to avoid arguments and use this proactive time to get things done. You may meet upbeat, motivated people. If you wish to make changes with your relationships, this could be the time to do it.

Taurus lunar eclipse

MAINTAIN SOLID FOUNDATIONS IN RELATIONSHIPS

You will find ways to get back to the foundation of your agreements so that you can make a more solid and stable commitment moving forward. But if a relationship has been at the breaking point, this eclipse could finally put you on separate paths.

Gemini lunar eclipse

FIND MORE FREEDOM

You are likely to feel restless at this time, and so may someone close to you. You must avoid making change for the sake of it, but you will gain the option to alter your career, general direction and/or status. Developments could also highlight a special venture or relationship that could point to a fresh arrangement in a commitment.

Cancer lunar eclipse

LOOK FOR A STRONG SUPPORT NETWORK

You could break new ground once you establish a stronger support network. Your understanding of a family member or organisation will proceed on a more solid footing once you have decided how best to approach your relationship. The crux of decisions may revolve around how well supported – or the opposite – you feel by someone.

Leo lunar eclipse

FIND SOLUTIONS TO LONG-STANDING PROBLEMS

If you consciously make plans to move forward this eclipse will be a blessing, even if events occur in unexpected ways. Say goodbye to one phase in your life and greet a fresh one in your usual daily routine or social circles. Be proactive about finding solutions to problems and you will revitalise your life.

SOLAR ECLIPSES:
making major changes run smoothly

Each solar eclipse signals a major turning point in your life that points to ongoing change for years to come. Find out here which solar eclipses will bring change in which areas of your life, and how to make the most of those changes.

Virgo solar eclipse
LIVE YOUR BEST LIFE

It's time to look honestly, long and hard at your life: are you living the way you always wanted to? If not this eclipse is a good time to make changes, especially if the eclipse falls before or on your birthday. If it falls after your birthday, moving forward will be about being healthier and working smarter.

Libra solar eclipse
INVEST IN PRIORITIES

A fresh chapter that reorients your values and expression of these may take place over several weeks or months, and will be an ideal time to take action with your priorities. For some the focus will be on people, while for others this eclipse will usher in a new financial situation. Consider what and who you value and act accordingly.

Scorpio solar eclipse
IMPROVE YOUR NEGOTIATION SKILLS

Be pragmatic, as the Scorpio solar eclipse could dredge up all kinds of dramas in your life. Keep your head and aim for your goals while also being adaptable. You will find a wonderful way to move forward by being methodical and practical with paperwork, taxes and at work.

Sagittarius solar eclipse

DEEPEN YOUR COMPASSION

Developments now have great healing potential, so even if situations are tiring consider the outcome in practical terms and be kind. Travel, study or generally broadening your horizons will appeal. Deeper understanding may come about through learning that someone is different from how you previously thought of them or that you yourself are changing.

Capricorn solar eclipse

KICK-START A FRESH DOMESTIC PHASE

You could make long-term commitments during this time that will feather your nest for some time to come. Avoid limiting your options or movements too much into the future, but be prepared to commit to a plan that will provide you with more stability. Anchor spiritual practices so you feel more supported.

Aquarius solar eclipse

RECONSIDER WORK AND HEALTH

This is a good time to look outside the box at your various options and to try something you've always wanted to do. This is a turning point within your everyday schedule; for many it will mean a new chapter at work and for others it will concern health. Changes in someone else's schedule could affect your own.

Pisces solar eclipse

EMBRACE MYSTERY

You may be struck by events that seem unusual or mysterious yet these will offer the chance to step up to a deeper sense of fulfilment in your daily life and interactions. As you grapple with new and interesting ways to get ahead, this eclipse will shed light on what and who is invaluable to you. Singles: keep an eye out as someone may appear out of nowhere!

Aries solar eclipse

FIND BALANCE IN AGREEMENTS

To gain more equality and balance, find ways to be assertive rather than antagonistic and dynamic in your relationships as opposed to bossy! You may find people (including you) are more aggressive during this phase. Consider how you share duties, finances and workloads, both at work and at home. Legal proceedings may be necessary if negotiations stall.

Taurus solar eclipse

FORGE AHEAD IN NEW AREAS

If you find forces beyond your control become an obstacle you must surge ahead intuitively into new terrain. This eclipse will present a fresh financial chapter or a new shared concern such as a change of duty or communal space. Stand your ground but avoid limiting your options for growth and adventure further down the line.

Gemini solar eclipse

CHOOSE A FRESH PATH

Travel, a creative project and deepening spirituality will all appeal. Take the initiative with collaborations, at work and in your personal life and make exciting plans. For some this eclipse points to relationships that have run their course, so you must opt for a new path.

Cancer solar eclipse

OPT FOR SECURITY AND NURTURANCE

You'll see the practicalities of maintaining good relationships that provide you with stability and security as a fresh chapter is about to begin within your career and/or family life. A friendship or love affair may deepen, or you may leave a familiar circumstance in a relationship. You may be drawn to join new groups.

Leo solar eclipse

PLAN A HAPPIER LIFE

Re-evaluate your life. How can you shine and feel accomplished both at work and in yourself? Be prepared to try something new, to work with people in dynamic ways and to take action in expressive ways to boost vitality that brings more of the qualities you want into your daily routine.

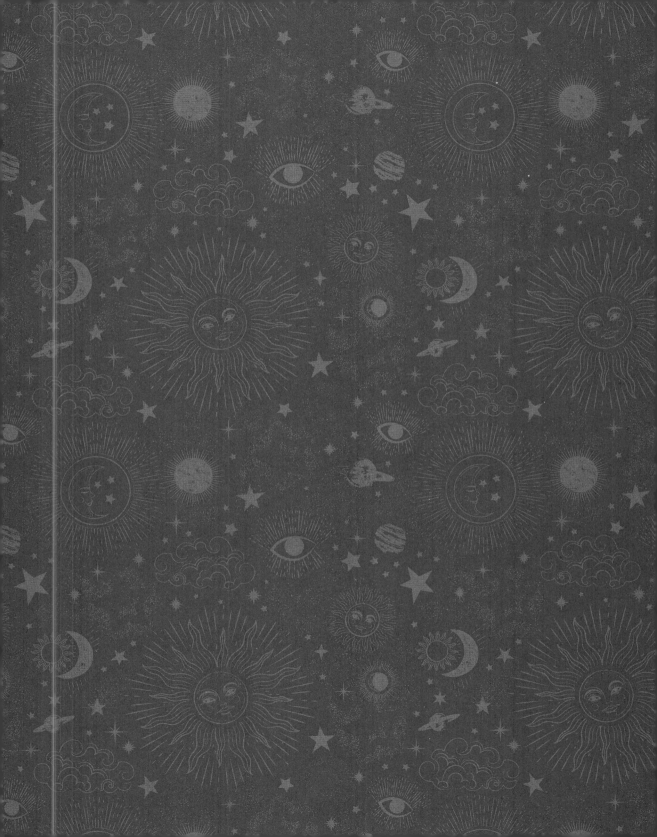

23 SEPTEMBER – 23 OCTOBER

SYMBOL
Scales

ELEMENT
Air

CONSTELLATION

LIBRA
SUN SIGN

INNER CALLING

Peace, harmony and togetherness make you feel the happiest, and if these qualities are not prevalent in your life it won't be through a lack of trying! Librans are most likely of all the sun signs to look for peace and balance in life, and to do so there has to be a perceived lack or you are not motivated to find it. Even once you gain a sense of balance and harmony in life you will always want more, but this sense of a lack in balance risks taking you away from your true calling in life: to feel happy.

Your sign's symbol – the scales – represents your wish for a harmonious and peaceful life, so it's important that you keep striving for these components as this will give you a sense of purpose even if you do feel a sense of lack. Love and money are the key areas in which striving to achieve positive results will most consume your energy and will be the areas in which you learn the greatest life lessons.

SELF-ESTEEM

With Venus as your sign's ruler you appear to have high self-esteem, as you exude natural calm and peace and appear to be balanced and calm. Many people with a strong Libran signature in their astrology chart have a heart-shaped face or a rounder shape with a pleasing form that invokes the notion of calmness and beauty. However, beneath the calm exterior can be myriad reasons you doubt yourself or have low self-esteem due to the underlying tension caused by continually seeking harmony. Scratch the surface and insecurities are aplenty, especially when you are young.

You can boost self-esteem by following your strict code of ethics and expressing them through your daily actions. As you accrue a sense of fulfilment, capability and accomplishment your self-esteem will slowly rise, but if you follow someone else's principles and morals you could realise they contradict your own and you are liable to sink deeper into a sense of inner conflict, leading only to lower self-esteem. Learn to trust your principles and values as these are linked with compassion and love. Your sign is ruled by Venus, the goddess of love, after all.

HOME LIFE

You will wish your home life to be a source of great pleasure, especially as you mature: you derive a sense of stability and security from your home and it is unlikely you live in a home that is ugly or worn down. As you mature and gain the resources to furnish your home luxuriously, it may even be difficult to prise you away from your domestic bliss.

Your family and children are important to you, as they are not only a source of pride but also of comfort and security. You will devote much time to your children and will also wish for a strong link with your parents, especially your mother. However, in your eternal search for balance and harmony you can tend to be critical of those with whom you share your home and must avoid promoting difficult circumstances due to your perceived lack of perfection. You could cause just what you don't want as a result: a lack of peace.

RELATIONSHIPS

Your desire for love is strong and you are unlikely to be a loner. You are outgoing and optimistic in your relationships, which are the area of your life where you most seek to establish peace, fulfilment and harmony. However, you are often attracted to dynamic and feisty characters and can feel a lack of balance in your life, as relationships are inevitably changeable or so fast moving and dynamic it's hard to keep up with them!

To overcome this anomaly, consider seeing your relationships as complementary to your quest for peace; see upbeat, feisty people as their yang to your ying. You may find then that a partner fulfils your lust for life while creating the complete big picture in the relationship you seek.

CREATIVITY

Your sign's ruler Venus governs beauty, so art and creativity are true interests for you. Even if you are not artistic you will enjoy creating an ambient atmosphere around you, for example through beautiful décor in your home or by being creative with your appearance and wardrobe. A love of fashion and beauty is a part of the Libran profile. Finding time to express your creativity will bring a sense of peace and calmness to your life.

Venus also rules music and you may find this a fulfilling way to express yourself, either joining in with the music of others or playing music yourself. You will enjoy attending music festivals and seeing artistic or dramatic performances.

You may find that your creativity is expressed through the ultimate act of creation: birthing children! You will enjoy being the central character in your own family and may also enjoy looking after other people's children during various phases of your life.

PITFALLS

You can tend to get caught in the vicious cycle of continuously wanting more, which can be a true pitfall for Librans. Your desires can be hard to curb, especially when you are looking for happiness in life, so it's important to direct your attention to realistic and healthy pursuits or you can feel you are constantly lacking. You'll find peace and harmony from inner calm rather than in the outside world or through money or passionate love. Meditation and other calming activities are true gifts to Librans for this reason.

Due to the fact you are constantly looking for balance in life you can tend to be indecisive as you strive for the best outcome. You can vacillate from one idea to the next, unable to make up your mind. This pitfall can be overcome by considering the practicalities first and then meshing these with your ideals and appreciation for beauty and meaning in life. Mix realities and dreams together and add a sprinkle of intuition, and you will make the right decisions and excel in life.

SOLAR TRANSITS:
harness the sun's power
every day of the year

The sun empowers you in different areas of your life as it travels through each zodiac sign from month to month. Find out here how to make the most of your strong points during each of the transits of the sun through the 12 signs.

Sun in Libra, September to October
BE PROACTIVE

The harmony and peace you're looking for can be attained, so make plans to create more balance in your life. A meeting of like minds or a romantic getaway could be therapeutic during this time. Aim to boost your appearance and also your kudos at work.

Sun in Scorpio, October to November
BOOST FINANCES AND SELF-ESTEEM

Your passions will rise and you can be super productive now, but you must double check your actions are in line with your values or you may regret your decisions. Maintain a healthy scepticism with new projects until you know the facts and then dive into them wholeheartedly but without being super impulsive.

Sun in Sagittarius, November to December
EXPRESS YOURSELF

Explore your values and principles: how do you express these? You may focus on money and self-expression through ownership or spending and may find retail therapy useful, but you must avoid overspending. You will be drawn to travel and will be chattier than usual as you find ways to explore your own interests and be happy.

Sun in Capricorn, December to January

INVEST IN DOMESTIC RELATIONSHIPS

You love to feel safe and secure, and this phase will spotlight the area where you most wish to feel happy: your relationships. You will feel the need to make solid agreements and may travel or be more communicative about making fresh arrangements that bring more security your way.

Sun in Aquarius, January to February

BRING VARIETY TO ROMANCE, FUN AND CREATIVITY

You will feel drawn to quirky or fun activities that bring your creativity out, such as home decoration, arts and crafts, dancing and music. Focus on having a more varied dynamic in your personal life, such as enjoying family outings and more socialising if you're single.

Sun in Pisces, February to March

BRING ROMANCE INTO YOUR DAILY LIFE

Your creative and romantic nature will rise to the surface. You may feel inspired to make changes at home or in your work environment so you feel more at ease and are able to express your need for balance and harmony in your daily life. Consider boosting your profile and wardrobe and including more comfort in your home.

Sun in Aries, March to April

REFRESH YOUR LOVE LIFE AND RELATIONSHIPS

You'll appreciate the opportunity to revitalise circumstances that alter your daily routine or environment and will easily channel energy into fun events. If developments are super busy or simply tiring and frustrating it will be because the people around you seem to lose their tempers or are more aggressive. Aim to establish peace as best you can.

Sun in Taurus, April to May

COLLABORATE AND CO-OPERATE

You'll feel motivated to collaborate better and will be more decisive. Your actions could also take effect more swiftly, and even if some obstacles arise these will stimulate your need for balance and harmony in your life and relationships. You will work harder to gain peace.

Sun in Gemini, May to June

EXPAND YOUR EXPERIENCES

Be prepared to embrace new experiences such as travel and study. Avoid being overly idealistic in business and research your options carefully, as you're liable to skim over the surface of agreements during this phase. Make plans for something special with your partner; if you're single you could meet someone special over the next few weeks.

Sun in Cancer, June to July

BOOST YOUR HAPPINESS

You are constantly on a search for harmony in life because life can be chaotic at times! During this phase sport, meditation, hobbies and modalities that relax your mind such as a lovely holiday to an inspiring and calm place will appeal. Your career could skyrocket the more you look after yourself; people will notice your sparkle!

Sun in Leo, July to August

SOCIALISE AND BOOST OPPORTUNITIES

You'll enjoy feeling upbeat about your connections with groups, organisations and friendships and may feel drawn to join new clubs and associations. Singles may feel more outgoing and wish to meet like-minded people. Working Librans may find this a particularly progressive time at work with new projects and opportunities to advance your career arising.

Sun in Virgo, August to September

FOCUS ON PRIORITIES AND HEALTH

You may enjoy altering your usual routine so you can accommodate your own and/or someone's health needs and negotiate a fresh work schedule in the name of well-being and health. This is a good time to investigate spiritual and psychological matters. You may be drawn to revisit the past.

LUNAR TRANSITS:
be calm and effective every day of the month

The moon spotlights different aspects of your emotional self as it travels each month through each zodiac sign, staying two days in each sign. When the moon is in each sign you gain the opportunity to express yourself more effectively in various areas of your life. Find out here how to make the most of your strong points during each of the two days each month.

Moon in Libra

GAIN EMOTIONAL BALANCE

You'll get the opportunity to come to grips with emotional and mental health and well-being and to focus on yourself to gain peace in life. The Libra moon will encourage you to find balance and harmony in situations that may test your resolve.

Moon in Scorpio

GAIN INSIGHT

While you generally aim to please, the Scorpio moon will spotlight your values and principles. If these differ from other people's you may feel a little uncompromising. You will nevertheless gain insight into your own situation and feelings and those of other people. On the positive side this could be a truly romantic time, so take advantage of these stars.

Moon in Sagittarius

PROGRESS WITH DECISIONS AND PLANS

The Sagittarian moon will encourage you to broach topics that are important to you and that involve someone close. Be positive and optimistic; you could make some great decisions and agreements both in your personal life and at work. This is a good time to take a short trip.

Moon in Capricorn
INCREASE DOMESTIC BLISS

Developments at home should provide stability and security, but if you feel circumstances are restrictive or tense then it's a good time to look for realistic ways to brighten up and revitalise your home life. Base your decisions on practicalities that will alleviate some of your tension.

Moon in Aquarius
REVITALISE TIRED RELATIONSHIPS

The Aquarian moon will spotlight your emotional needs from your family and home life. You may find developments here are upbeat, but if they are unusual or unsettling they may be destabilising. An upbeat or fun approach towards friends and lovers could revitalise relationships and create more calm.

Moon in Pisces
BE INSPIRED AT WORK AND HEALTH-WISE

You may feel particularly inspired at work but may also be absent-minded, so you must concentrate super hard! This is an excellent time to indulge yourself or someone close in a health and well-being treat. It is a good time for yoga, meditation, art, forest bathing and spiritual endeavours to boost peace and harmony in your life.

Moon in Aries
EXPRESS YOURSELF!

You'll feel motivated to be more expressive with those you love. Your ability to empathise with people can be a blessing as you are able to understand them easily; however, if someone's behaviour is truly unacceptable you must make a strong stance but must avoid escalating disagreements during the Aries moon.

Moon in Taurus
FOCUS ON ROMANCE AND SHARING

This is the ideal time to focus on those you love, especially partners. You'll appreciate creating a sumptuous atmosphere where romance will flourish. You may also get ahead with collaborations at work by being practical and realistic.

Moon in Gemini

BE ACTIVE

You may feel restless, so engage in physical exercise to dispel excess energy. You'll enjoy chatting and socialising and will feel drawn to doing something different such as travel or taking time out for a favourite hobby. Research and analysis will be productive.

Moon in Cancer

BE ASSERTIVE

Gather your thoughts and put yourself forward positively and with conviction, especially at work and in areas where you want your voice to be heard. You may feel ready to present your ideas to someone important or to make a statement. Trust your instincts for the right time and place to do so.

Moon in Leo

ENJOY THE COMPANY OF THOSE YOU LOVE

This is a good time to reach out to others, including work colleagues, and if you're looking for work it's a good time to circulate your resume. You may enjoy a fresh environment and socialising. It's a good time to make changes in your daily routine that are upbeat and therapeutic.

Moon in Virgo

SCHEDULE TIME FOR HEALTH AND HAPPINESS

This is a good time to rethink some of your schedules so they suit you better. You may consider a new daily routine or work schedule so you get more time for exercise, fitness and peace of mind, and more time for the people and activities you love.

FULL MOONS:
magnify your vibrant power

*Each full moon highlights different aspects of your power and vibrancy.
Find out here which full moons will be excellent times to turn a corner
in the various areas of your life to show just what you're made of.*

Full moon in Libra
BE DECISIVE IN YOUR PERSONAL LIFE

The beginning of a fresh phase in your personal life will involve a key decision, and the long-term benefits of being proactive will soon become evident. As several areas of your life will be affected it's wise to make solid, practical plans that lead to an optimistic upturn. Avoid conflict and taking someone else's moods personally.

Full moon in Scorpio
BOOST SELF-ESTEEM AND ABUNDANCE

You will turn a corner in a key financial or personal agreement, and this full moon will spotlight your feelings about circumstances. If you're making long-term decisions, take time out to maintain perspective and avoid allowing strong emotions to adversely affect your actions. Be ready for positive change.

Full moon in Sagittarius
UPGRADE COMMUNICATIONS OR TRANSPORT

The spotlight is on you: are you ready for an upgrade? It's time for a new communications device to boost a sense of fresh possibilities. Transport will also deserve attention to keep it up to date. If you experience any disappointments, focus on being optimistic and outgoing. Key financial matters will deserve attention so ensure you have the moolah to embark on a journey of discovery.

Full moon in Capricorn

BEGIN A FRESH CHAPTER AT HOME

You may need to make a tough call regarding your personal space versus work or duties. If disappointments arise, channel strong emotions into fun activities rather than allowing feelings of being hard done by to grow. Be practical with plans and conversations to ensure you maintain stability at home.

Full moon in Aquarius

REVITALISE ROMANCE, FUN AND CREATIVITY

Get set for a new chapter in your personal life or with family. Someone may need more freedom of expression; if it's you, find ways to be more expressive through art and creativity and to gain a deeper understanding of someone close. If you're single, this could be the time you meet someone new.

Full moon in Pisces

ADD SPARKLE TO WORK AND WELL-BEING

You may enjoy an increased sense of potential either at work or in your personal life, but if developments are mysterious and contribute to a feeling of disorientation ensure you get your feet back on the ground. You'll appreciate the chance to boost your health, beauty and well-being in inspired ways.

Full moon in Aries

TURN A CORNER IN RELATIONSHIPS

The chance to discuss your plans with someone close should be successful and productive as long as you avoid conflict. You may notice that you feel uncharacteristically feisty, or you may simply decide that someone's independence eclipses the relationship. Take things one step at a time to avoid arguments.

Full moon in Taurus
BOOST PASSIONS AND INTERESTS

This full moon is earthy and stimulates passion. It's a good time to make lasting commitments both to someone close and to a course of action at work. You may decide that certain ideas could work in a shared area or a financial investment; be practical for the best results.

Full moon in Gemini
EMBRACE MORE DIVERSITY

It's a good time to focus on ways to add more variety and spice to your life, such as fun pastimes and travel. Consider being more flexible in areas of your life you share such as duties, space at home and finances, and rearrange some agreements if necessary.

Full moon in Cancer
GROW YOUR CAREER OR STATUS

You'll appreciate the chance to turn a corner in your career or general circumstances that allows you to enjoy a little more nurturance and harmony in life, rather than feeling constantly as though you are the one who must provide nurturance to everyone else.

Full moon in Leo
PRIORITISE FAVOURITE ACTIVITIES

This full moon will put your values into the spotlight as you realise more fully what your priorities are, especially in connection with work, status, general direction, your personal life and those you love. It's not selfish to enjoy life, so schedule in love, fun and more love.

Full moon in Virgo
RESCHEDULE DAILY WORK AND HEALTH ROUTINES

Be practical and realistic about your daily life. Consider going to a gym or a nutritional or health class that boosts your vitality. A key development regarding a group or organisation could come full circle, enabling you to alter your everyday routine.

NEW MOONS:
start something fresh

Each new moon points to the start of something fresh for you in different areas of your life. Find out here which new moon to work with and how to make lasting change by starting something new, especially if you have been putting off change for some time.

New moon in Libra
MAKE LIFE MORE BEAUTIFUL

Look for peaceful ways to move ahead. This is a good new moon for improving your appearance, fitness and well-being or those of someone close. A moral dilemma or the need to make a key decision will kick-start a fresh chapter. Consider finances from a long-term perspective.

New moon in Scorpio
REBOOT FINANCES

Take the initiative and investigate new ideas and projects as you could make great progress, especially financially and work-wise. You may feel passionate about a principle and motivated to put your ideas into action, so this is a good time to look into the financial viability of your long-term plans.

New moon in Sagittarius
EMBRACE NEW OPPORTUNITIES

Keep an eye out for opportunities, but avoid gambling and overspending at the same time. You may be super generous right now and may tend to become stuck on a particular idea or principle, so ensure you maintain perspective. A new relationship or project could broaden your understanding of people and cultures.

New moon in Capricorn

MAKE A HAPPIER HOME

This is a good time to start something new with family or property or at home. It's also a good time to instigate plans that create a more stable and secure way of life at home, with family or property, but you must avoid limiting your abilities and may need to adapt to new parameters or restrictions.

New moon in Aquarius

STIMULATE ROMANCE, FUN AND CREATIVITY

If you're single this is a good time to plan for a quirkier and more fun time in your love life. Couples may enjoy trying a new approach to your partner to revitalise your relationship. Avoid gambling and making assumptions if making long-term decisions; you may not be on the same page as everyone else.

New moon in Pisces

KICK-START A FRESH DAILY ROUTINE

You will be looking to gain more meaning and relevance in your job and chores so a fresh daily routine may appeal. While drawing on inspiration and a need to have more purpose in your daily life, ensure at the same time you are realistic with work and domestic plans. You may adopt a new look.

New moon in Aries

REFRESH YOUR LOVE LIFE AND RELATIONSHIPS

A fresh start is on the way in a personal or business relationship that may take a little adjustment, so take things one step at a time. If you or someone close feels a little edgy during this phase, channel restlessness into fun activities and draw strength from activities you both love.

New moon in Taurus

EARTH RELATIONSHIPS AND MAKE COMMITMENTS

You will gain the opportunity now to move onto more solid ground, especially in your relationships. You must avoid impulsiveness and may need to be patient while reconfiguring some of your agreements, which could eventually transform your relationships.

New moon in Gemini

EXPLORE EXCITING HORIZONS

You'll enjoy allowing your fun-loving side to seek full expression. This is a good time to kick-start a new project or interest. Travel and the lure of the exotic or overseas will be hard to ignore. For some there will be a fresh collaboration to consider. Study, research and, on occasion, legal matters will deserve a fresh approach.

New moon in Cancer

NURTURE YOUR CAREER AND FINANCES

You're adept at finding peace and harmony in the least likely areas, and if anyone can create a peaceful mood it's you. You'll enjoy providing this influence with people you collaborate and share duties with. A change of circumstance could also be ideal, bringing a little breath of fresh air into your work life. Be imaginative.

New moon in Leo

BEGIN A MORE DYNAMIC PHASE

Prepare for a busy time. A change of routine could be ideal, and you'll enjoy broadening your horizons and being sociable. This new moon could provide direction at work or a renewed interest in your career. You'll enjoy being more dynamic but must avoid impulsiveness.

New moon in Virgo

FOCUS ON SPIRITUAL WELL-BEING

This is a good time to begin something new that involves planning, increased self-awareness and a little introspection, either concerning you or someone else. It's a good time to begin a fresh health routine and boost general vitality and balance and harmony in your daily life.

LUNAR ECLIPSES:
be strong during peak emotional changes

Each lunar eclipse signals a major turning point in your life and may bring about intense emotions. Eclipses point to circumstances that seem to disempower you and subsequently motivate you to address any imbalances, so keep an eye on those areas in which you lack control as that is where you can make the most changes and become strong. Find out here which lunar eclipse will bring change in which area of your life, and how to make the most of these changes.

Libra lunar eclipse
REINSTATE PEACE IN YOUR LIFE

Find ways to re-establish balance and be ready to adapt to circumstances as you may feel particularly emotional, especially if the eclipse falls on or near your birthday. If you were born after the date of the eclipse you may begin a fresh chapter at work or health-wise.

Scorpio lunar eclipse
BE DECISIVE ABOUT VALUES AND MONEY

Decisions will need to be made and yet topsy-turvy feelings make this difficult. Research facts to help with decision making. Check that your values and need for balance in life do not blind you to the reality of circumstances; be clear about your values and lead from there.

Sagittarius lunar eclipse
ESTABLISH FAIR PLAY AND JUSTICE

Values and ethics are important to you as you like to feel engaged in life on a moral level. You may feel driven to establish more fair play, either in your personal life or at work or regarding principles and human values in general. You may also be driven to improve your self-esteem and finances. For some this phase may involve legal matters in your search for fairness.

Capricorn lunar eclipse

LOOK FOR CALMNESS AT HOME OR WITH FAMILY

Domestic or family changes could turn your life upside down, but if you're diligent change could signal more security and peace ahead. You may need to make a tough call regarding your personal space, but you'll gain validation that you are making the right choices by monitoring small successes.

Aquarius lunar eclipse

WELCOME CHANGE

A lovely opportunity to bring change to your family, home life or property will add more innovation, beauty and luxury to these vital areas of your life. You may need to renegotiate an agreement as a fresh chapter will spotlight new priorities, for some due to changes outside your control such as those at work.

Pisces lunar eclipse

BE INSPIRED

You'll thrive by being creative and looking for projects at work that allow you to express yourself more fully. You may be drawn to more spiritual endeavours in your daily life and may be inspired by a way of life that brings more focus on well-being and health into your daily schedule. Put energy into sumptuous romance and love.

Aries lunar eclipse

BRING YOUR INNER PEACEMAKER OUT

Changes within an existing relationship will be long term. This eclipse will bring someone's tempers and tantrums out, so make arrangements to create a serene and comfortable atmosphere you can relax in. If you're single you may meet someone new, and couples could revitalise your relationship unless you feel it's time to go your separate ways.

Taurus lunar eclipse
ALTER COMMITMENTS

A positive course correction is on the way, even if drama arises in the process. This eclipse will shine a light on your true feelings about a commitment: you may be ready to make a fresh arrangement with a partner or will go your separate ways if the relationship has been on the rocks.

Gemini lunar eclipse
A FRESH PATH

Your horizons will broaden, but you will need to make new arrangements first or undergo negotiations that will permit you to move forward. Certain duties or finances may change as a result of legal matters. You may be drawn to travel, study or a busier time communications-wise. Avoid giving key commitments the flick in the process unless they have outgrown their purpose.

Cancer lunar eclipse
CHANGE YOUR STATUS OR FAMILY CIRCUMSTANCES

A period of adjustment will be necessary as it's all change within your general status and, for some, career. Domestic matters will require rearrangement as a result of developments in your status or profile. You may be drawn to particular family members and to ensuring you deepen your relationship.

Leo lunar eclipse
LOYALTIES CHANGE

A new social circle or organisation will put your focus in line with changing interests and priorities. A friendship or family arrangement may begin or end or alter footing. If you've been super sociable you may prefer to be a homebody for a while and vice versa.

Virgo lunar eclipse
HELP SOMEONE

Someone close may be in need of a little support or a health boost, and your help will be appreciated. Aim to be of service to others in need, and if you need more help yourself it will be available. For some this lunar eclipse is all about working hard and earning money even if a job or contract ends, so get ready!

SOLAR ECLIPSES:
making major changes run smoothly

*Each solar eclipse signals a major turning point in your life
that points to ongoing change for years to come. Find out
here which solar eclipses will bring change in which areas of
your life, and how to make the most of those changes.*

Libra solar eclipse
KICK-START A HAPPY LIFE

You want to be happy, so make it happen! Tact and diplomacy will go a long way towards securing long-term change. If a tough call must be made, you must avoid being too hard on yourself; keep communications clear for the best results. If you were born on the eclipse you will see change in your personal life, but if you were born after the eclipse it will be at work or health-wise.

Scorpio solar eclipse
A PASSIONATE CHANGE OF HEART

The Scorpio eclipse will kick-start a new phase in which there will be more clarity and passion in a personal partnership. You'll appreciate the sense of progress but must avoid dramas. You'll gain insight into your true feelings about a shared circumstance, such as space at home or taxes.

Sagittarius solar eclipse
INVEST WISELY

You may consider a large outlay or investment but must ensure you do not over- or underestimate your spending power. If you are in a relationship that is stuck, consider ways to spur it on. Singles may feel more proactive about finding a partner. For some this eclipse could point to a parting of ways, largely due to different values, and for some distance apart.

Capricorn solar eclipse
FIND MORE SUPPORT

This is a good time to look for more support from others and to build stronger foundations at home or at work. If an existing routine or way of life ends you will manage to create a new life that is stabilising and supports your needs.

Aquarius solar eclipse
BE MORE UPBEAT AND INSPIRED

Aim to be more resourceful and helpful; you may be asked for support or will need it yourself. Creative Librans may be truly inspired during this time, both in your everyday domestic or working life. For some Librans new circumstances may arise due to health matters; for others this eclipse signals a change in a close relationship.

Pisces solar eclipse
EMBRACE A NEW SCHEDULE

A fresh routine will arise due to matters outside your control. You may be increasingly drawn to spirituality and health and well-being modalities that boost your peace of mind. You may feel increasingly inspired and creative, and if you've been contemplating changes in a family context this could be the time to make them.

Aries solar eclipse
OPEN DOORS IN RELATIONSHIPS

A fresh dynamic in a relationship and a new work or health schedule will provide you with a greater sense of accomplishment. This phase may present as a missed opportunity or a situation that goes pear shaped, but new opportunities will arise that you may not yet see so be brave. Feisty people will have their say, so find key ways to minimise the effects of their anger on you.

Taurus solar eclipse
NEGOTIATE NEW ARRANGEMENTS

If you feel restricted by some commitments this is a good time to alter them. Avoid blocking opportunities to resolve issues, looking instead at ways to build bridges with those you must get along with. However, if you feel truly maligned it's time to take a fresh path.

Gemini solar eclipse

A SPOTLIGHT ON FREEDOM

You're ready to change some arrangements and feel freer, and if you have not been prepared to make changes in the name of peace this eclipse could bring long-overdue change into being. If you're single you may begin to feel prepared to commit; couples may consider a fresh understanding that involves more freedom of movement or travel.

Cancer solar eclipse

FIND MORE BALANCE IN LIFE

This is a good time to turn a corner in your career, status or direction. New activities will appeal. Look for more sustainability in your career, activities and interests: you may be drawn to update your skill set, travel or sign new contracts to alter your circumstances. A change of status from single to married or vice versa will draw on your inner resources, so be strong.

Leo solar eclipse

GAIN KUDOS

You'll enjoy being more assertive but must avoid conflict as you reveal a more proactive and outgoing you that some people may object to. Meetings and talks will deepen relationships with those you love and you'll come to understand which relationships sap your energy. Networking and socialising could be pivotal in boosting your status at this time.

Virgo solar eclipse

REBIRTH

This eclipse is simply about moving ahead as you have outgrown certain people in your life, such as groups and organisations, and your new affiliations will suit the new you that is emerging. For many, key changes will include the incubation of work and health schedules that are more the 'new you'.

23 OCTOBER - 22 NOVEMBER

SYMBOL
Scorpion

CONSTELLATION

ELEMENT
Water

SCORPIO
SUN SIGN

INNER CALLING

You need to feel that you have a goal and are effective in creating the life you desire, that you are not only the actor in your story but also the writer, director and producer. In this way your adventures become truly meaningful experiences and provide a sense of fulfilment, as they are the result of your vision, hard work, lust for life and productivity.

Because your sign is ruled by fiery and powerful Mars and Pluto you need to feel that you are the person who has the power, the person with the most proactive and dynamic personality. Rarely will you feel comfortable playing second fiddle in relationships, as for you to thrive and feel valued and confident relationships need to be fair and equal at the very least. This approach ripples out into your relationship with the world, as your calling is to feel thoroughly engaged with your activities. You will not give less than 110 per cent, otherwise you feel undervalued yourself. It's vital you find activities, a career and direction in life that are meaningful or your passionate character risks turning in on itself and becoming self-destructive.

You have a magnetic effect on others, who see you as being charismatic, charming and seductive. But not in a showy way: your charisma smoulders just beneath the surface of your skin and you don't need to show off as you are naturally charming and attractive. It's simply who you are; there is no effort needed to be beautiful, potent and intense.

You may not see this yourself, and this only adds to your charm. Your charisma is natural, like a fragrance that wafts from your pores! You attract people the way flowers attract bees, and this is an essential part of your inner calling: to interact with others in a creative, subliminal, non-conscious way so that your intense and creative essence is expressed through every interaction and action you take.

SELF-ESTEEM

You naturally possess high self-esteem, a self-assurance that forms part of your charm. However, all too easily when life throws you a curve ball you throw up your hands in surrender and your self-esteem evaporates and is replaced by your more negative traits: self-doubt, insecurity and anger. In reaction you can tend to lash out at those who seem to block your way, your reasoning being that it is they who are at fault because you never intended harm and therefore don't deserve any ill-luck.

When your self-esteem is dented it may take a while to rebuild it, so it's important to take the time to rebuild your self-confidence. It is a natural ability you possess, but if you are a volatile Scorpio then the more quickly you learn to restore your self-esteem the better for you. In this way you'll remain in control of your better qualities: loyalty, effectiveness and passion for all you do and experience in life.

HOME LIFE

Your home presents a treasure trove of opportunities to you throughout your life, from being a place of nurturance and togetherness to being a place of work or an interim resource as you prepare for exciting adventures. Your home life may be quirky in some ways, and you may have a family that is blended, unorthodox or different from that of other people.

You are likely to have an unusual home that encompasses unorthodox architecture. You may work from home, so your home may be partitioned into work and play areas more so than other people's homes.

As a parent you can be fiercely protective of your children and partner, which is something to be aware of, as your potency can easily be misconstrued as dominance rather than nurturance and protectiveness.

RELATIONSHIPS

You are seen as being a powerful, intense character and all the more so as people get to know you better. You may initially be seen as shy or even retiring, but once people get to know you the magnetic attraction becomes more intense. In intimate relationships you can be seen as a truly passionate character whose will is hard to resist once you are truly entwined in a relationship.

When you are crossed that famous sting in the tail emerges, and you can then be seen as spiteful, vengeful and destructive. You have relatively little self-control from other people's points of view and can be seen as dangerous. As you know, the sting in the tail is most likely to sting you, not your enemy, so the more you keep this destructive characteristic in check the better for all.

To enhance your charming attributes aim to show your loyal side and your wish to nurture and transform others more often, and demonstrate your ability to rise above drama and intrigue. In these ways you will rise like the phoenix ever strong from any flames of conflict.

CREATIVITY

Yours is one of the most creative signs of the zodiac as you have the power of transformation and self-transformation at your fingertips. Your sign's traditional ruler, the planet Pluto, is named after the Roman god of the underworld, who in turn was named after the Greek god Hades. As the ruler of the underworld, of life after death, Hades represents the ultimate power of transformation as he resides over the place we progress to from life to death and once more to life. Pluto astrologically represents the power of transformation, which is why in many zodiac symbols Pluto is equated with the phoenix that rises from the ashes.

Scorpio is a hugely creative sign on an elemental, natural, organic level. The Scorpio creativity is the creativity of life itself: birth and the fecundity and creation of life. Family, children and the cycle of life and death are likely to be of huge importance to you on some level.

On a daily level your creativity often stems from your own understanding of your ability to change your circumstances. You will not necessarily be the artist, craftsperson or musician who changes the world, but you are acutely aware that your everyday tasks are a manifestation of your own inner power and creativity and have an immediate and lasting effect on your reality, surroundings, circumstances and the people in your life, whether you create happy children or art or simply bring charm to the world.

PITFALLS

With Mars and Pluto running the show you have a vast amount of energy and dynamism at your disposal but you may also lack impulse control, especially when young. To ensure you make the most of your potential channel your energy into activities that have meaning for you, that resonate with your highest potential. Otherwise you can be easily seduced into activities that pander to your baser desires and could, if you take a wrong turn into drugs, alcohol or violence, lead to drama-fuelled events and self-destructive behaviour.

With two fiery, impulsive planets ruling your sign, anger and addictive, compulsive behaviour and gambling can be true pitfalls. You may find anger management and help with addictive behaviour a truly useful tool at various stages of your life.

Your true skills lie in self-transformation and in coaching others on their path to self-transformation. All this begins with work on yourself from a young age, and with witnessing for yourself how to turn negative behaviour patterns into positive ones.

SOLAR TRANSITS:
harness the sun's power
every day of the year

The sun empowers you in different areas of your life as it travels through each zodiac sign from month to month. Find out here how to make the most of your strong points during each of the transits of the sun through the 12 signs.

Sun in Scorpio, October to November

SHINE LIKE THE STAR YOU ARE

This phase will brighten your days, adding a sense of direction. You will experience a surge in passion, charm and energy, and your work and circumstances can improve as a result. Just avoid allowing your emotions and lust for life to cancel out your good sense, or you may find this phase leads you to being impulsive and short-sighted.

Sun in Sagittarius, November to December

EXPAND YOUR INFLUENCE

Your passionate side comes out during these four weeks. You may be drawn to express yourself flamboyantly or vibrantly through your appearance, and will enjoy new ideas, travel and fresh projects. You may seem larger than life, being the life and soul of the party, and may overindulge and overspend. Finances could be a focus and retail therapy will appeal.

Sun in Capricorn, December to January

BUILD STABILITY

Your need for comfort, sensuality and loyalty in your relationships will expand now. Building security and stability will appeal and take your focus. You may be particularly drawn to spend more money and energy on your own needs and those of others. This is a good time to organise a stable budget.

Sun in Aquarius, January to February
EXPLORE NEW IDEAS AND PLACES

Your restlessness and wanderlust will come out. This is a good time for travel and to make changes at home and in your environment, but you must avoid being too left field or you risk making changes for the sake of it. You'll enjoy being spontaneous with friends and family and updating décor, devices and even vehicles or travel routes.

Sun in Pisces, February to March
FOCUS ON ROMANCE AND CREATIVITY

You'll enjoy expressing your artistic side, so creative, romantic and musical Scorpios will find this a particularly productive time. Your interest in psychic, spiritual and esoteric matters will deepen. You may feel inspired to make changes domestically such as improving interpersonal dynamics or redecorating.

Sun in Aries, March to April
REGAIN YOUR VITALITY AND LUST FOR LIFE

You'll find these four weeks revitalising as you'll gain the chance to be more creative and spend time with those you love. This could be a passionate phase. If you're considering starting a family or adding to it, this is a positive time to take action!

Sun in Taurus, April to May
INVEST IN HAPPINESS AND RELATIONSHIPS

You'll enjoy the luxuries and sensuality of life. This is a good time to be practical with your actions, but if your emotions become intense ground them by being sensible and reasonable. You may feel drawn to someone special and to collaborating more, both at work and at home.

Sun in Gemini, May to June
ENJOY BEING LIGHT-HEARTED

Despite being busy you'll feel more light-hearted towards business and personal partners, which will create a fruitful and vibrant phase. However, some may see you as being elusive, so ensure you remind them of your loyalty. If you're inundated with work you'll get ahead by delegating.

Sun in Cancer, June to July

LET YOUR SPIRIT SOAR

You'll find expressing much of your motivation and energy is easier, especially your creative and romantic qualities. This is a good time for a holiday. You are likely to feel in your element, especially if you are engaged in spiritual, artistic and sporty activities or travel.

Sun in Leo, July to August

SHINE AT THE PEAK OF YOUR ABILITIES

The sun is at the top of your chart and is spotlighting your better qualities. Your dynamic, charming and positive self will be in full flight, and you'll enjoy demonstrating just how capable you are both at work and socially. You may be super charismatic, making this a good time for furthering your career and personal ventures and networking.

Sun in Virgo, August to September

CHOOSE THE COMPANY OF THOSE YOU LOVE

This phase will place focus on your social life, club memberships and organisations. You may be drawn to update your circle of friends or deepen loyalties and to a healthier lifestyle by joining a gym or spending more time on your health or that of someone close. For many Scorpios this is a good time to work hard as your efforts are likely to be rewarded.

Sun in Libra, September to October

EXPLORE YOUR DEEPER FEELINGS

This is a good time for personal exploration, such as spiritual enquiry and psychic development. Gaining psychological understanding of yourself will be easier at this time. Your work and health will be in the spotlight, and you could achieve more balance in both areas. A secret may be revealed that will add to your understanding of someone else or of yourself.

LUNAR TRANSITS:
be calm and effective every day of the month

The moon spotlights different aspects of your emotional self as it travels each month through each zodiac sign, staying two days in each sign. When the moon is in each sign you gain the opportunity to express yourself more effectively in various areas of your life. Find out here how to make the most of your strong points during each of the two days each month.

Moon in Scorpio

GET IN TOUCH WITH YOUR FEELINGS

This moon brings your inner feelings out and you'll feel more intense and invested in life. You'll enjoy spending time with like-minded people. Artistic Scorpios may be super productive, and if you're starting a family or adding to it this could be a fertile time. You'll enjoy music and dance, as your passionate side will demand expression.

Moon in Sagittarius

BUILD SELF-ESTEEM AND FINANCES

The moon in honest and frank Sagittarius will buoy your mood, and you'll feel optimistic and outgoing. Avoid speaking your mind too freely; the art of diplomacy is best employed during the Sagittarian moon, as you may otherwise speak first and think later. You may feel overly generous so must avoid overspending, especially if you are in debt.

Moon in Capricorn

ANCHOR YOUR ACTIVITIES

You're all about infusing your life with passion, so when some people don't move at your pace you feel frustrated. Take things one step at a time and avoid impulsiveness; find ways to anchor your activities with meetings and communications that lead to concrete results. It's a good time to set a solid financial budget in place.

Moon in Aquarius

INVEST IN DOMESTIC BLISS

You are likely to feel restless during this time. Talks, news and travel will gain your interest and may surprise you. Be careful with communications, as you may misunderstand someone else's intentions. Invest more in improving domestic dynamics; your effort will be appreciated. You may feel drawn to making changes at home such as redecorating.

Moon in Pisces

STIMULATE ROMANCE, FAMILY FUN AND SPIRITUALITY

Your romantic side gains expression, so plan romantic treats. Family matters may require more focus than usual. If you're artistic, this is a super-creative time as inspiration will flow. You'll love indulging in music, art, spirituality and dance, so plan favourite activities.

Moon in Aries

IMPROVE WORK AND HEALTH

You'll feel energetic and more emotionally engaged in your everyday activities and will be busy, but you also may appear intense. It's a good time to improve your emotional happiness, appearance and fitness. For some this will be an engaging time with family and friends and your love life, as you'll feel drawn to spend time with loved ones.

Moon in Taurus

INDULGE IN SENSUALITY

Singles: it's time to get out and meet someone who enjoys the same interests as you. Couples will enjoy deepening your romantic life. You'll be drawn to all things sensuous and self-indulgent, so you must avoid overindulgence especially if your budget is tight.

Moon in Gemini

RESEARCH COLLABORATIONS

You are less likely to get upset over issues, which will lead you to appear more light-hearted and easy going and will be ideal for making agreements. However, this may be an indecisive time so you must research facts and new ideas. Focus on paperwork, discussions and meetings but avoid being easily influenced by people who are fun but fundamentally superficial.

Moon in Cancer

FOLLOW YOUR DREAMS

You could truly make progress in a key area when the moon is in Cancer. Ensure, though, you have the right information and your charm and know-how will do the rest. You may be drawn to indulge in a favourite activity, to being creative or to booking a holiday. You'll feel inspired, and this is a good time to notice where your inspiration takes you.

Moon in Leo

BE ADVENTUROUS

Your daring side will seek expression, so be bold. But you will also appear more intense and dramatic to others, so avoid treading on their toes. You may be more generous and less inclined to worry about the consequences of your actions. If you tend to act first and worry later, remind yourself to think first then you could make great progress, especially at work.

Moon in Virgo

IMPROVE THE GROUP DYNAMIC

This is a good time for getting down to brass tacks with those you must collaborate and co-operate with, such as groups, friends and organisations, as you will be thinking and reasoning clearly. Avoid forcing new ideas at the drop of a hat, and aim to work collaboratively.

Moon in Libra

LISTEN TO YOUR HEART

Your sensitivities and insight are strong, especially regarding someone close who requires help and support. Make time for them and avoid taking their issues personally. You may need to rebalance a situation such as your arrangement with a group, organisation or friend.

FULL MOONS:
magnify your vibrant power

*Each full moon highlights different aspects of your power and vibrancy.
Find out here which full moons will be excellent times to turn a corner
in the various areas of your life to show just what you're made of.*

Full moon in Scorpio
TRANSFORM YOUR APPROACH TO LIFE

Considerable changes point to your need to change your approach to the areas undergoing most change. Frank talks will help you to understand someone special. A change of routine or a work development could be ideal, but will also need an adjustment in attitude so be more adaptable. A new look may appeal.

Full moon in Sagittarius
FOCUS ON FACTS

Key decisions will revolve around money and your values, principles and self-esteem. Avoid making assumptions. A particular agreement or relationship may hit a pinnacle. If the end is on the cards, rest assured a new relationship phase will involve self-discovery and adventure.

Full moon in Capricorn
BE PRACTICAL WITH COMMUNICATIONS AND TRAVEL

Important conversations or travel will bring your emotions out or feel intense; however, even if developments tug at your heart strings they will be transformative and character building in the long term. A fresh understanding with someone close could open doors to activities you'll enjoy and to the company of like-minded people.

Full moon in Aquarius
EMBRACE FRESH IDEAS AT HOME AND WORK

The Aquarian full moon signals new opportunities and a fresh chapter in your work, family life, a creative project or regarding property. Look for innovative options to broaden your influence in these key areas and to accommodate fresh and invigorating ideas.

Full moon in Pisces
ENJOY ROMANCE AND CREATIVITY

You may feel particularly idealistic and romantic, which you'll enjoy, but you must keep your feet on the ground to avoid conflict further down the line due to having had unrealistic expectations. Be wary of being forgetful and overindulgent, especially as socialising and networking will be appealing.

Full moon in Aries
BOOST WORK, STATUS AND WELL-BEING

Now is the time to change things, especially if you are fed up with your work or daily routine. Ask where you could be more proactive and dynamic. Health-wise, a fresh diet through better nutrition and a boost in vitality will become more important to you.

Full moon in Taurus
BOOST YOUR LOVE LIFE AND RELATIONSHIPS

This full moon will help you end a chapter that no longer serves your higher purpose; you may decide to change your work and health routines and personal matters. This could open new doors for you to create more stability. Be prepared to let old habits go if they no longer truly support your growth, be these in your personal life or at work.

Full moon in Gemini
FIND TIME TO NEGOTIATE AND COLLABORATE

This is a good time to include more fun and variety in your relationships. Meetings and discussions will be productive as you'll get the chance to improve some of your agreements, but you must avoid reacting adversely to other people's behaviour as you may be seen as aggressive. Be prepared to negotiate and you could make solid progress financially and at work.

Full moon in Cancer
A CALL TO NURTURANCE

You may wish to reconnect with someone who has a nurturing link with you such as a parent or child. For some a new way to share duties or finances will mark a turning point in a key relationship. This Cancer full moon represents a fresh start with a favourite activity or interest. You may be drawn to travel or to engage in nurturing activities.

Full moon in Leo
SHOW OFF YOUR BEST SIDE!

Be prepared to turn a corner principally in your direction or work life as you become more dynamic and proactive, set a good example and assume a leadership role. And if a career or job ends, rest assured events will open a door that ultimately will benefit you if you embrace learning and self-improvement.

Full moon in Virgo
CONSIDER A FRESH APPROACH TO OTHERS

Aim to move your relationships forward. Avoid overanalysing circumstances, especially if someone is super sensitive, and trust your instincts. You may make a key commitment to someone or to a group at work. This full moon will spotlight how best to progress in practical, realistic ways, especially health-wise.

Full moon in Libra
ESTABLISH WORK/LIFE BALANCE

You'll realise you need balance and harmony in your daily routine, health and well-being. To find it, a change in work hours and a refreshing healthy schedule may be necessary. You may touch base socially with like-minded people and develop creative skills.

NEW MOONS:
start something fresh

Each new moon points to the start of something fresh for you in different areas of your life. Find out here which new moon to work with and how to make lasting change by starting something new, especially if you have been putting off change for some time.

New moon in Scorpio
REVOLUTIONISE YOUR LIFE

The Scorpio new moon is a great time for a fresh start. If it's your birthday at or before the new moon a fresh start is likely to take in your personal life; if you were born later it'll be at work and health-wise. On a deep level you are ready to revolutionise your life but you must take things one step at a time to avoid impulsive moves. Follow your gut instincts; they will not lead you astray.

New moon in Sagittarius
INVEST IN YOURSELF

You'll appreciate the fun-loving and revitalising effect of this new moon phase as it will resonate throughout your life and bring more variety and the chance to boost your personal life, self-esteem and finances. You may be more generous than usual and must avoid overinvesting if you are making large purchases.

New moon in Capricorn
BE PRACTICAL ABOUT COMMITMENTS

If some relationships have been up in the air or you have been in a whirlwind of adventure and change, the new moon in Capricorn will help you to get your feet back on the ground and make practical decisions about commitments and loyalties.

New moon in Aquarius

KICK-START A UNIQUE PHASE AT HOME

Consider fresh territory at home. The circumstances of those around you may alter at this new moon and will stimulate discussion about developments that may be quirky or out of the ordinary. To make valid decisions, do your research and avoid impulsiveness; it could land you in hot water.

New moon in Pisces

DEEPEN SPIRITUALITY AND BRING JOY INTO YOUR LIFE

This is a great time to begin a new project and inject more creativity, laughter and love into your life. You may feel super romantic; singles could meet a romantic character. Creative and spiritual Scorpios will be inspired; however, you may be inclined to overindulge, so ensure you also kick-start a healthy routine at this new moon.

New moon in Aries

BEGIN A NEW PROJECT OR HEALTH ROUTINE

Take action to improve your daily life: this is a good time to begin a new project, health routine or personal relationship. It is likely to be a fast-moving project or relationship, so hang on to your hat! Avoid snap decisions. If conflict has been simmering with someone close, find ways to bring peace to circumstances.

New moon in Taurus

MAKE A COMMITMENT

This new moon is a good time to start a new business or personal partnership and to make fresh agreements within existing relationships. To make progress you may need to focus on finances and your need for stability. It's certainly a good time to create more cohesion in your life.

New moon in Gemini

REVITALISE RELATIONSHIPS

Consider approaching those you share space and duties with in a new way during this time. If you're single you may kick-start a light-hearted relationship, while couples may rediscover the fun aspect of your relationship. You may find you are more adaptable than you believe, so embrace change.

New moon in Cancer

DEEPEN RELATIONSHIPS AND KEY INTERESTS

A fresh, more nurturing approach to the areas you share in life and to the people you share space with could benefit you. How could you be a little more supportive of someone? How could shared projects be more mutually enhancing? A trip such as a holiday will be a nurturing time. This new moon is an excellent time to discuss finances in a supportive way.

New moon in Leo

KICK-START VENTURES

You could propel yourself forward by making a key decision at work or financially. Ask yourself where in life such as work or family you feel most accomplished. A fresh activity or commitment could capture your attention in this light. Avoid making changes for the sake of it; look for revitalising activities that appeal to your deeper purpose.

New moon in Virgo

ENHANCE TEAMWORK

Could you revitalise the spirit of teamwork both at work and at home? This is a good time to plan ahead for a happier, healthier future and to take practical steps to reinvigorate areas of your life that have become stale or disconnected.

New moon in Libra

CARRY OUT A HEALTH CHECK

Consider a new health plan that supports you psychologically. You are a passionate character who can be quick to anger. This new moon may bring your frustrations to the surface, so avoid impulsiveness and consider finding ways to be less reactive. Avoid secrecy or you risk leading yourself and others into uncertain territory.

LUNAR ECLIPSES:
be strong during peak emotional changes

Each lunar eclipse signals a major turning point in your life and may bring about intense emotions. Eclipses point to circumstances that seem to disempower you and subsequently motivate you to address any imbalances, so keep an eye on those areas in which you lack control as that is where you can make the most changes and become strong. Find out here which lunar eclipse will bring change in which area of your life, and how to make the most of these changes.

Scorpio lunar eclipse

PERSONAL GROWTH

Deep emotions may surface, so if life is tense it's a good time for psychoanalysis or other deeply self-transformative modalities. Self-transformation could arise from a big change in a close relationship if you were born on or before the eclipse. If you were born after the eclipse you may begin a fresh daily work or health routine.

Sagittarius lunar eclipse

RECONSIDER YOUR PRINCIPLES AND VALUES

As a passionate and intense character you can become obsessed once you decide to back a cause. During this eclipse phase you may feel particularly passionate about principles and may need to dig deep to find perspective and establish fair play as you move forward.

Capricorn lunar eclipse

INVEST IN PRACTICALITIES

Communications will be intense, however, even if developments tug at your heart strings or anger you they will be transformative in the long term. You may need to invest in practicalities such as a more secure communications device or find ways to be assertive rather than aggressive.

Aquarius lunar eclipse
REFOCUS YOUR PRIORITIES, LOYALTIES AND VALUES

You will wish to voice your opinions, especially in the domestic arena and at work. You may wish to make changes due to humanitarian values or simply due to your principles. A fresh outlook or agreement could arise that alters the way you communicate, learn or see others.

Pisces lunar eclipse
RE-INVENT YOUR PERSONAL LIFE

Family-minded Scorpios will experience a creative and fertile phase, so if you're looking to start a family this is a good time to try. However, if relationships or projects have been tense you may go separate ways. For some this eclipse will point to the end of a family phase as you face an empty nest. Artistic Scorpios could see a turning point with a creative project.

Aries lunar eclipse
CHANGE EMPHASIS AT WORK AND HEALTH-WISE

You will be inclined to look for activities that resonate on a deeper level and feel propelled to make relevant changes in your life. You may feel more ambitious and therefore able to work harder. For some this eclipse will spotlight your feelings about the behaviour of someone in particular: it may be time to part ways.

Taurus lunar eclipse
ALTER COMMITMENTS

A fresh circumstance will begin and the decision may be out of your hands. Be practical with the commitments you make as they will be long term. This eclipse signals a new agreement or arrangement in a personal relationship for Scorpios with birthdays on or before this eclipse; for those born later it will be at work or health-wise.

Gemini lunar eclipse
RECONSIDER SHARED CONCERNS

As your deepest feelings rise you may react by behaving dismissively towards others or to circumstances. However, being tactful in your communications will serve you better, so aim to discover a more light-hearted but still heart-centred way to communicate. This eclipse will spotlight shared finances, duties and partnerships.

Cancer lunar eclipse

TRUST YOUR INTUITION

This phase may feel like a spiritual test in that you wonder who you can trust and whether or not you can trust your own instincts. Yes, you can, hence the feeling you're undergoing a test! You may be drawn to deepen your connection with someone or to finally say goodbye if the relationship has been tense. You will put new ideas and rules in place regarding shared projects.

Leo lunar eclipse

RELEARN COMPASSION

You may feel overshadowed by someone else, so take things one step at a time and re-align with your power base to avoid reacting with angry outbursts. A fresh circumstance is waiting in the wings in association with a group or friend or at work. If you're single you may meet a dynamic character; if you're married more independence may appeal.

Virgo lunar eclipse

GET ORGANISED

It's a good time to discuss your long-term plans with those they affect such as family and employers. If you're looking for a promotion make an appointment with your boss; if you're looking for a new job send out your resume. A fresh phase will begin with an organisation or loved one. Be prepared to hear home truths but also to excel.

Libra lunar eclipse

RESET EMOTIONALLY

Where do you find balance and harmony in your life? This eclipse is a good time to boost the feel-good factor in your life through hobbies, romance and family time. You may feel more inclined to socialise, or if you've been super sociable to relax at home more often. Use a change of circumstance to your benefit: invest in yourself.

SOLAR ECLIPSES:
making major changes run smoothly

*Each solar eclipse signals a major turning point in your life
that points to ongoing change for years to come. Find out
here which solar eclipses will bring change in which areas of
your life, and how to make the most of those changes.*

Scorpio solar eclipse

SET A NEW BENCHMARK

Don't see this eclipse as a punctuation mark in a chapter of your life; aim to start a new book! Keep an eye on developments as you will make great life changes and will manage to bend with circumstances. You are ready to reinvigorate your personal life, taking on more empowering activities, and to kick-start key work or personal projects.

Sagittarius solar eclipse

FIND MORE FULFILMENT

Consider your personal and financial investments: are they fulfilling? If not, make changes now! Perhaps your personal life merits more romance and connection. Some Scorpios will be drawn to being more independent and sociable as travel, study and generally improving your self-esteem will appeal.

Capricorn solar eclipse

FIND NEW WAYS TO COMMUNICATE

A negotiation, trip or new understanding could bring more responsibility your way, so choose your commitments carefully and make decisions that provide stronger foundations. You may need to update your communications devices or learn a new language or skill set so you can get on better with people.

Aquarius solar eclipse

THINK LATERALLY

The Aquarian solar eclipse suggests you are ready for new beginnings in your personal life, and the more you think outside the box about your options and developments the better for you. Avoid an argumentative approach; be adaptable.

Pisces solar eclipse

BUILD ON YOUR SUCCESS

There is merit in maintaining the success you have already achieved, so avoid underestimating your achievements. This is an inspiring phase, but you must avoid being overindulgent. This is an excellent time to develop your intuitive, psychic and creative abilities, both at work and at home; however, you may be easily influenced so be practical as well.

Aries solar eclipse

A NEW START AT WORK

Your inner dragon may be stirred into action, so you will be busy but must avoid conflict as you may be liable to burn bridges. This eclipse could feel cumbersome at first but it will ultimately provide a sense of purpose and direction. For some a new development in your personal life will be the focus, and for many a new path in your daily routine will appeal.

Taurus solar eclipse

AGREE TO DISAGREE

Create a more authentic, calmer and peaceful life according to your morals and values, and allow the commitments in your life to reflect these. Be prepared for a new chapter at work, at home or in your daily life. If you've been poorly, ensure you self-nurture and seek expert advice if fatigue continues.

Gemini solar eclipse

TURN A CORNER WITH NEGOTIATIONS

You are ready for a new arrangement in your personal life or professionally. Your finances could see great change, so take the initiative with talks and negotiations. Some communications and shared financial matters will require patience and attention to detail, making this an excellent time to improve your communication skills.

Cancer solar eclipse
EMBRACE NEW OPPORTUNITIES

New opportunities are on the way, even if these come about through dramatic change. A more stable phase will be possible as a result, as you'll initiate change in your activities and in the way you share duties. You may wish for more nurturance in your relationships and may undergo a key financial change; some Scorpios may even receive an inheritance.

Leo solar eclipse
CHOOSE SUCCESS AND HAPPINESS

You are ambitious and willing to go the extra mile to achieve success, and your hard work will pay off. Work towards results that resonate with your heart. If you experience a disappointment, avoid feeling downcast: learn from the experience and find ways to boost morale in inspired ways that include your favourite interests and activities, friends and family.

Virgo solar eclipse
PLAN YOUR LIFE DIRECTION

Your career, general direction and everyday life come under the microscope, and you may need to make a tough call that will involve being responsible, dutiful and diligent. And while you are more a passionate and less a cold, hard reasoning character, there will be merit in planning during this phase.

Libra solar eclipse
LET THE PAST GO

The Libran solar eclipse represents your opportunity to turn a new leaf. Be positive and take action. Be bold at work with networking and socialising, as the more outgoing you are the more likely doors will open into new avenues that suit your stage in life.

22 NOVEMBER - 21 DECEMBER

SYMBOL
Archer

CONSTELLATION

ELEMENT
Fire

SAGITTARIUS
SUN SIGN

INNER CALLING

Your sign's symbol, the Archer, points to the inner you: you aim high in life and generally reach your target. You use your skills to serve a fulfilling purpose as your generosity of spirit, optimism and sense of adventure all combine to paint a positive picture. You are good at learning and keep up to date with new developments – unless, that is, you lose track of your goals or allow yourself to be easily distracted.

Your penchant for learning begins at a young age, but for a minority of Archers it will kick in when you're a little more mature. Long-distance travel, which is a conduit for learning about other cultures and peoples, will appeal to you. You will be the one in high school who wishes to: learn more about life in general, religion and languages; see more of the world; travel and study through higher education; and assimilate as much as you can in terms of wisdom, experience and education. You are also likely to enjoy teaching, which may be in a learning institution or more broad ly by sharing your experiences in life with those you love.

You love socialising and engaging in activities with like-minded people, but will also seek the company of people from a different upbringing or cultural heritage. You are curious, and curiosity as you know has a tendency to kill the cat. Luckily, cats have nine lives, and because you like to learn you will always learn from your mistakes and gain strength, wisdom and knowledge in the process.

Any form of upset or challenge will serve to ultimately pave the way to a deeper understanding of who you are and strengthen your capabilities. You are in a sense the true alchemist of the zodiac, as you transform even negative experiences into positive ones purely through your inherently positive mindset.

SELF-ESTEEM

You'll appreciate the belief that you gain your sense of self-esteem from being outgoing and adventurous, yet your self-esteem comes from feeling secure in your life. For you, feeling secure will come from all kinds of sources and at different times in your life. For some, a sense of security will come via a financial safety net, for others via a relationship and for others via success at work or in your status.

A strong foundation is necessary for you so that you're able to be outgoing and adventurous, because with your feet on the ground you can be daring in other areas of your life: through your hobbies, through travel or through your ideas and beliefs. In other words, a strong foundation is what will give you the chance to aim high and try new and different ideas and courses of action, all of which will enable you to complete sometimes hazardous tasks to boost your self-esteem. Although it may initially appear counter-intuitive to create a solid foundation and security in life, remember that stability becomes your springboard for excitement and success. Feelings of stability truly boost your sense of self and help you to aim high and be adventurous.

You also gain self-esteem from sharing your wisdom and experience; and from the sense that you can help others to enjoy life in the same way you do. You love sharing grand schemes such as planning long-distance travel and daredevil experiences like mountain climbing, snowboarding, skydiving and speed racing. You are likely to be sporty and to have had the chance at school to show just how athletic you are. You'll prefer team games as you enjoy a sense of togetherness and the strong bonds forged in teamwork.

HOME LIFE

Your home life can provide you with the stability you need to up and leave to indulge in your ambitions and projects. Your need to succeed comes from the emotional core that motivates you to leave your comfort zone, to be gregarious and bold beyond even your own understanding. You may even wonder sometimes where your strong motivation comes from, but it's an emotional need that will be hard to suppress. Parents of Sagittarian children may find containing you within four walls a real chore as you enjoy the outdoors, sport and fun.

Because your true sense of strength comes from having a solid foundation in life it's important to establish a sense of security so that your need for adventure doesn't leave you vulnerable and without a safety net as an adult. Your home life can provide this and will reflect your interest in other cultures and people; there may even be a bohemian or other-worldly feel to the décor, with mystical or mood lighting to reflect your interest in spirituality and exploration. You may be tempted to move often, but your home will be a main driver of where you can put down roots. You may, however, tend to throw caution to the wind and never settle anywhere for long, so it's important to realise your home is your true source of inspiration and strength.

You can be generous to a fault and may tend to overinvest in your home, so be realistic about what you can and can't afford. You'll be generous with space at home, with welcoming friends and family, but will benefit from a large space yourself so you must avoid hemming yourself in.

RELATIONSHIPS

People see you in a good-natured, positive light, and your optimism is catching. Your good sense of humour enables you to maintain a positive approach to life, and people see a confident, accomplished person in you. You understand deep down that a positive mindset can free the mind and therefore can improve relationships, yet your carefree attitude can appear to others as superficial. Your predilection for favouring adventure and excitement may contribute to some feeling you are unlikely to commit, especially when you're young.

As you mature you see that your ideas play out through the actions you take, so when you have positive ideas it's important to take action as very little results from an idea alone. You love freedom of movement and independent thought. As a partner you can seem difficult to tie down as you are constantly on the go or perpetually planning new adventures.

You appreciate a bright and chatty partner who gives you the intellectual connection you crave. Good communication skills and a meeting of minds are the hallmarks of a successful relationship for Archers, and for this reason you will attract like-minded people. Your main pitfall in your relationships is that you are so honest you can be seen as blunt and, worse, uncaring or even uncompromising.

CREATIVITY

Your playful side brings out your most creative qualities, and you're likely to express your creativity through dance, sports and music or through actions that aren't necessarily seen as being traditionally creative, such as romance. Yet your ebullience can be mistaken for a lack of seriousness and, on occasion, of sincerity. To counteract this impression, aim to be clear to delineate when you are joking and when you are serious, when you are playing and when you're working. To you the difference is clear, but to some people it's less so and they won't know the difference until they get to know you better.

Your largesse translates well into generosity, both financially and of spirit. You have also a keen mind that rarely lets you down, enabling you to learn and subsequently teach subjects you are passionate about. Your generosity of spirit adds to the general impression that you are a kind-hearted individual and that kindness and love are the most creative of qualities in life.

PITFALLS

People can find your ebullient, larger than life personality overbearing and even invasive, so be aware you can be seen as someone who transgresses personal boundaries and be mindful of them. Aim also to be tactful to avoid seeming brutally blunt.

Another pitfall is that you can be easily led and distracted by unimportant aspects of other people's lives, so it's important you remain well informed about whichever new adventure or fresh terrain you enter or you risk being led astray. Information really is your best friend, as it enables a learning curve in areas that excite you and stretches your capabilities and imagination so that you feel you live an exciting life of discovery, exploration and reward.

SOLAR TRANSITS:
harness the sun's power
every day of the year

The sun empowers you in different areas of your life as it travels through each zodiac sign from month to month. Find out here how to make the most of your strong points during each of the transits of the sun through the 12 signs.

Sun in Sagittarius, November to December

EXPAND YOUR SKILL SET

The sun in your sign is an ideal time to focus on your own abilities and desires. Optimistically consider your best path forward, especially in your personal life and at work. Work on your communication skills to avoid appearing blunt, especially in sensitive circumstances.

Sun in Capricorn, December to January

IMPROVE FINANCES AND COMMITMENTS

You are one of the more generous sun signs and can tend to overspend. During this phase you may need to devise a fresh budget and discover new ways to get out of debt. You may also feel more prepared to commit to particular ventures, people and relationships after due research.

Sun in Aquarius, January to February

EMBRACE ADVENTURE

This is an upbeat, fun time of the year and you'll enjoy expressing your outgoing qualities and need for adventure, variety and spice in life. Organise fun trips and get-togethers and learn new skills. You may be drawn towards new digital or technological devices or to repair a vehicle. This is a good time to get up to date with a financial plan.

Sun in Pisces, February to March

INVEST IN YOUR HOME LIFE

You will be inspired to take your goals a step further in the domestic realm. Consider the benefits of a stable roof over your head: a solid foundation for personal growth. This is a good time to infuse your home with more comfort and to boost your interests in spirituality and psychology. You may be drawn to visit the homes of others through travel.

Sun in Aries, March to April

RELISH ROMANCE, FUN AND CREATIVITY

This is an excellent phase to boost your personal life and home as your energy levels are likely to be high. As a fire sign you like to take action, and updating décor and undertaking DIY projects may appeal; however, you must pick your battles carefully or you may be prone to fire up over every little thing.

Sun in Taurus, April to May

IMPROVE WORK AND HEALTH

The sun in Taurus will help you to get things done both at work and in your personal life, so be practical and realistic in those areas for the best results. If obstacles arise they will stimulate your need for success and to express your innermost values, including fair play, in your daily life.

Sun in Gemini, May to June

EMBRACE VARIETY

You'll appreciate the opportunity to revitalise the fun aspects of your relationships and will also enjoy building a happier and more upbeat schedule in your everyday life. You may find your daily duties will include more variety, and you'll keep on top of a busy schedule.

Sun in Cancer, June to July

DEEPEN YOUR UNDERSTANDING OF OTHERS

Your focus will now be on other people. Shared areas of your life such as finances and joint duties will require more focus. Consider bringing your caring, nurturing qualities to bear in your key decisions. People will respond well to your kind side.

Sun in Leo, July to August

BROADEN YOUR HORIZONS

This is an ideal phase to take a break or go on a holiday and to investigate new pastimes and activities. The more audacious the better, as these will appeal to your inner adventurer: anything from rock climbing and long-distance travel to spiritual inquiry.

Sun in Virgo, August to September

PLAN A BRIGHT FUTURE

Make hay while the sun shines, as you could make great progress. If you're looking for a change in your career this is a good time to initiate it, as change is likely to be for the best. You may be drawn to broaden your horizons through travel or study, and may be extra busy and in demand.

Sun in Libra, September to October

GAIN BALANCE AND HARMONY

This phase will remind you to establish balance in your life by ensuring you're not becoming a hermit on the one hand or a work horse on the other. You may wish to join clubs and to socialise more and could be drawn to a more peaceful work environment or even to cut your work hours. If you've been working fewer hours you may wish to ramp them up.

Sun in Scorpio, October to November

FOCUS ON YOUR PURPOSE

The sun in Scorpio is a good time to go within and check you are still on the right path for your own interests, especially at work. You may benefit from an introspective spiritual phase or even psychological insight. For mid-December–born Sagittarians this phase will be super sociable and passionate and could also be romantic!

LUNAR TRANSITS:
be calm and effective every day of the month

The moon spotlights different aspects of your emotional self as it travels each month through each zodiac sign, staying two days in each sign. When the moon is in each sign you gain the opportunity to express yourself more effectively in various areas of your life. Find out here how to make the most of your strong points during each of the two days each month.

Moon in Sagittarius
BE POSITIVE AND GET THINGS DONE

You'll feel optimistic and could make great progress in all areas. Take the time to try something new and be proactive. Avoid oversharing your opinions and being super blunt or you'll lose friends, as sensitive people may find you overbearing.

Moon in Capricorn
GAIN MORE STABILITY AND SECURITY

Take the time to slow down and consider your feelings: could you infuse your daily life with more certainty and stability? Financial or personal matters will be resolved with a realistic approach. You are in a practical mindset, enabling you to overcome conundrums.

Moon in Aquarius
BE PROACTIVE AND INQUIRING

You may feel restless, so aim to channel that restlessness into upbeat activities: you may be surprised by the circumstances you find yourself in. A fresh environment, new people to meet, a trip or financial transactions may bring something or someone quirky your way.

Moon in Pisces

INCREASE DOMESTIC BLISS

A little luxury or splash of colour at home will raise morale and help you express your creative side. You'll appreciate the opportunity to focus on improving dynamics at home or with family. Spiritually minded Sagittarians will appreciate deepening your understanding of the mysteries of life.

Moon in Aries

EMBRACE ROMANCE, FAMILY FUN AND CREATIVITY

This is an energy-fuelled two days, so aim to spend time boosting domestic well-being, family dynamics and your sense of creativity. Avoid making changes where they are not yet warranted, and find ways to relax at home. You must avoid gambling, both financially and emotionally.

Moon in Taurus

INDULGE IN YOUR SENSUAL SIDE

A fresh environment or change of routine that feeds your predilection for good food and activities that boost your looks, health and vitality will appeal. You may enjoy relaxation techniques that take the stress away from everyday living. This is also a good time to take practical steps to improve work.

Moon in Gemini

STRENGTHEN YOUR LOVE LIFE AND RELATIONSHIPS

You're likely to be more talkative and may be particularly drawn to discuss your ideas with colleagues or a partner. New plans may be exciting and will soon come together with due research. Singles may feel flirtatious and couples more fun-loving, so organise a treat!

Moon in Cancer

INVEST IN COLLABORATIONS

This is a good time to draw on inspiration and bring new projects and ideas into being. It is also a good time to reset and re-organise priorities, especially to do with your favourite projects, collaborations and shared finances. Be guided by fulfilling duties and by nurturing those you love and yourself.

Moon in Leo
RESEARCH EXCITING VENTURES

The Leo moon will encourage you to be outgoing and enjoy travel, meetings and your favourite activities. This is a chatty time, so if communications have been tense make that extra effort to smooth a way forward. Your upbeat vibe will be catching and will help you to overcome any differences of opinion.

Moon in Virgo
BOOST YOUR PROFILE

This is a good time to invest in your public profile and to make progress at work and with your financial aspirations. Take the initiative, as you're likely to produce positive results at work and with your favourite projects. Pay attention to details, and be practical and realistic to boost your status.

Moon in Libra
REGAIN A SENSE OF ORDER

The Libran moon will shine a light on areas of your life that are slightly out of balance, so for example issues at home, socially or at work may seem more intense. This should inspire you to take the initiative and change circumstances for the better that are no longer making complete sense.

Moon in Scorpio
FOCUS ON IMPROVING MOODS

You'll improve your daily life by focusing on your spiritual, mental and psychological well-being. If emotions are overpowering, consider meditation to calm your mind. You're more likely to act on impulse now, which can mean a more spontaneous and upbeat time, but you must avoid making rash decisions.

FULL MOONS:
magnify your vibrant power

Each full moon highlights different aspects of your power and vibrancy.
Find out here which full moons will be excellent times to turn a corner
in the various areas of your life to show just what you're made of.

Full moon in Sagittarius
EMBRACE PERSONAL GROWTH

There will be key developments in your personal life as a crucial chapter comes full circle. This may also involve finances. You may decide it's time for a new look, fresh haircut or outfit. You'll appreciate the opportunity to express your creative and adventurous side. Be daring and excel.

Full moon in Capricorn
EXAMINE FINANCES AND SELF-ESTEEM

A fresh financial or personal commitment will begin, and you'll need to weigh up your options carefully or must make a tough call. You may need to negotiate the way you share space or duties with family or a work colleague. Be practical and aim to establish more stability and security.

Full moon in Aquarius
SPRUCE UP YOUR LIFESTYLE

Look afresh at some of your relationships, loyalties and activities. This full moon offers the chance to re-evaluate your priorities, and if life has become stale it is the ideal time to research how to spruce up your general lifestyle. You may be drawn to travel or study and to updating a device or vehicle.

Full moon in Pisces

TURN A CORNER WITH FAMILY OR PROPERTY

Developments may be ideal, but if they fall short of your goals avoid trying to push events to fit into your preconception or trying to coerce others. There is a better future that you can't quite see yet. For some the most marked developments will be at work and in your general direction, impacting on home and relationships.

Full moon in Aries

BE ADVENTUROUS IN YOUR PERSONAL LIFE

You're not afraid of a little adventure and excitement, so you'll feel less restless around an Aries full moon than other less adaptable signs. Be prepared to take positive action when a change in your family or personal life arises. The people who admire you will feel supported by you and vice versa.

Full moon in Taurus

REFINE YOUR DAILY SCHEDULE

How much consideration do you give to your own happiness? Consider your loyalty to your own purpose and fulfilment, and ask how you could boost your sense of accomplishment in practical ways or how a fresh phase could steer you in a new direction, both in your personal life and professionally. Then take action.

Full moon in Gemini

NEGOTIATE AND COMPROMISE

Be prepared to negotiate and compromise with both personal and business partnerships. You'll be pleased to embrace more variety and spice in your schedule as you get the chance to make financial matters work better for you through, for example, a fresh work phase or daily routine.

Full moon in Cancer

BE PRACTICAL WITH JOINT DECISIONS

You may feel super romantic or sentimental during this time, so be careful with the practicalities concerning a shared matter both in your personal life and at work, especially concerning finances or who must fulfil which duty.

Full moon in Leo

A CALL TO ADVENTURE

Be positive, as this full moon will stimulate your joie de vivre even if you can only see the end of a cycle. An exciting new chapter is waiting in the wings, and events may already provide you with an idea of them. For some developments may revolve around a thrilling relationship; for others around travel, a venture or plan that comes to an end, allowing space for something new.

Full moon in Virgo

RE-ORIENT YOUR GOALS

You may be ready to turn a corner in your career, goals and status. For some a change in a favourite activity or venture such as a trip or legal matter will come full circle, and this full moon will show the most realistic way forward. Avoid feeling you must be perfect, as you will make great progress now simply by doing your best.

Full moon in Libra

ENJOY THE COMPANY OF LIKE-MINDED PEOPLE

You may feel ready to make a commitment to a group, friend or idea, which will involve some soul searching. People with humanitarian interests may be particularly appealing. Be ready to back up your inspired ideas with hard work and you'll be looking at success.

Full moon in Scorpio

LOOK AFTER YOUR EMOTIONAL HEALTH

There is likely to be a lot going on in the background psychologically and in your emotional and spiritual lives, so ensure you pace yourself and avoid allowing destructive feelings to run your life. Consider gaining more psychological and spiritual insight into yourself or someone close if you encounter obstacles. Move on from the past via a fresh health or work routine.

NEW MOONS:
start something fresh

Each new moon points to the start of something fresh for you in different areas of your life. Find out here which new moon to work with and how to make lasting change by starting something new, especially if you have been putting off change for some time.

New moon in Sagittarius
START SOMETHING NEW

This new moon is particularly potent if it's your birthday. Look out for a wonderful opportunity to revitalise your personal life, health and well-being. For all Sagittarians this new moon will be a call to action to create the space for something new in your life.

New moon in Capricorn
MAKE COMMITMENTS

For some Sagittarians this new moon will introduce a more stable phase in your personal life, so if you'd like to ask someone for a commitment now is the time. However, you must be ready yourself to commit! For most the Capricorn new moon will help you to devise a budget that suits your needs.

New moon in Aquarius
UPDATE YOUR COMMUNICATION SKILLS

A trip, visit or exciting venture will open your eyes to new people, discussions, ideas and even cultures. Your communications will become quirkier and different, and you may meet all kinds of interesting people. Because you will be in a fresh environment or will meet new people, focus on good communication skills or you may experience misunderstandings.

New moon in Pisces

REBOOT DOMESTIC DYNAMICS AND SPIRITUALITY

This is an excellent new moon to consider how you might beautify or even change altogether your domestic circumstances. Spiritual Sagittarians may find this an especially inspiring and uplifting time. Investment in yourself and your environment will be enriching, so be inspired by new ways to boost your circumstances.

New moon in Aries

START A CREATIVE OR PERSONAL VENTURE

The Aries new moon feels revitalising in your personal life and also creatively; however, you may tend to jump into projects feet first, especially regarding domestic matters or your love life, so ensure you base your actions on facts and then enjoy the newfound vitality!

New moon in Taurus

KICK-START A NEW DAILY ROUTINE

This is a good time to review your daily routine and put a clever new schedule in place. This Taurus new moon points to a fresh chapter that may entail considerable change, for some Sagittarians at work and for others in your personal life. You will gain increased security even if at first some change is disruptive.

New moon in Gemini

REVITALISE YOUR LOVE LIFE AND RELATIONSHIPS

This is a good time to kick-start a more varied and upbeat health regime that will boost vitality and relationships. It's also a good time to begin a new job, a light-hearted venture or a communications-based project at work. It will be a busy and chatty time, and you may begin a fresh relationship. Singles: look out for exciting partners!

New moon in Cancer

MAKE A FRESH AGREEMENT

This new moon suggests a relationship would benefit from more nurturance and support so you can better share duties or finances. A fair go, an equal outcome and the chance to speak the truth are all qualities that will encourage you to speak up. Approach discussions carefully rather than tactlessly or you could create conflict, the opposite of your desired outcome.

New moon in Leo
BEGIN AN EXCITING PROJECT

The Leo new moon suggests you will be ready to branch out and consider your own needs first, considering who does what and what's fair and make new agreements on that basis. A new project will be exciting. A fresh financial or work agreement may be made.

New moon in Virgo
LAUNCH FRESH INCENTIVES AND IDEAS

You may feel inspired to begin a new project at work or a venture such as study or travel. For some this new moon will be all about your status as those you love and work with begin to see you in a different light. Aim to shine by spotlighting your ability to concentrate and pay attention to detail.

New moon in Libra
JOIN A NEW CLUB AND MAKE FRIENDS

You're ready to meet new people, socialise, network and bring like-minded people into your circle. This may be a natural progression as you wish to mingle with people who have the same values and mindset. You may begin a fresh project with a group, friend or organisation.

New moon in Scorpio
GAIN MEANING THROUGH WORK AND HEALTH

This new moon could bring you up to date with your own deeper feelings about what must be done now, especially regarding work and your daily life and health. You may be ready to reveal your secret plans to those they impact. For some mid-December–born Sagittarians this new moon will kick-start a more passionate and sociable phase.

LUNAR ECLIPSES:
be strong during peak emotional changes

Each lunar eclipse signals a major turning point in your life and may bring about intense emotions. Eclipses point to circumstances that seem to disempower you and subsequently motivate you to address any imbalances, so keep an eye on those areas in which you lack control as that is where you can make the most changes and become strong. Find out here which lunar eclipse will bring change in which area of your life, and how to make the most of these changes.

Sagittarius lunar eclipse
EMBRACE INDEPENDENCE

The Sagittarian lunar eclipse signifies a completely new chapter in your life. Singles may be drawn to a similarly independent partner and a commitment may be made. Couples may wish for more time apart. For some a new daily routine will begin due to work or health factors.

Capricorn lunar eclipse
REFRESH FINANCIAL OR PERSONAL COMMITMENTS

You may feel frustrated by situations that are stuck, so it's important to establish a new status quo rather than simply throwing caution to the wind. You may need to weigh up your options carefully or must make a choice. A personal or financial matter may come to a head. Think long term.

Aquarius lunar eclipse
INNOVATE AND STIMULATE IDEAS

This eclipse will highlight the lengths you are prepared to go to be innovative with agreements and relationships. You may have a true opportunity to boost your career, finances, personal life or status, so ensure you grasp opportunities and if none seem forthcoming then look for ways to broaden your horizons in exciting ways.

Pisces lunar eclipse
ACCOMMODATE DOMESTIC CHANGES

A change of circumstance at home may result from changes at work, and you will need to accommodate change domestically. For some the focus will be more on your status, general direction and career, so look for new opportunities there. Be inspired to find more peace at home.

Aries lunar eclipse
MAKE CHANGES IN YOUR PERSONAL LIFE

A proactive, 'I've got this' frame of mind will propel you into new territory. However, you must avoid giving in to pressure and being distracted by the impatient demands of other people and by conflict. Focus on action rather than sentiment. You could make great progress and long-term change with family, domestic life and creativity.

Taurus lunar eclipse
BE MOTIVATED BY HAPPINESS

If you're miserable in any aspect of your life such as your job, this eclipse is likely to motivate you to move on; and if your love life could be more fulfilling you'll feel motivated to make changes there. Avoid feeling overwhelmed by emotions or overindulging in food or drink as a way to avoid emotions. Take action.

Gemini lunar eclipse
RECOGNISE YOU NEED VARIETY IN YOUR LIFE

Get set to turn a corner in a major relationship as new financial or interpersonal agreements will be made during this phase. If you've been single a long time you may decide you would like a commitment. Couples may seek more freedom in your relationship. A fresh perspective towards your work or health routine will bring more variety your way.

Cancer lunar eclipse
INVESTIGATE YOUR FEELINGS

Consider your true loyalties and priorities and use your intuition before committing to new investments, whether emotionally or financially. Finances are best considered in the long term as decisions you make now could bring into being a fresh cycle, especially concerning your taxes, an inheritance, shared space at home or duties. Avoid sudden decisions.

Leo lunar eclipse
BE PRODUCTIVE AND LOOK FOR OPPORTUNITIES

Look for ways to ring in the changes, as an alteration in status or circumstance awaits you. Dynamic learning opportunities will arise such as study, work opportunities, travel or a new learning curve in a relationship.

Virgo lunar eclipse
STRATEGISE TO IMPROVE YOUR CAREER AND STATUS

You'll appreciate the chance to put some great strategies into action and, ultimately, to boost your circumstances, so ensure you research your ideas and take practical steps especially if you must alter your career, status or interests. A change at home could mean new horizons beckon.

Libra lunar eclipse
RETHINK YOUR CIRCUMSTANCES

Take things one step at a time with a view to creating more harmony. You may be drawn to fight for your rights or for fair play, but if conflict is around you avoid being caught in someone else's battle. You may wish to relate with groups, a friend or organisations in a new way, especially if relationships seem unbalanced or unfulfilling.

Scorpio lunar eclipse
CLEAR A BACKLOG OF WORK AND BAD HABITS

It's time to eliminate aspects of your daily routine or work that no longer resonate with you on a deep level. You'll enjoy focusing on rebooting your mental, physical and spiritual well-being. A detox may be necessary. You may feel uncharacteristically moody, so some psychological insight may be beneficial.

SOLAR ECLIPSES:
making major changes run smoothly

Each solar eclipse signals a major turning point in your life that points to ongoing change for years to come. Find out here which solar eclipses will bring change in which areas of your life, and how to make the most of those changes.

Sagittarius solar eclipse
BELIEVE IN YOURSELF DESPITE DISRUPTIONS

The solar eclipse signals a positive new phase in your personal life, although change may initially be disruptive. Avoid knee-jerk reactions; think things through. If it's your birthday on or before the eclipse date, changes may affect a relationship; if you were born after the eclipse a fresh health or work routine will arise.

Capricorn solar eclipse
BUILD STRONG FOUNDATIONS

Key decisions merit care and attention, and you may ask if a commitment you've made or are contemplating is too restrictive. If so, make new agreements. If you find this a trying time financially it will nevertheless provide you with the opportunity to build strong foundations for moving forward.

Aquarius solar eclipse
RENEW COMMUNICATIONS AND TRAVEL

A new approach to communications will offer you the chance to improve relationships and work. Travel may appeal, or if you travel a lot a restless phase will end. Consider investing in technology to boost your efficiency. You may be drawn to digital work or will find ways to be more technically minded.

Pisces solar eclipse

REVAMP DOMESTIC AND FAMILY DYNAMICS

Be inspired, but in the process maintain a practical and methodical outlook or you may be inclined to feel inundated by events or demands in your personal life. A friend, family member or group may be super useful or will contribute to your circumstances. You may be inspired by art, music and dance and must avoid gambling.

Aries solar eclipse

NEGOTIATE CHANGE GENTLY

Be prepared for change as it may bring sensitivities out. Aim to put vulnerabilities aside. For some a fresh start will occur domestically or with family. You may feel fired up emotionally and must guard against impulsiveness, especially if you feel under pressure or under someone's thumb. Aim to negotiate change gently.

Taurus solar eclipse

BE PRACTICAL ABOUT LONG-TERM CHANGE

You will find the support you need during this time, so reach out to trusted resources. Avoid gambling and ensure you research your circumstances carefully. A fresh chapter at work or with family or a new financial arrangement will begin.

Gemini solar eclipse

BRING VARIETY AND SPICE INTO YOUR DAILY LIFE

You may experience a work or financial development that resonates into the future. A fresh daily schedule may begin, and a more varied health schedule will appeal. If your birthday is on or either side of the eclipse date you may meet someone new if you're single, while couples will undergo a key development.

Cancer solar eclipse

ADOPT A FRESH APPROACH TO SOMEONE CLOSE

A fresh agreement or a new understanding, for many involving finances or your personal life, will be a catalyst for change. A fresh approach to a business or personal partner could foster improved dynamics within the relationship if it presents problems. You may need to consider how to provide more comfort and nurturance to someone, or how to gain more yourself.

Leo solar eclipse

BOOST SELF-ESTEEM AND SHINE

Be prepared to step into new territory, to broaden your horizons and meet new people even if someone steels your thunder. Developments will encourage you to see yourself in a new light and shine in a new arena. You may feel more proactive about study and learning a new skill. A key relationship may undergo change.

Virgo solar eclipse

A CHANGE OF DIRECTION

Even if change is the last thing on your mind it has been waiting in the wings, and you'll gain insight over the coming days and weeks about how best to progress. You may need to learn a new skill, begin a new career or alter your home life to better suit your needs.

Libra solar eclipse

WELCOME NEW PEOPLE, IDEAS AND ADVENTURES

A beautiful relationship can blossom, but if you feel it's stuck in a rut this solar eclipse will open your eyes to ways to revitalise your relationships or to finally choose to go on separate paths. You'll meet new people and broaden your horizons.

Scorpio solar eclipse

RE-INVENT YOURSELF

This is an excellent time to shed your skin, to lose old ways that are holding you back, and you'll appreciate the sense that you can begin a fresh chapter. For many it will be due to changes at work, while for others it will concern your health. A fresh schedule and approach to work may begin, especially if you've wanted to alter your routine for some time.

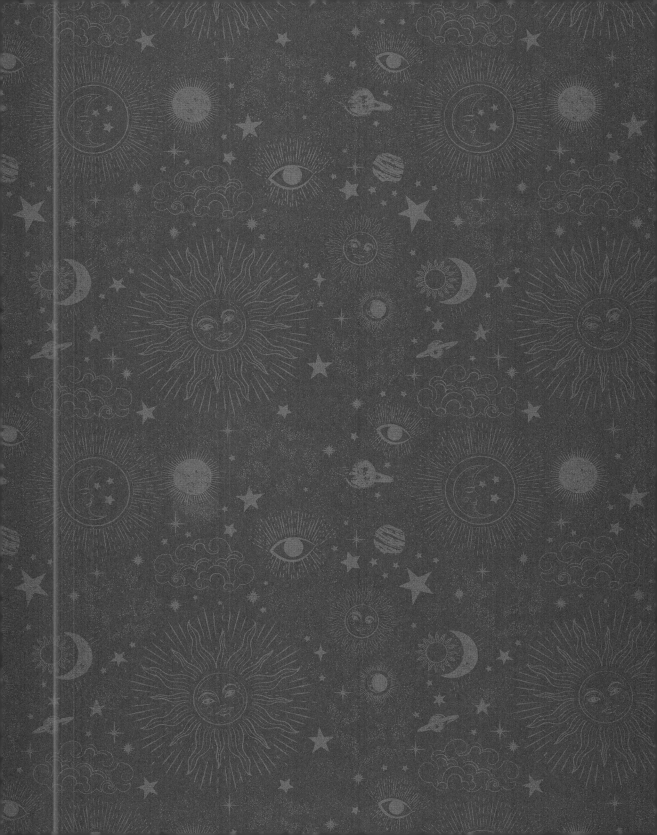

21 DECEMBER – 20 JANUARY

SYMBOL
Goat

CONSTELLATION

ELEMENT
Earth

CAPRICORN
SUN SIGN

INNER CALLING

You must feel that you are a success, yet the qualities that spell success will alter as you progress through life. To a degree, despite the fact you are an earth sign best known for being a little set in your ways, you are in fact constantly evolving and are adaptable as a result.

You are essentially a goal-oriented person, so very little will get in the way as your inner mountain goat (your sign's symbol) strives towards your desired outcomes and the pinnacle of your abilities. However, to achieve your goals you are unlikely to rush your activities and seldom seem pressured in your strategy; rather, you will appear to progress slowly one step at a time. Your measured progress, however, belies your tenacity: slowly but surely you attain your goals and do so unfailingly and regardless of any obstacles that stand in your way.

You will attain your aims even if your projects require true diligence and application. You are focused, and it's very hard to put you off your stride once you have a goal in mind.

You have a calm, understated demeanour even if excitement and motivation linger just beneath yourexterior. You are adventurous and love to try new ideas, especially in the fields of work and health. It's partly this underlying thirst for adventure that feeds your ability to remain focused, as you need fresh experiences just the same as you need air. You continue relentlessly with your aims and goals, pursuing them because you are driven to do so.

Capricorn gets a bad rap as being boring and staid due to their intractability, yet there is drive that sizzles just below the surface. Those who get to know you deeply realise this and appreciate your depths.

SELF-ESTEEM

Your self-esteem increases in measure with your perceived success in life, so the more successful you are in terms of what is considered to be success in your culture the higher will be your self-esteem. Because the modern world's idea of success revolves around money and career so too does your idea of success revolve around money, status and career and you will seek to excel in these areas. However, as you progress through life, starting a family for example where kindness, compassion and companionship are the most valuable qualities, then these are the qualities you will embrace so that you feel you are a success. You are adaptable; it's just that when you have a goal in mind very little will deter you and this will give you a reputation for being inflexible.

Your self-esteem takes a dive when your abilities go unappreciated. For example, when you visit a country where your achievements are disrespected you will see this as nonsensical at best and a personal affront at worst, an assault on your self-esteem. You take the opinions of other people personally, which can be a real pitfall as you will react according to their values. You can work on this by providing yourself with an enduring sense of worth regardless of what other people feel is valuable in society.

When you are guided by your heart, by love, compassion and mutual respect, you will not stray far from a path of happiness as you will feel the rewards of your actions in your heart and will no longer depend on the admiration of others.

HOME LIFE

You're a traditionalist at heart, so family and upholding values will be important to you. You are a sensuous, earthy character but may appear reserved or shy at first. You are dependable and will not let people down, unless you have a restless moon sign or ascendant. You are fundamentally the most dependable character in the zodiac, even if you do seem focused on career, status or earnings at various times of your life.

Your home life may be changeable, especially when you are young. You will like to be the one in control at home and may have a strong personality in one of your parents. You are not afraid to take the initiative to build a happy home, although you may experience opposition to the way you rule the roost. Aim to ease your stance at home, as your softer side will seek expression there.

RELATIONSHIPS

As those who love you will confirm, your ability to commit to values, people and relationships is a favourite quality. Your dependability and reliability are positive attributes. You are more able than many other zodiac signs to create and live with strong, stable relationships; however, you will not suffer fools gladly and your pragmatic character will not hold back from expressing any misgivings that may arise in relationships. You are strong, and will ensure you do not remain in circumstances that lack respect or dignity. You raise the bar for those you are in relationships with, and when they rise with you the security and love you experience as a result provide strong foundations for happiness.

You can be seen as obstinate and also inflexible even if your dependability is acknowledged. Others may believe you're unrelenting in the pursuit of your goals and uncompromising when your path is blocked or your will opposed. You can also be seen as reserved or distant, largely because you are slow to commit to ideas, people and ventures. But once you do you are one of the most steadfast and loyal individuals, and your reputation for reliability, constancy and dependability will grow the more you retain your self-respect and stand your ground. It may simply take people a while to see the positive aspects of your methods.

You can be seen more as a social climber and as someone who focuses on wealth and outer forms of success rather than on inner spiritual fortitude and domestic happiness. You are the sign most likely to follow in your father's footsteps and are seen as a social stalwart.

CREATIVITY

Art, music and creativity have an earthy and sensual attraction for you. You will enjoy your life all the more when surrounded by beauty in the form of music, art, great architecture, environments or people. This is where you find your inspiration and is what drives you to keep your feet on the ground, knowing that true beauty, art and creativity come from deep within, from the ground and from nature and people themselves.

You have an appreciation of creativity in others even if you do not make art or music yourself, and appreciate the magic inherent in beauty, art and music. Your heart soars in dance and sensuality and being in nature and in love. Your creation of family and providing security is your highest form of self-expression, the one that keeps you grounded and happy.

PITFALLS

You can be seen as being obstinate by others as your staid personality can on occasion prevent you from adjusting to circumstances or going with the flow, yet you have a deep appreciation of life and a streak of adventure that, when you engage it and express it more often, gives you a more open frame of mind. People who love you appreciate your dry sense of humour and understated love of life.

SOLAR TRANSITS:
harness the sun's power
every day of the year

*The sun empowers you in different areas of your life as it
travels through each zodiac sign from month to month. Find
out here how to make the most of your strong points during
each of the transits of the sun through the 12 signs.*

Sun in Capricorn, December to January
WHEN YOU FEEL THE STRONGEST

You'll find that many of your past efforts will come to fruition and that your slow but steady progress is paying off, especially in your personal life and at work. Try to see any disappointments as a course correction that offers more insight and direction so your path becomes clearer moving forward.

Sun in Aquarius, January to February
RE-EVALUATE IDEAS AND FINANCES

Quirky, unorthodox and fun ideas will spark ventures into new territory. For some this phase will bring a fresh period in your personal life as you or someone close may feel a need for independence, freedom and variety. Avoid overspending, as you may make impulsive decisions around money.

Sun in Pisces, February to March
IMPROVE COMMUNICATIONS AND TRAVEL

You will be inclined to view the world and relationships uncharacteristically in an idealistic manner, so remember to be realistic especially with negotiations, travel and business. Combine your organisational skills with your hopes and ideals and you'll make great progress.

Sun in Aries, March to April
BE PROACTIVE AT HOME

You'll feel more in the zone when it comes to getting things done at home, with family or even DIY projects. People may respond well to your ideas over the coming weeks, making this an ideal time to plan ahead, but if someone opposes your plans take the time to persuade them of their merits rather than starting conflict.

Sun in Taurus, April to May
EXPRESS YOURSELF!

You may be particularly productive with creative and artistic work and will enjoy the company of family and friends more, so this is a good time to schedule get-togethers. You'll feel motivated to do home improvements and relish being romantic and indulging in favourite meals, music and dance.

Sun in Gemini, May to June
DIVERSIFY AT WORK AND HEALTH-WISE

You will feel more light-hearted and enjoy experiencing new activities in life, at work and in your daily schedule. This is a good time for a holiday, and your love of children and family may be a focus. A change of circumstance with family or someone special may introduce a fresh dynamic into your personal life.

Sun in Cancer, June to July
NURTURE YOUR LOVE LIFE AND RELATIONSHIPS

Your business or personal partner will be more responsive to your ideas or will catch your attention more than usual. They may verbalise their emotional needs more or confide in you more. For some this phase points to the need to look after yourself or someone close, and is a lovely time to organise a holiday and nurturing activities.

Sun in Leo, July to August

REVITALISE COLLABORATIONS

While this is an upbeat time for collaborations, some developments may appear to proceed too quickly for your liking so ensure you know how to apply the brakes in tactful ways. Then you'll enjoy a sunny outcome with relationships, including romance.

Sun in Virgo, August to September

ATTAIN YOUR GOALS

This is a good time to work hard and to embrace new ventures, collaborations and projects. You may be drawn to long-distance travel and study and to improving your personal life. Relationships could flourish, so take the initiative but avoid being demanding and a perfectionist.

Sun in Libra, September to October

REGAIN BALANCE IN YOUR CAREER AND DIRECTION

You're a hard worker and are diligent about your work, but sometimes your hard work and goal-setting mindset can take over your life. This phase will help you to include fun activities and favourite hobbies, and a holiday, short break or adventure may appeal and will restore balance.

Sun in Scorpio, October to November

BOOST YOUR SOCIAL LIFE

These four weeks will ramp up your lust for life, which you'll enjoy. Have you ever thrown caution to the wind? This is the phase when you're most likely to! Be practical for the best results or you may find that your head is turned by activities that you'd generally consider unrealistic or impractical.

Sun in Sagittarius, November to December

ACT CONFIDENTLY WITH WORK AND HEALTH

This is a good time to work super confidently behind the scenes to develop work and health ventures, as you'll feel more enthusiastic about your projects. If you're drawn to spiritual or psychological enquiry you could make a great deal of headway.

LUNAR TRANSITS:
be calm and effective every day of the month

The moon spotlights different aspects of your emotional self as it travels each month through each zodiac sign, staying two days in each sign. When the moon is in each sign you gain the opportunity to express yourself more effectively in various areas of your life. Find out here how to make the most of your strong points during each of the two days each month.

Moon in Capricorn
WHEN YOU FEEL MOST PRACTICAL

The Capricorn moon will help you to stride ahead confidently and make realistic plans everyone can work with. You'll get things done methodically over these two days, and positive talks and meetings will be productive.

Moon in Aquarius
OPEN YOUR MIND TO DIFFERENT VALUES

Open your mind to different values and principles: you may, for example, entertain fresh strategies and financial plans. You will be drawn to investigating ideas, so it's a good time to go out on a limb if you're considering new projects. However, you must avoid being unreliable.

Moon in Pisces
BE INSPIRED

People you love will inspire you both at home and at work. You may be drawn to travel or study. However, you can tend to be an idealist and may see someone or a conundrum through rose-coloured glasses. Take a step back and be practical.

Moon in Aries

INVEST IN DOMESTIC BLISS

This is a good time to improve your home life but you may feel feisty or restless, so you must establish balance at home to avoid conflict. If you decide to make changes at home don't take on too many chores or you could cause arguments through feeling unsettled.

Moon in Taurus

INDULGE IN ROMANCE, FAMILY FUN AND CREATIVITY

You'll enjoy get-togethers and the chance to be creative. If work or other responsibilities seem to eat into your personal time, ensure you plan ahead to schedule in favourite events as these two days will feed your desire for sensuality and romance.

Moon in Gemini

PACE YOURSELF AT WORK

You prefer life at a set pace, as too many changes can be disorienting and you then need time to adjust. Events will ask that you think on your feet, and life can seem to speed up. Being busy is exciting for you, but when a fast phase spans a few days it can also be tiring so ensure you rest when you can.

Moon in Cancer

SCHEDULE NURTURING TIMES AND ROMANCE

Relaxing and nurturing activities will help soothe nerves during this phase. You or your partner may feel particularly romantic, and you or someone close may feel inspired and imaginative. The more practical you can be yet also the more resourceful the better will be the outcome.

Moon in Leo

ENJOY AN UPBEAT PACE

Some get-togethers will be ideal at this time, as you could infuse a light and fun-loving touch to interactions that people will respond well to. Adopt an upbeat tone in your relationships and people will follow your example.

Moon in Virgo

POWER AHEAD WITH VENTURES

You're in a position to see your activities and projects fall into place. Be methodical, especially with long-term projects and collaborations, and you could see excellent results from your hard work.

Moon in Libra

LOOK FOR HARMONY AND A FAIR GO AT WORK

You can excel at this time, although this moon at the zenith of your chart may put your heart on your sleeve and you may see the world through purely emotional eyes. Seek balance and look for solutions to problems.

Moon in Scorpio

ENJOY THE COMPANY OF THOSE YOU LOVE

You'll feel more passionate about your activities and motivated to make changes. You'll enjoy socialising, and there's also a feel-good focus on health, well-being and networking. Take time out to make positive changes. Look for inspiring activities, as these will lighten your mood.

Moon in Sagittarius

LEAN INTO PRIORITIES AND HEALTH

You'll enjoy the company of special friends and colleagues and also enjoy networking. Take the time to explore new ideas, but only if you're ready. You may feel more energised at work or drawn to an upbeat fitness program.

FULL MOONS:
magnify your vibrant power

Each full moon highlights different aspects of your power and vibrancy.
Find out here which full moons will be excellent times to turn a corner
in the various areas of your life to show just what you're made of.

Full moon in Capricorn
TIE UP LOOSE ENDS

This full moon signals the beginning of a new cycle in your life. Events may be intense, especially regarding relationships, work or finances, so ensure you pace yourself. The key to progress lies in being able to discuss circumstances and options with someone close and to tie up loose ends in practical ways.

Full moon in Aquarius
FOCUS ON FINANCES AND SELF-ESTEEM

A personal or financial matter will come to a head that may be unexpected or out of the ordinary. Weigh up your options carefully around a commitment. You may need to negotiate the way you share space, finances or duties, so be realistic and research your options carefully.

Full moon in Pisces
RE-IMAGINE COMMUNICATIONS AND TRAVEL

Get set to turn a corner in a relationship. Be innovative: you may even surprise yourself with insightful and inspired ways to add more excitement to your life. Some years this full moon will spotlight an important trip. A fresh agreement may be on the cards, especially regarding shared duties, collaborations, finances or taxes.

Full moon in Aries

BOOST YOUR ENVIRONMENT

Make concrete plans for success in the environment you spend most time in and with the key people there. Communications and meetings could kick-start a fresh agreement or project, but you must ensure joint projects are up to speed with your own goals and principles. Be clear with communications to avoid having to backtrack later.

Full moon in Taurus

GAIN PERSPECTIVE IN YOUR PERSONAL LIFE

Be prepared to turn a corner with the people you love and to gain a sense of purpose. A development at home or work or regarding family will highlight how you feel about your home. If some relationships seem more difficult than others, take time out to gain perspective and aim for compromise in talks.

Full moon in Gemini

IMPROVE WORK CONDITIONS AND CREATIVITY

A new understanding with someone will begin that may lead you to needing more security or to making a commitment one way or another. Avoid feeling you must always agree with everyone, as sometimes it's wiser to agree to disagree and to allow for a degree of freedom.

Full moon in Cancer

STRENGTHEN RELATIONSHIPS

This is a good time to raise morale, both at work and in your personal life. Key talks could lay the groundwork for better communications, so be prepared to broaden your skill set through adopting a compassionate and supportive approach to those you work with or love.

Full moon in Leo

LOOK FOR FRESH UNDERSTANDING

Consider how to be more upbeat with your collaborations and boost your sense of fulfilment and achievement. Your interactions with a friend or organisation may be more relevant than usual as your talks could lead to a fresh understanding.

Full moon in Virgo

CHOOSE YOUR INTERESTS AND ACTIVITIES

Choose interests and activities you love! This may sound simple, but sometimes you just follow the crowd. Find practical ways ahead but avoid overanalysing options and be realistic, optimistic and proactive. Embrace activities that provide a sense of stability, nurturance and growth and be supported by like-minded people.

Full moon in Libra

REBALANCE YOUR LIFE

A career move or the end of a chapter regarding your status – from single to married or vice versa, for example – may occur. Key decisions will merit careful focus. How could you set fresh boundaries in your relationships and expedite paperwork? Look for fair play and balance and avoid gambling on a supposed outcome.

Full moon in Scorpio

ADOPT A NEW ROLE WITHIN A GROUP OR WITH A FRIEND

You may be more inclined during this time to express your humanitarian views; joining a new group or organisation may appeal. If you've been quiet socially prepare for a busier time, but if you've been burning the candle at both ends prepare for a quieter time.

Full moon in Sagittarius

RESEARCH INFORMATION

You may discover information that points to a better way forward. Ensure that your health and work routines support your personal growth, and avoid overwork and a poor diet. If work has hit a speed bump look for pursuits that have a purpose.

NEW MOONS:
start something fresh

*Each new moon points to the start of something fresh for you in
different areas of your life. Find out here which new moon to work
with and how to make lasting change by starting something new,
especially if you have been putting off change for some time.*

New moon in Capricorn
KICK-START A MORE STABLE LIFE

The Capricorn new moon offers you the chance to kick-start a fresh cycle in your personal life,
especially if it's your birthday. Get set to turn a corner to where you can work in a more relaxed
and stable environment and can minimise the level of unpredictability in your personal life by
planning and communicating your long-term goals with those you love.

New moon in Aquarius
THINK LATERALLY ABOUT INVESTMENTS

Be ready to step into the new with your personal or financial investments. A fresh budget could
be the key to a better daily life. For some this new moon will be all about a new place and
environment that will stimulate your enjoyment in life and raise morale.

New moon in Pisces
EMBRACE YOUR DREAMS

You may need to change some aspects of your life to ensure you attain a sense of fulfilment.
Talks, a trip or negotiations during this new moon could set the ball rolling to a more inspired
life. Avoid overspending and idealism, as these could trip you up. Infuse communications and
relationships with more inspiration and verve.

New moon in Aries

A BUSY CHAPTER AT HOME

Careful talks and negotiations will lead to the domestic results you seek. A trip to somewhere beautiful will appeal both to you and someone special as it will feel revitalising or will signify a fresh start. DIY projects, home decoration or even a move or starting a family will be upbeat and suggest a busy time.

New moon in Taurus

EMBRACE SENSUALITY

You'll welcome more sensuality in your life due to more romance or simply due to a beautiful environment, good food and lovely company. Singles could meet an alluring character and couples deepen intimacy, so plan ahead! This is a good time to schedule a family holiday or retreat or to renew marriage vows.

New moon in Gemini

BEGIN FRESH WORK AND HEALTH ROUTINES

This is a good time to begin fresh projects and schedules. Avoid being impulsive with people who try your patience, as this is a good time for research at work and with well-being. A fun venture with friends or family may be a success, so think outside the box and spruce up your daily life.

New moon in Cancer

KICK-START A NURTURING RELATIONSHIP PHASE

Adopt a sensitive and nurturing approach to your relationships and they will blossom. For some Capricorns the focus will be on a fresh chapter in your daily routine, work or health matters. This is a good time to revitalise your diet and self-care.

New moon in Leo

MAKE PROGRESSIVE, PRODUCTIVE NEW AGREEMENTS

Aim to ring in exciting changes in a business or personal partnership. The changes may come from out of the blue or will feel revitalising. Be optimistic, as a positive outcome will then develop. Be dynamic, proactive and responsible with your arrangements.

New moon in Virgo
BROADEN YOUR HORIZONS

A new, detailed approach to your various interests and activities will be productive as a fresh phase will see your status and direction change. The key to happiness will lie in finding time for all areas of your life in practical, methodical ways. Avoid perfectionism, especially in relationships; be realistic.

New moon in Libra
OVERHAUL YOUR CAREER AND STATUS

This is a good time to overhaul your outlook, to find more fairness and equality in your life so you can work towards better circumstances. The key to success is to avoid an ego battle. You may enter new terrain at work or socially or with a special project. You may need to be more adaptable or, conversely, to uphold your convictions if you have been overly compromising.

New moon in Scorpio
START A PASSION PROJECT OR NEW ALLIANCE

You'll feel more upbeat and outgoing. Your status, career and direction could soar as you are likely to feel more passionate about your projects. Get set for a fresh social and networking circle as you will be drawn to meet and greet all kinds of adventurous people.

New moon in Sagittarius
FOCUS ON BEING POSITIVE AND PRODUCTIVE

Being such a methodical person, a buoyant Sagittarian new moon can feel unsettling unless you focus on its benefits, which will encourage you to be more optimistic and outgoing. You'll enjoy the sense of embracing new possibilities and expressing your full potential, especially at work.

LUNAR ECLIPSES:
be strong during peak emotional changes

Each lunar eclipse signals a major turning point in your life and may bring about intense emotions. Eclipses point to circumstances that seem to disempower you and subsequently motivate you to address any imbalances, so keep an eye on those areas in which you lack control as that is where you can make the most changes and become strong. Find out here which lunar eclipse will bring change in which area of your life, and how to make the most of these changes.

Capricorn lunar eclipse
A MAJOR NEW LIFE CYCLE

Events may be intense, especially regarding relationships and finances, so pace yourself and take things one step at a time. The key to progress lies in being able to talk through your feelings and discussing your circumstances and options. Some Capricorns may undergo a change at work or health-wise.

Aquarius lunar eclipse
TRANSFORM YOUR FINANCES AND PERSONAL LIFE

As major emotional or financial investments take a turn you may feel torn between sticking with the usual, with tradition and with what you already know versus pushing the boundaries forward and choosing a new role. Weigh up the odds and be guided by your values to make informed choices.

Pisces lunar eclipse
BUILD SOLID COMMUNICATIONS

This phase could be disorienting, but developments will open your mind to fresh dynamics such as a new romantic involvement or travel or work that takes you into new territory. This eclipse demands good communication skills to avoid misunderstandings in crucial talks.

Aries lunar eclipse
ACT ON YOUR INTUITION AT HOME

You are ready to make changes with property or a domestic circumstance even if you feel under pressure. Spiritual Capricorns may experience an awakening. Some Capricorns will find certain relationships change footing, potentially due to travel, a new environment or a move. Be positive and adaptable and avoid obstinacy.

Taurus lunar eclipse
EMBRACE FRESH DYNAMICS

Family circumstances are likely to change for some Capricorns and domestic circumstances for others. Artistic Capricorns will enjoy a creative phase. The eclipse will encourage you to be more affectionate with your partner or family and, if you're single, you'll feel willing to look for someone as a companion and potentially to make a commitment.

Gemini lunar eclipse
EMBRACE A MORE VARIED DAILY ROUTINE

You are ready for something new that brings more variety into your everyday life. Aim to broaden your skills and discuss exciting options. You may make or break a key commitment but must be clear about your feelings and intentions. For some this lunar eclipse will bring a distracted phase or ambivalent feelings. Find ways to earth yourself.

Cancer lunar eclipse
TURN A CORNER IN A KEY RELATIONSHIP

Be practical, realistic and adaptable during this potentially emotional time. Someone close may have key news or will reveal a change of circumstance or of heart. For some Capricorns the lunar eclipse will end a major work or health cycle and reveal a new chapter.

Leo lunar eclipse
ADJUST TO SHARED DUTIES OR FINANCES

A fresh phase will begin in communal circumstances such as shared commitments, finances and space. Change may occur due to matters beyond your control, but the more dynamic you are about adapting to new circumstances the better it will be for you, as exciting opportunities will arise. Avoid being obstinate.

Virgo lunar eclipse

PACE YOURSELF

Events will represent considerable change in your activities and interests. You like to attain goals in your own time – the tortoise and the hare come to mind! A practical as opposed to emotional approach to life's ups and downs will pay off, and by the end of the eclipse phase you'll be tapping your foot at the finishing line way ahead of late-arrival hares!

Libra lunar eclipse

DEFUSE TENSION IN YOUR CAREER AND DIRECTION

Look for realistic ways to move towards a more harmonious phase as you restore a sense of balance and fair play in your career or general direction. Be prepared to adjust to circumstances and to make changes at home or financially. Someone may seem aggressive, so aim to defuse tension.

Scorpio lunar eclipse

MAINTAIN PERSPECTIVE ABOUT STATUS AND GOALS

Emotions you have ignored or rationalised will rise up, especially around your status or social circles and your general direction in life. You may feel super passionate about your status and goals work-wise. This is a motivational phase, but you must keep an eye on maintaining perspective to avoid making rash decisions.

Sagittarius lunar eclipse

PLAN TO BE HAPPIER

A key chapter in your daily routine will come to an end. Get set to begin a new chapter even if it draws on your emotions and demands that you step into new territory. You may be drawn to humanitarian or volunteer work or will wish to boost your physical health.

SOLAR ECLIPSES:
making major changes run smoothly

Each solar eclipse signals a major turning point in your life that points to ongoing change for years to come. Find out here which solar eclipses will bring change in which areas of your life, and how to make the most of those changes.

Capricorn solar eclipse
CHANGE YOUR LIFE

A key decision or commitment could change your life, especially if you were born before or on the eclipse. Avoid restricting yourself too much within the agreements you make; instead, look for stability and security. If you were born after the eclipse a key new daily routine will begin either due to work or to health developments.

Aquarius solar eclipse
BE INNOVATIVE, ESPECIALLY FINANCIALLY

Fresh financial arrangements could put you in a strong position moving forward. Consider how you might manage your budget in ground-breaking ways to make your dollar stretch further on a daily basis; you may, for example, be drawn to internet banking or investments. Think imaginatively, but avoid investing in super-risky schemes.

Pisces solar eclipse
PLAY BY NEW RULES

Aim to consolidate your circumstances and finances as you may be surprised or simply must face an unprecedented circumstance and need to draw on your communication and negotiation skills. If you find yourself in uncharted waters, gain independent expert advice.

Aries solar eclipse
MAKE A TOUGH CALL AT HOME

A fresh domestic arrangement is likely to gather momentum. You may need to make a difficult decision but must look after your own interests first, even if you feel conflicted in doing so. You and the people around you may feel more feisty than usual, so aim to find clever ways to diffuse anger and unreasonable behaviour.

Taurus solar eclipse
THINK CREATIVELY

A key decision in your love life or with a creative matter or family will come down to practicalities rather than emotions. A change of circumstance such as children arriving or leaving home may arise. Avoid seeing only what is lacking in your life and find ways to experience more stability in crucial areas: your home, security and family.

Gemini solar eclipse
BE ADAPTABLE WITH YOUR WORK/LIFE BALANCE

It's a good time to discuss your ideas and think outside the square, and to adjust your perspective and preconceived ideas. Get set to turn a corner at work or to change your daily schedule and health to boost the work/life balance. Maintain an adaptable frame of mind and embrace a diverse set of activities even if a schedule change is disruptive, as it will usher in new times.

Cancer solar eclipse
A MAJOR CHANGE IN A PARTNERSHIP

A work or personal partner, boss or colleague will have a significant bearing on your circumstances as a new chapter is about to begin in your relationship. If health has been a concern this solar eclipse will spur you on to improve it. Take time to nurture yourself and others for more supportive relationships.

Leo solar eclipse
BE COURAGEOUS WITH AGREEMENTS

A fresh agreement will help you turn a corner in a key area; you may simply begin to relate to someone important in a new way. Events could point to a legal document that will enable you to move forward. Avoid being pushed into a corner: be bold but avoid conflict, as it's likely to escalate.

Virgo solar eclipse
PLAN A BREAK, EXCITING VENTURE OR ACTIVITY

Expect a change of atmosphere, of pace or of place. Plan a trip, as it will shine a light on activities that strike a chord with you. You'll be in a good position to make the necessary changes to accommodate new interests. Key talks will signal a fresh understanding of someone close. Legal matters deserve attention to detail.

Libra solar eclipse
DARE TO STEP INTO SOMETHING NEW

A change of status, such as from single to married or vice versa, or a fresh career, profile or outlook will be what motivates you to make further changes in your life. You may feel trepidation at taking steps into a new direction, but if you aim for a peaceful outlook you'll create a more balanced and harmonious life.

Scorpio solar eclipse
TURN A CORNER WITH A GROUP OR ORGANISATION

Changes you make to your work or social life will have a positive effect on your personal life. If you have been reluctant to make changes in your love life or your social circle you will be able to do so now. You may meet or leave a significant person in your life.

Sagittarius solar eclipse
ASK FOR AND OFFER HELP

You'll appreciate the help of a loyal friend or organisation. You may feel particularly drawn to humanitarian work, and some of your plans may be truly grandiose but merit research as they may have great potential. This eclipse sheds light on the importance of honesty.

20 JANUARY – 18 FEBRUARY

SYMBOL
Water bearer

ELEMENT
Air

CONSTELLATION

AQUARIUS
SUN SIGN

INNER CALLING

Your inner calling is to find the truth about life – about people, relationships and the big-picture meaning of human existence – which will initially be expressed through your search for meaning in your immediate environment, home life or neighbourhood. You understand the underlying paradox of life and death, the inner tension that spawns existence and creation. On a day-to-day level this translates as inner tension between two different approaches to life: the reasonable, practical approach on the one hand and the wish to bring something new and exciting into your life on the other.

This underlying tension is largely because your sign is co-ruled by two very different planets and energies: Saturn and Uranus. In ancient mythology Saturn (Kronos in Ancient Greek) is the son of Uranus. Saturn overcame his father during a fight and discarded his body into the ocean. This myth symbolises the new order (embodied in Saturn, the son) that overthrows the old order (in the shape of Uranus).

In your sign of Aquarius there is an ongoing fight within you about how to evolve and how best to move forward in innovative ways without recourse to completely overthrowing and destroying your previous ideas or lifestyle. This constant battle can lead to great stress and indecision from weighing up the relative merits of embracing the new versus keeping the old, and you will frequently need to decide whether to hold on to the past or welcome the new in radical ways. You can consequently seem to others to be irrational and quirky, and to change your mind frequently.

Your indecision also comes from the need to overcome the past in some way, and a struggle may seem inevitable in order to do so. However, it needn't be a struggle if you can reconcile your need for change with your reliance on the status quo. You will always need to move forward and overthrow the past, but not necessarily in such a destructive way as the gods whose planets rule your sign.

SELF-ESTEEM

Your self-esteem can take a battering when you're under stress, as this is when the inner tension that pulls you this way then another is most likely to emerge. Your key to improved self-esteem is in maintaining a calm and stress-free life. You'll find benefit in the study of philosophy, spirituality, art, music, creativity and similar activities that build a sense of peace and relaxation. You also gain a sense of support via collaborations and team spirit, so sport and volunteer work will be appealing as a way to gain confidence.

When you focus on upbeat and calming activities such as sport and meditation you'll gain a sense of achievement from having directed restless energy into form and function, and will feel fulfilled when you realise your actions have resulted in positive results. Humanitarian endeavours and collaborative efforts at work and socially will certainly lead to the sense you are achieving results in your world, and will feed back to you as a rewarding sense of accomplishment.

HOME LIFE

Through your home life you'll find a way to embrace both your inner traditionalist and your innovative side. Your home represents security and stability on the one hand but can also facilitate your outgoing and eccentric nature on the other so you can be spontaneous and dependable at the same time. This is who you are! Embrace your inner tension rather than allowing it to become a problem.

Your home is likely to be eclectic as you are intrinsically a maverick. Technical and digital media will be attractive to you and your home is likely to feature impressive technology. However, a real pitfall for you is overstimulation of your mind to the degree you become confused or frustrated by additional input over and above the already raging undercurrent of deep-down tension, so it's important your home life also includes relaxation space.

RELATIONSHIPS

You can be seen as a truly eccentric character, someone who is outside the norm. Many Aquarians, though, are no more oddball than anyone else but people may point out the anomalies in your rationale (especially if you're under pressure) where you see none at all. Bear in mind that you're a bit of an enigma, so if you prefer to be seen in a stable light then take the time to reassure others of your constancy within relationships.

This is especially important as your wish to retain independence within relationships can feel frustrating to those you hold dear. There is, however, a degree of independence you will not surrender, which can make you hugely attractive to partners or it can make you seem the opposite: frustrating in your seeming lack of commitment. Once again, if you wish to project a sense of dependability ensure you make the additional effort to show just how reliable you really are.

CREATIVITY

Your inner tension can lead to an incredible sense of creativity, so you must find ways to channel your restlessness into productive activities. You have a great deal of power in your creative understanding of the world, and if you take steps to channel this level of understanding into the work you create on a daily basis your compassion for the absurdity of human life will result in clever and kind work. This will be appreciated by those in your immediate family and also those you work with and help.

You are an air sign, and there's no doubt you have a smart mind. Feed and nurture your mind with interesting and diverse activities and your mind will, in turn, work at its optimum capacity, opening doors to rewarding insights and experiences that will increasingly nurture your spirit.

PITFALLS

Your inner tension and search for the ultimate truth in a paradoxical world can lead to great insecurity and to others seeing you as eccentric and, at worst, erratic and unreliable. Some people may not understand you, still less your quirky sense of humour. You will nevertheless have a peace of mind and self-assuredness that others find difficult to attain.

On occasion you feel conflicted about what you should do and even wonder who you are, as you have the two paradoxical impulses regarding the old order and the new order running concurrently inside you. This can lead to inaction and especially in relationships, for example, if you are in a loving relationship that provides status quo but does not feel as though it is progressing you will feel frustrated. An inner debate will arise about the relative value between stability and security versus the new and moving forward.

As a progressive character you need stimulation and can sometimes let excellent situations go simply because you need change. It's vital to have a set of checks and balances so you do not allow one or the other of your dominant characteristics to take the lead. Wishing things to stay the same while also wishing for freedom and independence can lead to the magical sweet spot of inspired living you so crave.

SOLAR TRANSITS:
harness the sun's power
every day of the year

The sun empowers you in different areas of your life as it travels through each zodiac sign from month to month. Find out here how to make the most of your strong points during each of the transits of the sun through the 12 signs.

Sun in Aquarius, January to February
LET YOUR INNER REBEL OUT!

Give full flight to your more unusual ideas as you can effectively combine your natural sense of rebellion with your understanding of the need for traditional boundaries and restrictions. It's a good time to innovate and make changes, especially at work and in your personal life, but you must also keep an eye on practicalities.

Sun in Pisces, February to March
INVEST IN YOUR DREAMS

You may make a deeper commitment romantically or financially and it may be perfect; however, you could be super idealistic about life and therefore must set realistic expectations. Consider approaching your priorities in a new way; be prepared to be inspired by others and to travel and meet and greet.

Sun in Aries, March to April
BE PROACTIVE AND GAIN VALUE IN LIFE

Look for more value in your life, which may be derived from a happier home or more fulfilment in your work. Now is the time to find it. You may appear more feisty than usual or someone at home may need more independence, so also aim to collaborate.

Sun in Taurus, April to May
BOOST DYNAMISM AND DOMESTIC LIFE

You need to be grounded and practical with your various interactions and plans to make them succeed. You may dislike the sluggishness with which some communications progress, but you will as a result manage to put in place solid agreements. You will enjoy travel and indulging your senses.

Sun in Gemini, May to June
ENJOY TRAVEL, ROMANCE, FUN AND CREATIVITY

Travel will appeal, and it's a good time to receive visitors. You may be inclined to invest in your home environment and health via comfortable décor and better interpersonal dynamics. Good communication skills will pave the way to better understanding, so if you must broach thorny topics a light-hearted yet concise approach will work.

Sun in Cancer, June to July
INVEST IN WORK, HOME AND HEALTH

You are a matter-of-fact but also quirky character, so you can be slightly distracted or even exasperated by the needs of others who are less self-sufficient than you. Take the time to be more considerate of the failings of other people. Step up to the plate if work is busy, as your good deeds won't go unnoticed.

Sun in Leo, July to August
RELISH RELATIONSHIPS

You'll feel attracted to upbeat people who come your way and will attract prospective partners if you're single. Couples will find fun and dynamic ways to infuse your relationship with more zing. Working Aquarians may be super productive during this time, so take the initiative.

Sun in Virgo, August to September
HONE RELATIONSHIP SKILLS

This is a good time to practise your negotiation and relationship skills. Your shared duties, investments, key relationships and communal space such as at home will be in the spotlight as you must come to new agreements. Pay attention to details; this is a good time for research.

Sun in Libra, September to October

RESTORE PEACE

A holiday, long-distance trip or study and furthering your spiritual understanding will appeal. You'll appreciate finding the time for people you love. If you've been at loggerheads with someone or work has been trying, this phase could restore peace but you must take the initiative.

Sun in Scorpio, October to November

SEIZE OPPORTUNITIES

Enjoy the new opportunities coming your way! You may be surprised by developments, but must be innovative and embrace change. Be aware that you are likely to feel more passionate about your work and general direction and may even become overzealous about beliefs and activities.

Sun in Sagittarius, November to December

EXPAND YOUR INFLUENCE

You'll appreciate the opportunity to expand your social circle and work experience. You will feel optimistic about your aims and goals. Groups, clubs and organisations may be particularly helpful.

Sun in Capricorn, December to January

BRING YOUR INNER RESOURCEFULNESS OUT

Matters that are stuck could come to light during this time, giving you the opportunity to move them forward. Are you an easy-going Aquarian, or are you obstinate when things don't go your way? This phase will spotlight your default reactions, giving you the chance to improve them.

LUNAR TRANSITS:
be calm and effective every day of the month

The moon spotlights different aspects of your emotional self as it travels each month through each zodiac sign, staying two days in each sign. When the moon is in each sign you gain the opportunity to express yourself more effectively in various areas of your life. Find out here how to make the most of your strong points during each of the two days each month.

Moon in Aquarius

EXPRESS YOURSELF

You'll feel adventurous and optimistic and will be drawn to express your quirky side more than usual. If you tend to be eccentric, your more traditional or staid side may emerge at this time to redress the balance. A fun new look, health regime or outfit may appeal.

Moon in Pisces

BOOST SELF-CONFIDENCE AND BELIEVE IN YOURSELF

To experience a better sense of self you must avoid romanticising your situation. Be bold and inspired, but think of the bigger-picture situation in realistic ways as both personal and financial matters are best approached in practical, methodical terms.

Moon in Aries

BE PRODUCTIVE AND FOCUSED

You will feel more productive. Avoid being sidetracked by changeable logistics and focus on the facts to avoid snap decisions.Retail therapy will appeal as a way to celebrate a sense of progress, and you may be prone to overinvesting and overestimating your potential.

Moon in Taurus

ENHANCE DOMESTIC BLISS

You will be drawn to sumptuous décor and good food and treating yourself and others to the fine things in life. You'll enjoy good company and cocooning and spending time improving your domestic circumstances by sprucing up your environment and interpersonal dynamics.

Moon in Gemini

CHANNEL RESTLESSNESS INTO SOLID PLANS

This phase could bring about a chop-and-change atmosphere and you may feel restless. To counteract changeability, trust your ability to innovate and plan ahead as this will help you progress through this phase despite restlessness or abrupt change beyond your control.

Moon in Cancer

IMPROVE WORK AND HEALTH SCHEDULES

Find more time to relax by researching how to be more efficient in your daily schedule and at work. Health and self-nurturance will capture your imagination; it's a good time to look for ways to boost your well-being.

Moon in Leo

EMBRACE DIVERSITY

You have two sides: you can be a traditionalist and an eccentric, but during the Leo moon your more oddball, outgoing side will gain expression as you may be ready for something different or fun! You love good company, but if you are at loggerheads with someone this is a good time to re-establish common ground.

Moon in Virgo

CONSIDER THE FEELINGS OF OTHERS

Be sensible and reasonable and you'll make headway with relationships and collaborations. If being sensible isn't your usual approach you may learn some of its benefits during this phase by default. Attention to detail and careful attention to the feelings of others will pay off.

Moon in Libra

ENJOY LIFE

While you'll enjoy a sense of excitement about your projects and ventures you can be sensitive just like everyone else. You may see developments purely from an emotional point of view during this phase, so take a moment to be analytical to gain a sense of proportion.

Moon in Scorpio

INVEST IN YOUR CAREER

You'll feel super motivated about your work and general direction in life, so this is a good time to boost your career. However, things can be intense so you must avoid getting caught in someone else's drama, especially at work. Luckily you can trust your instincts during this phase.

Moon in Sagittarius

SOCIALISE AND NETWORK

You can boost your circumstances but must guard against seeing life through rose-coloured glasses. Maintain a professional stance at work and avoid exaggeratedly high expectations. This is an excellent phase to make headway at work, in your career or in your general direction.

Moon in Capricorn

BUILD A SOLID FOUNDATION

Are your ideas practical or idealistic? Start planning realistic solutions to work issues. This can be a good time to consider a fresh health regime and to methodically get ahead at work.

FULL MOONS:
magnify your vibrant power

Each full moon highlights different aspects of your power and vibrancy.
Find out here which full moons will be excellent times to turn a corner
in the various areas of your life to show just what you're made of.

Full moon in Aquarius
SEE YOURSELF IN A NEW LIGHT

You will see yourself through someone else's eyes. If a relationship has undergone difficulties this full moon may signal a key turning point. You will be drawn to doing something very different with your appearance, and to travel, broadening your horizons and meeting new people. Consider how to reboot work and health if necessary.

Full moon in Pisces
BE INSPIRED AND PRACTICAL

A fresh chapter in your personal life or finances will begin, so it may be time to consider how you share your finances and duties. For some Aquarians there will be romance galore, but you must avoid glorifying people and circumstances and will benefit from maintaining perspective.

Full moon in Aries
INITIATE TALKS AND NEGOTIATIONS

A new agreement or change of location will open your mind to fresh options and infuse your life with renewed direction. If you're unable to travel be prepared for a visit or a change of atmosphere that feels refreshing. You may need to be flexible with negotiations and discussions.

Full moon in Taurus

A TURNING POINT IN A DOMESTIC CIRCUMSTANCE

Personal developments at home or with family or due to business and travel will demand you be practical and down to earth. A tough decision may be called for. Avoid impulsiveness, but be ready for the new. Careful planning will lead you to success.

Full moon in Gemini

BE VERSATILE WITH ROMANCE, FUN AND CREATIVITY

The more adaptable you are the better the outcome, both at work and in your personal life. Key talks will spur you on to great heights unless you succumb to pressure or distractions, as you may be busy. Focus is the key to success. Determine who and what has the most priority in your life and aim to be creative, fun and upbeat.

Full moon in Cancer

LET YOUR INNER NURTURER OUT

Get set to turn a corner as it's a good time to invest more in your health and well-being. You could be asked to help someone else. You may be passionate about the direction your work is taking, but if you feel that it's not on track you must make changes.

Full moon in Leo

BE BOLD IN YOUR LOVE LIFE AND RELATIONSHIPS

Someone special will be on your mind, if not in your heart. Some Aquarians may experience a change of pace at work or in your daily schedule; prioritising your various activities will provide the recipe for success. Be bold and assertive and willing to take on new projects.

Full moon in Virgo

BE DISCERNING ABOUT COLLABORATIONS

You may need to renegotiate a financial or personal agreement. Avoid making assumptions and do adequate research or mistakes could be made. This full moon will help you to decide which people you'll hold close and which you'll hold at arm's length.

Full moon in Libra

BRING MORE BALANCE INTO YOUR LIFE

Beauty, art, film, music and romance will appeal. You'll appreciate the opportunity to look at exciting travel, consider study or simply broaden your horizons to create more balance in your life. You may wish to establish more give and take within a business or personal relationship and enable fair play and justice.

Full moon in Scorpio

RE-INVENT YOUR STATUS

Be prepared to reinvent an aspect of yourself involving your career, home, status or direction in life. You may feel passionate about a new direction, so be ready to implement changes. A new circumstance such as a change in status may arise, for example from single to married or vice versa.

Full moon in Sagittarius

MEET NEW PEOPLE

During this phase you're likely to feel outgoing and will wish to broaden your influence into new areas. You may be drawn to a new social or sports group, for example, or will wish to deepen your interest in humanitarian projects. Be positive and upbeat; cast your net wide with new interests you'll enjoy.

Full moon in Capricorn

RE-ORGANISE YOUR DAILY LIFE OR HEALTH ROUTINE

You're ready to close a door to your past; you may let a bad habit or unfulfilling job go. Changes will be part of a bigger-picture clearing, making way for improvements. A change of pace will boost your feel-good factor, even if some elements of change are logistically complex or seem stuck.

NEW MOONS:
start something fresh

Each new moon points to the start of something fresh for you in different areas of your life. Find out here which new moon to work with and how to make lasting change by starting something new, especially if you have been putting off change for some time.

New moon in Aquarius
GRASP FRESH OPPORTUNITIES

You are ready for a change of direction and for something entirely new, but if you find the cogs are sticking as you attempt to change gear take the time to work out a plan. This time is rife with opportunity to improve your life, both at work and personally, so seize any opportunities after carrying out due research.

New moon in Pisces
ANCHOR YOUR PLANS AND FINANCES

The Pisces new moon could bring new opportunities for financial and personal investments but you must establish a solid budget rather than allowing money to randomly flow in and out. Avoid get-rich-quick schemes. A development in your personal life may be ideal, but if you experience a disappointment focus on building a solid foundation.

New moon in Aries
REVITALISE COMMUNICATIONS AND RELATIONSHIPS

A new chapter due to a contract, agreement or relationship will arise at the Aries new moon, putting you on track for a refreshing and rewarding chapter. A trip somewhere new is likely to be revitalising, so consider where you would like to be. This could be a re-energising time that is ideal for a holiday or short break.

New moon in Taurus

CREATE A HAPPIER, MORE STABLE HOME LIFE

A new agreement may arise from developments at home, with family or property. You'll enjoy feeling motivated by your various projects and ideas. A trip, visit or conversation could kick-start fresh agreements, ideas and plans, so investigate projects and aim for more stability.

New moon in Gemini

LEARN TO JUGGLE!

You may need to juggle family life with your projects, keeping many balls in the air. You'll feel ready to take a creative or work project to the next level, but it's important to avoid putting the cart before the horse. You'll ultimately be happier with plans and projects that have all their components in place before stepping up to begin a new chapter.

New moon in Cancer

START A NEW PASSION PROJECT

This is an excellent time to start a new job or project. A written or imaginative work of art may kick-start a more visionary phase, so this is a good time to develop your creativity. Your nurturing abilities will seek expression, and projects aimed to help others will thrive if begun now. Remember to also begin a healthy schedule for yourself.

New moon in Leo

BE PROACTIVE IN YOUR LOVE LIFE AND RELATIONSHIPS

This is a lovely new moon to kick-start a more vibrant phase in your relationships. It's also a good time to boost your health through upbeat fitness programs as you may experience a surge of energy. Avoid overwork, as you may be super busy. If you're single, look for upbeat, entertaining people. A relationship begun now will include a dynamic, fun aspect.

New moon in Virgo

INVEST IN COLLABORATIONS

This is a good time to begin a new relationship and to make deeper commitments to an existing one. You could gain a sense of belonging, so aim to anchor relationships and agreements. The new moon will help you to organise your plans and paperwork for the future.

New moon in Libra

INITIATE NEW VENTURES

It's time for something new such as a project or personal arrangement; you'll gain the information you need to set sail on a new course. Look for activities that bring a sense of peace and channel your feelings into productive and unifying pursuits. If you don't, tempers could arise out of frustration as you leave a stale situation behind.

New moon in Scorpio

TRANSFORM YOUR STATUS

This is a good time to kick-start a fresh project in your career and to venture forward into a new relationship status. Get set to transform how you appear to others through your presentation and abilities. Teaching, study, travel or adventure should be truly fulfilling. You may experience a boost in self-esteem.

New moon in Sagittarius

EMBRACE HUMANITARIAN SKILLS

It's a good time to invest in humanitarian interests. You may feel super extroverted, so you must be discerning about which activities you choose. Opportunities to boost your career and status may knock, so prepare for an outgoing and upbeat time. Be inspired but avoid making change just for the sake of it.

New moon in Capricorn

SUPPORT YOUR OWN INTERESTS

A new chapter will begin in the realms of work and health. Aim to hold on to activities you cherish, but if work represents too many limitations this new moon will help you to get things back on a more reasonable basis in practical ways.

LUNAR ECLIPSES:
be strong during peak emotional changes

Each lunar eclipse signals a major turning point in your life and may bring about intense emotions. Eclipses point to circumstances that seem to disempower you and subsequently motivate you to address any imbalances, so keep an eye on those areas in which you lack control as that is where you can make the most changes and become strong. Find out here which lunar eclipse will bring change in which area of your life, and how to make the most of these changes.

Aquarius lunar eclipse
REDESIGN YOUR LIFE

You are now beginning an entirely new chapter. Evaluate where you must place your focus; you may even wish for a completely new life. If you were born at or before the eclipse date aim to make changes in your personal life; if you were born later make those changes at work. This is an excellent time to focus on improving health and well-being and also your work life. Take the initiative.

Pisces lunar eclipse
RECONSIDER YOUR AGREEMENTS AND ARRANGEMENTS

A new agreement is in the cards, especially regarding shared duties, collaborations or taxes. Look afresh at some of your relationships, loyalties and activities, as this eclipse signals the chance to re-orient your priorities and especially your projects and affiliations. Be clear and avoid being overly idealistic or emotional, as it's likely to bite back.

Aries lunar eclipse

BE BOLD WITH COMMUNICATIONS

This is a good time to be proactive and get ahead with paperwork and communications, but you must avoid conflict as you or someone close may be on a short fuse. Your feelings may change considerably about who and what is important to you. Travel may appeal, and you'll enjoy broadening your horizons in other ways as well such as study.

Taurus lunar eclipse

RECONFIGURE YOUR COMMITMENTS

Your closest relationships and commitments will change, for some Aquarians due to developments at home or due to travel. Changes will revolve around how to better keep in touch with people, and you may need to update your car or technological devices to do so. Business people may discover more viable ways to make money.

Gemini lunar eclipse

BRING YOUR INNER CREATIVITY OUT

You may wish to have more freedom of expression or of movement, so think laterally and be inspired. For some, major developments will revolve around domestic matters such as children. If you are at odds with someone find ways to clear disagreements and debts so you can sail ahead more freely.

Cancer lunar eclipse

DRAW ON YOUR RESOURCES

This is a good time to seek more nurturance and support from those you love, and to offer more yourself. Developments will draw on your inner resources and you may need to pull a rabbit from a hat during emotional times. Communications may need sensitivity, so be calm and opt for ways to defuse tension at work, with family and health-wise.

Leo lunar eclipse

TAKE A FRESH DIRECTION IN A KEY RELATIONSHIP

Be positive and proactive about changes in relationships: consider new partnerships as opportunities to bring your inner dynamism to the surface. A partner may wish for more independence or you may wish to be more independent yourself.

Virgo lunar eclipse

REARRANGE SHARED FINANCES AND DUTIES

Shine a light on financial matters as a fresh approach will be useful, not only for your own budget but also for budgets you share with others such as partners or the taxation department. Other areas you share such as space at home, projects or duties will also come up for review, and you will gain the chance to rearrange them.

Libra lunar eclipse

LOOK FOR FAIR PLAY

You may need to redress the balance in a shared situation such as communal office or domestic space, or to redress the balance in a marriage or financial circumstance. Avoid power plays and find fair ways to move ahead. If it's been all work and no play for a while, aim to broaden your activities during this eclipse phase into activities that relax your mind and feed your soul.

Scorpio lunar eclipse

CONSIDER A CHANGE OF DIRECTION

You know how to combine clever planning with imaginative solutions, and your unique ability to be both practical and innovative will serve you well. A change of status or direction could impact on developments at home or with property. You will gain the chance to sort out areas of uncertainty such as finances.

Sagittarius lunar eclipse

EMBRACE ADVENTURE

Bring your inventive, innovative side out. You may feel drawn to quirky or adventurous new projects at work and to going it alone more in your own career. This eclipse could also bring out an independent streak, but you must be careful to avoid burning bridges with those who provide stability in your life.

Capricorn lunar eclipse

LET GO OF BAD HABITS

Be willing to let an aspect of your life go such as an unfulfilling job or bad relationship. Changes that arise are part of a bigger-picture clearing that makes way for improvements. For some the eclipse points to a new relationship or loyalty to a new organisation, group or friend.

SOLAR ECLIPSES:
making major changes run smoothly

Each solar eclipse signals a major turning point in your life that points to ongoing change for years to come. Find out here which solar eclipses will bring change in which areas of your life, and how to make the most of those changes.

Aquarius solar eclipse
BE UNIQUE!

This is your chance to gain more purpose and meaning in life and to celebrate and emphasise what makes you unique, especially if it's your birthday at the eclipse or just before. Be prepared to let go of habits that no longer serve your bigger-picture purpose and consider a new look or health routine as an adjunct to finding your unique place in life.

Pisces solar eclipse
CHOOSE LOYALTIES CAREFULLY

It's time to make changes. If you feel your personal life merits some extra work, this is an excellent time to focus on it. An overhaul of your priorities and finances may also appeal; however, this eclipse can feel disorienting and emotionally overwhelming. Choose your personal loyalties carefully. You may begin or end a relationship.

Aries solar eclipse
BE ASSERTIVE AND GAIN STRENGTH

You may see yourself or someone close to you in a new light. If your vulnerabilities surface it may be because someone is attempting to steal your thunder. You will find new ways to settle arguments. Travel, study or a fresh interest will motivate you to start a new project.

Taurus solar eclipse

BE OPEN TO NEW EXPERIENCES

This eclipse phase will spotlight particular conversations, news and events that will mean you must be practical and down to earth. For some this will be regarding finances, while for others it will be about domestic life, travel and communications in general. You may need to open your heart to new ideas, values and other cultures or languages.

Gemini solar eclipse

GAIN PERSPECTIVE IN YOUR PERSONAL CIRCUMSTANCES

If your creativity or family or personal life have been a little lacklustre you'll enjoy the chance to bring a more vivacious atmosphere to these areas of your life so you don't feel stuck. Consider new options carefully: avoid seeing only the superficial in circumstances and consider their long-term impact in practical terms. This is a good time to learn how to manage your emotions.

Cancer solar eclipse

STAND UP FOR YOUR PRINCIPLES

You may need to make a stand and back up your opinions with facts. You may begin a fresh daily schedule or will wish to incorporate more health and fitness into your everyday routine. Aim to nurture relationships with those you love and you will reap the rewards, feeling yourself to be more supported by others in return.

Leo solar eclipse

CONSIDER A FRESH APPROACH TO RELATIONSHIPS

What can you do to feel more fulfilled in your personal and business relationships? A relationship may require more attention from you or will respond well to a change of scenery. You may need to look after yourself or someone close more actively and be assertive if someone attempts to diminish your self-esteem.

Virgo solar eclipse

BE METICULOUS WITH SHARED CONCERNS

During this phase, analysis, research and planning will put you in a strong position. Endeavour to make detailed arrangements that provide a solid platform for moving forward. Go over areas you share, such as finances, duties and taxes, and relationships with a fine-toothed comb but avoid being perfectionist and overly critical.

Libra solar eclipse

CHOOSE ACTIVITIES THAT BOOST CONFIDENCE

Find ways to boost your confidence and kudos so you can move ahead more confidently; this may be through reading, research and study, for example. Choose activities that revolve around

your values to boost self-esteem. Writing, collaborations, spirituality and travel will all excite your senses and motivate you to leave your comfort zone.

Scorpio solar eclipse

LEAVE YOUR COMFORT ZONE

This eclipse may feel intense as it has the potential to alter your status, earning power and home life, so pragmatically manage changes in one or all of these areas. As one door closes in your life you must avoid fuelling drama; in retrospect you will see events as being the transformation you always needed.

Sagittarius solar eclipse

BROADEN YOUR EXPERIENCES

You'll appreciate trying something new in your social life, at work or within your interests. A social group may be influential, and you'll discover how following your beliefs improves your self-esteem and values. Not everyone will agree with you about the changes you make, but you will get the chance to boost your circumstances in adventurous and upbeat ways.

Capricorn solar eclipse

EXPLORE IDEAS THAT RESONATE DEEPLY

Due to your beliefs or personal circumstances you may be drawn to changing jobs or focusing on a healthier diet and management of your well-being or that of someone else. This is a good phase to put in place a solid foundation for your future health and wealth, choosing your activities carefully in line with your deep interests and beliefs.

18 FEBRUARY - 20 MARCH

SYMBOL
Fish

CONSTELLATION

ELEMENT
Water

PISCES
SUN SIGN

INNER CALLING

Your inner calling is to understand the big picture in life. You can be exhausted by details and distractions, so you must always ensure you maintain sight of your long-term destination and goals as otherwise you can be taken off course. This can be a difficult task, as you will frequently not know your true destination and need to focus on details to progress in life. Your sign's symbol is two fish swimming in opposite directions, a symbol that characterises the inner tension Pisces embodies: tension between the need for stability in your life and a sense of the limitless possibilities.

Your inner tension concerns, specifically, your lust for life, drive to succeed and wish for knowledge versus your desire to simply let things be, to float away in reveries. This highlights a major Piscean pitfall: you would ideally float through life irrespective of realities and duties. This can of course contribute to an escapist mindset, because life involves challenges, responsibilities and difficulties that form part of your learning curve.

Philosophy, literature, debate, human rights, social work and creativity all attract you at various times in your life as these are areas that involve an appraisal of the human condition and offer a model to work with.

You love to daydream, to be inspired and to create, but you can tend to appear vague as a result. However, you are the zodiac's true artist and creator, able to bring into being ideas that are beyond the understanding of others as you allow your mind to plumb the depths and heights of mysticism. You are a practical person when you need to be. Jupiter, your sign's co-ruler with Neptune, keeps your feet on the ground even when you are reaching out to broaden your knowledge and experience in mind-expanding and heart-warming ways.

SELF-ESTEEM

The impression initially is often that Pisces is a sensitive character prone to inner conflict between the ideals and realities in life and with a tendency towards daydreaming, yet the picture isn't complete without mention of Pisces' generally high self-esteem. You are not afraid to put yourself in a position of vulnerability, chiefly because of the appeal of expansion and knowledge but also because there is a boldness in you that is not always apparent on first meeting. There is great courage and determination in the Piscean make-up to face the inevitable in life and to sail fearlessly into unknown territory.

Pisces is associated with the cycle of learning through adversity, victimhood and sacrifice, so for some Pisces self-esteem can plunge truly low and a real pitfall is falling into the victim-martyr role. When adversity strikes – and adversity is your chief bridge to learning – it is vital that you shore up your self-esteem and avoid buying into other people's opinions of you as a victim or martyr. Be bold, be strong and seek always to expand your horizons.

HOME LIFE

Your home life is likely to be as fluid as the water your symbol, the Fish, inhabits yet you prefer to have an anchor in life, so if you work hard at creating a solid platform for yourself you will certainly attain one. But if your priorities are elsewhere in life you may find, especially when young, that your home life undergoes many changes, from house moves to various people entering and leaving your domestic realm as if swimming into your terrain and then leaving it equally as easily, rather like fish in the sea.

Your décor is likely to be inspired and romantic and maintain an edge of design, form and function, combining your appreciation for art with your appreciation for the functionality of furniture and the house itself.

RELATIONSHIPS

As you are instinctive and intuitive you can pick up subtle undercurrents and may be seen as unusual in your understanding of circumstances: an understanding that goes way beyond the abilities of other signs. In relationships you are adept at picking up on people's moods that perhaps they are themselves unaware of. You can be super sensitive and people may see you as being different, therefore you can tend to be marginalised or feel alienated. This can lead to a sense of being victimised or made to feel different, which will alienate you further and you can then be seen as being weak. You are prone to co-dependent relationships due to the victim-martyr role you tend to adopt, so be sure to keep healthy boundaries in relationships.

You have the unique ability to rise above the kind of behaviour that would marginalise, alienate and shame you. You are a much wiser person than many other people, and your compassion for those who seek to discredit you will help you rise above adversity in relationships.

CREATIVITY

You have a vivid imagination and artistic and creative abilities. When you develop these you will open up a new world that facilitates your learning and development in beautiful and soul-nourishing ways.

You are inherently spiritual and are conscious of the existence of higher powers. You will be innately aware of your connection with nature, the universe and god consciousness, and this will suffice for many Pisces. The creator's creativity is something you know no one can mimic, so your creativity resides in your spirituality.

PITFALLS

When you go through difficult times in life, drugs, alcohol and other addictive substances and behaviours may appeal to you as an easy way to dull your heightened sensitivity. But when you dull your senses you mute your intuition, which is your true source of wisdom and support. This is counterproductive.

To counteract your predisposition towards addictive behaviour use your considerable intuitive abilities. Your intuition links you with spirit, with great wisdom and knowledge. It is a fundamental Piscean quality that many other zodiac signs simply do not possess. Use your intuition in your everyday life; it will not let you down if you clear your mind to allow this invaluable quality to guide you.

SOLAR TRANSITS:
harness the sun's power
every day of the year

The sun empowers you in different areas of your life as it travels through each zodiac sign from month to month. Find out here how to make the most of your strong points during each of the transits of the sun through the 12 signs.

Sun in Pisces, February to March

SEEK INSPIRATION

Your intuition is strong during this phase, so trust it. You're known to be intuitive yet you can feel lost in emotion, and daydreaming during this time will lead to forgetfulness. Aim to improve your work and career prospects by boosting your appearance and presentation. The sun in Pisces will spotlight your interest in mysticism, so it's a good time to develop spirituality.

Sun in Aries, March to April

IMPROVE YOUR FINANCES AND SELF-ESTEEM

You'll feel increasingly focused in the areas of money, motivation and self-esteem, and the next four weeks are ideal for boosting your personal life. You may feel more energised than usual, but if people appear more aggressive avoid taking things personally.

Sun in Taurus, April to May

ENJOY LIFE!

Focus on establishing solid and reliable relationships and a secure financial budget. You'll enjoy the luxuries and comforts in life and indulging in good food and drink. If you're on a diet or saving for a big expenditure, beware of this phase as you may blow your budget or break your diet. Enjoy life!

Sun in Gemini, May to June

ZHUZH UP YOUR HOME LIFE

It's a good time to spruce up your home life. Your inner chatterbox will come out, and you may be more inquisitive than usual and will enjoy getting together with neighbours and receiving visitors and being engaged in community efforts. You may also be drawn to new ways to communicate through travel, different devices and technology.

Sun in Cancer, June to July

BE INSPIRED BY LOVE, COMFORT AND SPIRITUALITY

Focus on your personal life and self-development. Creative Pisces will be super inspired. If you're thinking of starting a family or adding to your existing one, this is a fertile time. Your home life may take much of your attention, but if you must travel or are away this phase will remind you of the importance of a comfortable home life.

Sun in Leo, July to August
BOOST YOUR WORK, HAPPINESS AND HEALTH

You will feel more dynamic and enjoy updating your health routine, appearance and well-being. You'll be productive at work. Romantic Pisces may have more time and inclination to spend with someone special; family time could also blossom.

Sun in Virgo, August to September
ENJOY YOUR LOVE LIFE AND RELATIONSHIPS

Romance will flourish; however, you may be a little more critical and self-critical during this phase. Take criticism on board if it's merited, otherwise avoid being a martyr. You may need to adjust unrealistic expectations during this time to fit with reality.

Sun in Libra, September to October
PROMOTE TEAMWORK

This is a good time for teamwork, for collaborations and for romance. Your skill set as a mediator and peacemaker will be strong during this time, so aim to build bridges and find peace in diplomatic ways. This is also a good time to find a partner if you're single and to revitalise romance if you're a couple.

Sun in Scorpio, October to November
FOLLOW YOUR DREAMS

Use your intuition as it will be super strong. This is a good time for psychic development, dream work and self-improvement. You will enjoy activities that take you out of your usual terrain, such as travel and study. If you are unsure of your feelings take things one step at a time and consult your gut instincts. Avoid conflict; find peaceful solutions instead as strong emotions will come out.

Sun in Sagittarius, November to December
ADVANCE YOUR CAREER AND ACTIVITIES

This is an outgoing phase and you'll feel more adventurous at work and could boost your profile. Your attraction to daring and upbeat ventures, travel and spirituality will peak, and embracing your courageous qualities will feel rewarding.

Sun in Capricorn, December to January

BE SOCIABLE AND MAKE COMMITMENTS

You'll welcome the opportunity to make commitments that could be long term, both at work and in your personal life. You may find forging agreements with people more rewarding or easier to make. If you're looking for stability this four-week–long vibe will help you gain a stronger foundation.

Sun in Aquarius, January to February

INVEST IN YOURSELF

You may feel restless during this phase and will be drawn to re-orient some of your beliefs and interests so they are expressed better in your daily life and work. A minor awakening could occur, and your interest in the esoteric such as astrology and psychic phenomena will become stronger.

LUNAR TRANSITS:
be calm and effective every day of the month

The moon spotlights different aspects of your emotional self as it travels each month through each zodiac sign, staying two days in each sign. When the moon is in each sign you gain the opportunity to express yourself more effectively in various areas of your life. Find out here how to make the most of your strong points during each of the two days each month.

Moon in Pisces
EXPRESS YOURSELF

The Pisces moon will bring your inner romantic and mystic out. You'll enjoy expressing your creative and loving sides; however, you may need to knuckle down to chores at work or consider matters in a factual light as you may be easily distracted and feel a little idealistic.

Moon in Aries
BE DYNAMIC AND PRACTICAL

The Aries moon may shake things up, so maintain a level-headed approach. Restlessness and rebellion may rise to the surface during these two days, so ensure you have a structured plan of action especially at work and stick to it! Otherwise you may be distracted by arguments. It's a good time to work hard and make money, but you may be inclined to also spend fast.

Moon in Taurus
SPEAK FROM THE HEART

Meetings, calls, catch-ups and reunions will all appeal, as will travel and treats. Be guided by your compassion and talks will proceed well. You may be in demand, and people will respond to your earthy and sentimental side.

Moon in Gemini

INCREASE DOMESTIC BLISS

Dig deep and decide what you want at home, and if you already have it you'll enjoy it all the more! If not, these two days will provide insight into how to change the domestic arena so it is more to your liking. Think laterally for the best results.

Moon in Cancer

BE CREATIVE

Reading, art, music and romance will inspire you. You are likely to feel creative but also on occasion nostalgic. Trust your instincts: they're sparking on all cylinders. Spiritually minded Pisces will find this phase particularly insightful and inspiring.

Moon in Leo

GET BUSY

Be prepared for busy days. If you love what you do at work you'll love the Leo moon, as you'll get to truly engage with your work. But if you don't annoyances could get the better of you, so be patient. You'll enjoy doing something upbeat in the evenings and boosting health.

Moon in Virgo

MAKE PLANS WITH SOMEONE SPECIAL

This is a good time to be practical about your plans with personal and business partners. Plan something special for the upcoming days if you have nothing on the horizon yet. It's also a good time for strategising and making arrangements, so consider enlisting the help of someone trustworthy and dependable at work or at home, as together you could move mountains.

Moon in Libra

FIND COMMON GROUND

It's an excellent time to look for ways to bring more balance and harmony into your life, especially in your collaborations. However, the Libran moon may bring your sensitivities to the surface and someone close may be more sensitive or emotional, so take things one step at a time.

Moon in Scorpio

TRUST YOUR INSTINCTS

Your passions, intuition and instincts will to be strong and you will be drawn to deep and introspective people and your favourite activities. Consider the logistics of your plans, especially concerning travel, study, legal matters and relationships, as you may have your head in the clouds.

Moon in Sagittarius

BE ADVENTUROUS

You're inspired, which will serve you well at work, but your idealistic views may be at counterpoint with some of the practicalities you must attend to within your various projects. Be adventurous, not reckless; be outgoing, not fanatical!

Moon in Capricorn

GET THINGS DONE

You may have a passionate and motivated stance to some of your activities and the people you mingle with during this phase, but you must avoid being obstinate about your ideas. Aim to collaborate and you could excel with projects. Be rational. You may need to prioritise health concerns at this time.

Moon in Aquarius

GAIN INSIGHT INTO WORK AND HEALTH

You have some wonderful plans and ideas, and it's a case of getting these into some sort of manageable order. The Aquarian moon will help you to organise your work, but you must avoid distractions and focus on realistic and practical plans while enabling inspiration to flow. Meditation and yoga will boost your inner health and provide insight.

FULL MOONS:
magnify your vibrant power

*Each full moon highlights different aspects of your power and vibrancy.
Find out here which full moons will be excellent times to turn a corner
in the various areas of your life to show just what you're made of.*

Full moon in Pisces
EMPOWER YOURSELF

Prepare for a fresh cycle in your life. Meditation, art and spiritual endeavours will help you to move on. Romance could blossom, but if you are idealistic about relationships and frequently disappointed then you must be practical. For some a fresh work or health project could be birthed at this time.

Full moon in Aries
BOOST PRODUCTIVITY

If finances, energy levels and your ego have been in a slump, prepare to gain more vitality and stability. Your hard work will be rewarding, especially if you are proactive about turning a corner to sustain improved self-esteem and energy levels.

Full moon in Taurus
FOLLOW A SAFE PATH

Look for a smooth path ahead via a practical plan of action and good communication skills. Don't be surprised if a revelation arises. For some Pisces this will be to do with money and for others to do with your personal life. It could open doors.

Full moon in Gemini

CHOOSE YOUR PRIORITIES AT HOME

A change in your status or relationships will lead to a new chapter at home or with family. You may feel drawn to more independence or to a sense of possibility and variety, but if this is at the cost of security and stability your choices must come down to practicalities. Travel may appeal as a way to broaden your horizons.

Full moon in Cancer

TURN A CORNER SPIRITUALLY AND CREATIVELY

You'll appreciate the opportunity to lose yourself in some of your interests. If cocooning is what you want rest assured your home can become a true source of nurturance. Developments could boost your creativity or time spent with family or someone you love. Spiritual Pisces may experience an epiphany.

Full moon in Leo

GAIN CLARITY AT WORK AND WITH YOUR STATUS

A fresh incentive or new chapter will arise and your interests will slowly change. For some a new horizon awaits in your personal life concerning family, health or your creative ventures. Be proactive and boost self-esteem to stimulate change.

Full moon in Virgo

UNCOMPLICATE YOUR RELATIONSHIPS

A fresh agreement or relationship arrangement will arise. Be realistic rather than idealistic, as the more you attend to logistics the better. You may make a fresh commitment to an agreement, either within an existing relationship or with a new one. It may simply be time for a clear out of your address book.

Full moon in Libra

CREATE MORE BEAUTY AND HARMONY

Bring beauty, flowers, scents and romance into your life to boost your well-being. Increase whatever brings value to your life. For some Pisces a partnership may come to an end, but an amicable outcome can be arranged with a view towards fair play and harmony. A new relationship can be forged and romance could blossom.

Full moon in Scorpio
SHINE A LIGHT ON FRESH INTERESTS

You will gain insight into new interests in such diverse areas as travel, study, spirituality, marriage, career and kudos. Key news may signal a change within an agreement or arrangement and developments should seal a deal that has been up in the air.

Full moon in Sagittarius
BE DECISIVE IN YOUR CAREER AND STATUS

You'll appreciate the opportunity to be more outgoing in your life through your career or a change in status such as marriage, and by pursuing your goals. News will enable you to make a key decision that involves a friend or organisation, but you must do your research so you don't make mistakes. Avoid biting off more than you can chew.

Full moon in Capricorn
GAIN STABILITY IN YOUR SUPPORT NETWORKS

Your involvement with someone at work or a career matter may be under a microscope and come full circle. Be practical and realistic at work and with long-term decisions. For some, developments will revolve around romance and passion. This could be an intense time, so pace yourself.

Full moon in Aquarius
RECONSIDER PRIORITIES AND HEALTH PRACTICES

You may be drawn to investigate new ways to boost your well-being. Complementary health or alternative remedies may appeal, and you may decide to try something different at work. For some this full moon spotlights new groups and organisations you'd like to join.

NEW MOONS:
start something fresh

Each new moon points to the start of something fresh for you in different areas of your life. Find out here which new moon to work with and how to make lasting change by starting something new, especially if you have been putting off change for some time.

New moon in Pisces

KICK-START AN INSPIRING CHAPTER

This is a good time to launch a creative or imaginative project. You may begin an inspiring phase in a relationship. Aim to boost your appearance, profile, well-being and romantic life, as in the process you may find out if you've been unrealistic about someone or a venture. If you have been, you'll get the chance to build more independence and security.

New moon in Aries

REGENERATE FINANCES AND SELF-ESTEEM

Be positive: you can turn a corner with a work or personal plan. Finances could improve. Avoid being super idealistic and impractical, as you could make great progress by combining your creative abilities with hard work and your drive to succeed.

New moon in Taurus

INITIATE NEGOTIATIONS

You may feel upbeat about initiating changes and, most importantly, you'll be at your practical best so it's an ideal time to make concrete alterations to arrangements. Keep your values uppermost in your mind as these will guide you to making the right decisions.

New moon in Gemini

START A PROJECT AT HOME

DIY projects, renovations, a move or an addition to the family will take well. Coincidentally, this may be a time you choose to travel to visit family at their home or to receive guests. This is an excellent time to begin new enterprises that concern your domestic life and family happiness.

New moon in Cancer

INVEST IN LOVE, SPIRITUALITY AND FAMILY

This is a good time to consider how your intuition and caring nature can help boost relationships and domestic dynamics and create a more supportive atmosphere at home. It is also an ideal time to develop your spiritual beliefs. You will be more motivated to indulge in romance, so singles: mingle!

New moon in Leo

START A NEW JOB OR HEALTH KICK

You'll enjoy a more varied, creative and artistic cycle that will begin at this new moon: it will be a busy period. It's a good time to begin a new work or health schedule and could also be a therapeutic time that is ideal for appointments with medical professionals, beauty therapists and work colleagues.

New moon in Virgo

ANCHOR YOUR LOVE LIFE AND RELATIONSHIPS

A new, more settled phase is about to begin in a key relationship, although it may involve a little soul searching first. Be positive; avoid playing the martyr. A new job offer, change of pace or promotion could present fresh horizons to be conquered – which you will, in your inimitable way. Just avoid being super self-critical and critical of others.

New moon in Libra

PROMOTE MORE EQUALITY AND TEAMWORK

This new moon will encourage you to look for more equality in a shared circumstance such as a financial or domestic arrangement that is ready for a fresh agreement. Avoid taking people's agendas or abrupt comments personally and establish common ground instead.

New moon in Scorpio

START A PASSION PROJECT

You'll be fuelled by a passion for adventure and research and broadening your horizons and will gain a true sense of purpose as a result. You'll be driven also to collaborate more by someone you love or admire. A long-distance trip and the pursuit of knowledge will be rewarding, so plan ahead.

New moon in Sagittarius

BEGIN ADVENTUROUS OR SPIRITUAL PROJECTS

The Sagittarian new moon will encourage you to embrace adventure. For some this may include a fresh direction in your career, while for others it will be a new study course or sporting opportunity. A fresh attitude to someone close may be productive. You may be ready to delve more deeply into your spiritual quests or to embrace your creative side.

New moon in Capricorn

EXTEND YOUR LEARNING CURVE

You like to learn and grow on life's journey, and this new moon will provide you with the opportunity to do so. A venture could blossom and help broaden or ground your learning base. A friend or organisation may be helpful. A fresh cycle will begin where the people you count on for support will offer an increased sense of security and belonging.

New moon in Aquarius

RENEW HEALTH AND VITALITY

Get set to reinvigorate your life, which will involve fresh health plans or a new work ethic. A fresh opportunity in one or both of these areas could be ideal, but you will need to be ready to ditch preconceived ideas and move forward. Above all, avoid impulsive decisions; be spontaneous instead and dispense with bad habits in innovative ways.

LUNAR ECLIPSES:
be strong during peak emotional changes

Each lunar eclipse signals a major turning point in your life and may bring about intense emotions. Eclipses point to circumstances that seem to disempower you and subsequently motivate you to address any imbalances, so keep an eye on those areas in which you lack control as that is where you can make the most changes and become strong. Find out here which lunar eclipse will bring change in which area of your life, and how to make the most of these changes.

Pisces lunar eclipse
TIME FOR SELF-REFLECTION

Be prepared to alter the way you see your daily life and yourself. This is an excellent time to think laterally, as new ideas and opportunities are likely to arise as if from out of the blue. For some Pisces this lunar eclipse will completely revolutionise your personal life, and you may as a result find yourself in different circumstances within six months either side of the eclipse.

Aries lunar eclipse
REARRANGE YOUR FINANCES AND PRIORITIES

The Aries lunar eclipse is a good time to get things done, especially paperwork and financial matters. Someone's views may differ considerably from yours; you must avoid a clash and aim to negotiate even if you would rather fiercely stand your ground. Finances or your personal situation will change as a result of negotiation.

Taurus lunar eclipse

RETHINK YOUR VALUES AND COMMUNICATIONS

You may be drawn to reconsider some of your principles and values, and a shared circumstance such as a marriage or businessagreement could be subject to change. You may be ready to invest in something new and to spend a lot of money on a particular outlay.

Gemini lunar eclipse

ACCLIMATISE TO NEW CIRCUMSTANCES

You'll enjoy improving décor or acclimatising to a new environment such as a new housemate or family developments. You or someone at home may need to move or need more freedom. If your domestic situation is unclear, get the information you need. For some this lunar eclipse will alter key relationships or your neighbourhood. You'll be drawn to update devices or transport.

Cancer lunar eclipse

BRING PEACE TO YOUR LIFE

Consider letting go of a past circumstance you feel strongly about. A change within your family may be poignant. This is an excellent time to develop your intuitive and psychic abilities and to find ways to experience a sense of belonging at home and in your personal space. Be creative.

Leo lunar eclipse

CONSIDER A FRESH TIMETABLE

A fresh approach to health and work will appeal. Build your dreams with the benefit of feasible plans. For some a fresh romantic or family circumstance will arise. You may feel particularly emotional at this time, so the more constructive and proactive you are about creating new circumstances for yourself the better.

Virgo lunar eclipse

PRIORITISE YOUR LOVE LIFE AND RELATIONSHIPS

The Virgo lunar eclipse will highlight your emotions or those of someone close, so if you have been feeling a little moody you now know why! More importantly, this eclipse will spotlight relationships at home or at work, and a fresh approach will benefit you over time. Organise get-togethers and plan for relaxing talks to build a sense of security and belonging.

Libra lunar eclipse
ESTABLISH A CALMER MINDSET

Difficult circumstances or aggressive people may eclipse your sense of well-being. The key to better relationships may lie in finding new ways to share duties or finances. Stand firm in your own power while also showing compassion and a willingness to collaborate.

Scorpio lunar eclipse
GAIN INSIGHT INTO YOURSELF AND OTHERS

You may wish to change tack with a relationship or activity. As you are philosophical you can tend to leave major decisions to fate, yet you do have free will! Attention to details and research will help you to make decisions although you may feel forgetful or super sensitive. If you have developed your psychic abilities you will be super intuitive, so trust your instincts. You may be drawn to psychology.

Sagittarius lunar eclipse
BE PREPARED TO ALTER PLANS

The key to success lies in researching your circumstances, as they may change due to matters beyond your control. Travel plans, study, visits, relationships and even legal matters may require additional focus. Be prepared to look outside the square at ways to broaden your horizons even if you feel your will has been eclipsed by someone else's.

Capricorn lunar eclipse
REBUILD YOUR STATUS, CAREER AND STABILITY

This could be an intense time, so take things one step at a time. The spotlight will be on your career, general direction and status. You may feel emotional about the end of a job or phase in your life, yet this is a perfect time to rebuild those areas where you would like to see more stability and security.

Aquarius lunar eclipse
ADOPT A FRESH APPROACH TO YOUR WELL-BEING

Aim to turn a leaf so your daily schedule better supports your needs. A group, organisation, friend or someone close may have a strong influence. Think laterally regarding new opportunities and consider ideas that seem counter-intuitive: they may suit your stage in life. Find clever ways to create a more upbeat daily routine.

SOLAR ECLIPSES:
making major changes run smoothly

Each solar eclipse signals a major turning point in your life that points to ongoing change for years to come. Find out here which solar eclipses will bring change in which areas of your life, and how to make the most of those changes.

Pisces solar eclipse
REBOOT YOUR PERSONAL LIFE

The Pisces solar eclipse will be most potent for birthday Pisces and Pisces with birthdays before the eclipse as you kick-start a fresh relationship or leave someone behind. Those born after the eclipse date will begin a fresh health or work chapter as your daily routine is due to undergo considerable developments. Be inspired, trust your intuition and be strong.

Aries solar eclipse
IMPLEMENT WELL-LAID PLANS

The feisty, dynamic energy around this eclipse may feel unsettling, but it is a good time to initiate new financial and personal plans as you'll be motivated to express your values and ideas through action. However, you must avoid appearing aggressive. You may make a new commitment in your personal life or financially. Avoid taking developments personally if someone lets you down.

Taurus solar eclipse
GROW YOUR INFLUENCE

Take a moment and consider where in your life you'd like to see new opportunities: for some this will be financially, for some through travel and for others at work. Make a wish, as it's likely to take because this is a powerful new moon. Be methodical and look at the practicalities and the realities of life rather than having unrealistic hopes.

Gemini solar eclipse

MOVE FORWARD DOMESTICALLY

Specific meetings and talks will provide the clarity you need to move forward in the domestic realm. Spiritual Fish may reach an epiphany. A change within your domestic dynamics may be bittersweet and will ask you to boost your communication skills. A trip or visit may be ideal but also may draw on your reserves.

Cancer solar eclipse

NURTURE YOURSELF AND THOSE CLOSE TO YOU

A change of status may affect your home life. If you're single you may meet someone new, and couples will undergo considerable changes within the family and concerning issues to do with support. Tune in to your more nurturing, supportive self. You will feel assertive and have strong opinions at this time so you will need to defuse any tension this may cause.

Leo solar eclipse

LET YOUR INNER HERO OUT

You'll attain a goal in ways that may surprise you, as your inner hero will seek expression. You are likely to be more outspoken and proactive. A fresh work or health routine or a new environment will point to the way ahead. However, you may need to first overcome a challenge or exert yourself in ways that stretch your abilities.

Virgo solar eclipse

MAKE A COMMITMENT

Be prepared to make a commitment to a new future. A relationship is due a change, especially if you were born on or before the eclipse date. If you were born afterwards you'll begin a fresh work or health routine: either yours or that of someone close. Hold your ground and seek calmness if a storm is brewing – and, above all, be practical and realistic with duties and commitments. Ditch bad relationships and work habits.

Libra solar eclipse
ESTABLISH A FAIR GO

A great deal of focus will be on someone else, so this will be a great time to work on more equal ways to share duties, romance, love and mutual support. With frank discussion any hiccups can be worked out. Be ready to alter some shared financial arrangements and devise a fairer plan.

Scorpio solar eclipse
ALTER PRECONCEIVED IDEAS

This eclipse will mark the end of a key learning curve or even a key relationship. Your approach to life may become more intense, or you will simply become more philosophical as changes will mean you must alter some notions. Plans may need to be rearranged. It's a good time to delve more deeply into spiritual and psychological matters.

Sagittarius solar eclipse
BE BRAVE WITH YOUR CAREER, STATUS AND ACTIVITIES

The eclipse will bring your sense of adventure to the surface, which will be expressed in more upbeat activities and interests ranging from travel to sports and from study to human rights. You will feel drawn to promote a cause and take action in areas you usually dream about.

Capricorn solar eclipse
REVEAL YOUR INNER STRENGTH

You are ready to turn a corner and be seen as the authority you are. You may benefit from a promotion at work or a fresh direction. If you experience a disappointment, see it as a chance to try something different in a new arena at work or to learn a new skill. If you feel eclipsed by authority figures find the time to improve your confidence and assertiveness.

Aquarius solar eclipse
FOCUS ON SELF-DEVELOPMENT

This is an excellent time to let go of ingrained bad habits. You will appreciate the chance to revitalise your health and fitness. A change at work could be on the cards, and you may be particularly drawn to humanitarian and spiritual work. Self-development will appeal as you try new modalities to feel more fulfilled in life.

NEW MOONS, FULL MOONS AND LUNAR AND SOLAR ECLIPSES UNTIL 2050

NEW MOONS

2021 NEW MOON IN:	
Virgo	7 September
Libra	6 October
Scorpio	4 November
Sagittarius	4 December

2022 NEW MOON IN:	
Capricorn	2 January
Aquarius	1 February
Pisces	2 March
Aries	1 April
Taurus	30 April
Gemini	30 May
Cancer	29 June
Leo	28 July
Virgo	27 August
Libra	25 September
Scorpio	25 October
Sagittarius	23 November
Capricorn	23 December

2023 NEW MOON IN:	
Aquarius	21 January
Pisces	20 February
Aries	21 March and 20 April
Taurus	19 May
Gemini	18 June
Cancer	17 July
Leo	16 August
Virgo	15 September
Libra	14 October
Scorpio	13 November
Sagittarius	12 December

Note: all dates are in Greenwich Mean Time (GMT).

2024 NEW MOON IN:

Capricorn	11 January
Aquarius	9 February
Pisces	10 March
Aries	8 April
Taurus	8 May
Gemini	6 June
Cancer	5 July
Leo	4 August
Virgo	3 September
Libra	2 October
Scorpio	1 November
Sagittarius	1 December
Capricorn	30 December

2025 NEW MOON IN:

Aquarius	29 January
Pisces	28 February
Aries	29 March
Taurus	27 April
Gemini	27 May
Cancer	25 June
Leo	24 July
Virgo	23 August and 21 September
Libra	21 October
Scorpio	20 November
Sagittarius	20 December

2026 NEW MOON IN:

Capricorn	18 January
Aquarius	17 February
Pisces	19 March
Aries	17 April
Taurus	16 May
Gemini	15 June
Cancer	14 July
Leo	12 August
Virgo	11 September
Libra	10 October
Scorpio	9 November
Sagittarius	9 December

2027 NEW MOON IN:

Capricorn	7 January
Aquarius	6 February
Pisces	8 March
Aries	6 April
Taurus	6 May
Gemini	4 June
Cancer	4 July
Leo	2 August
Virgo	31 August
Libra	30 September
Scorpio	29 October
Sagittarius	28 November
Capricorn	27 December

2028 NEW MOON IN:

Aquarius	26 January
Pisces	25 February
Aries	26 March
Taurus	24 April
Gemini	24 May
Cancer	22 June and 22 July
Leo	20 August
Virgo	18 September
Libra	18 October
Scorpio	16 November
Sagittarius	16 December

2029 NEW MOON IN:

Capricorn	14 January
Aquarius	13 February
Pisces	15 March
Aries	13 April
Taurus	13 May
Gemini	12 June
Cancer	11 July
Leo	10 August
Virgo	8 September
Libra	7 October
Scorpio	6 November
Sagittarius	5 December

2030 NEW MOON IN:

Capricorn	4 January
Aquarius	2 February
Pisces	4 March
Aries	2 April
Taurus	2 May
Gemini	1 June
Cancer	30 June
Leo	30 July
Virgo	28 August
Libra	27 September
Scorpio	26 October
Sagittarius	25 November
Capricorn	24 December

2031 NEW MOON IN:

Aquarius	23 January
Pisces	21 February
Aries	23 March
Taurus	21 April
Gemini	21 May and 19 June
Cancer	19 July
Leo	18 August
Virgo	16 September
Libra	16 October
Scorpio	14 November
Sagittarius	14 December

2032 NEW MOON IN:

Capricorn	12 January
Aquarius	11 February
Pisces	11 March
Aries	10 April
Taurus	9 May
Gemini	8 June
Cancer	7 July
Leo	6 August
Virgo	4 September
Libra	4 October
Scorpio	3 November
Sagittarius	2 December

2033 NEW MOON IN:

Capricorn	1 January
Aquarius	30 January
Pisces	1 March
Aries	30 March
Taurus	29 April
Gemini	28 May
Cancer	26 June
Leo	26 July
Virgo	24 August
Libra	23 September
Scorpio	23 October
Sagittarius	22 November
Capricorn	21 December

2034 NEW MOON IN:

Aquarius	20 January
Pisces	18 February and 20 March
Aries	18 April
Taurus	18 May
Gemini	16 June
Cancer	15 July
Leo	14 August
Virgo	12 September
Libra	12 October
Scorpio	11 November
Sagittarius	10 December

2035 NEW MOON IN:

Capricorn	9 January
Aquarius	8 February
Pisces	9 March
Aries	8 April
Taurus	7 May
Gemini	6 June
Cancer	5 July
Leo	3 August
Virgo	2 September
Libra	1 October
Scorpio	31 October
Sagittarius	29 November
Capricorn	29 December

2036 NEW MOON IN:

Aquarius	28 January
Pisces	27 February
Aries	27 March
Taurus	26 April
Gemini	25 May
Cancer	24 June
Leo	23 July and 21 August
Virgo	20 September
Libra	19 October
Scorpio	18 November
Sagittarius	17 December

2037 NEW MOON IN:

Capricorn	16 January
Aquarius	15 February
Pisces	16 March
Aries	15 April
Taurus	15 May
Gemini	13 June
Cancer	13 July
Leo	11 August
Virgo	9 September
Libra	9 October
Scorpio	7 November
Sagittarius	6 December

2038 NEW MOON IN:

Capricorn	5 January
Aquarius	4 February
Pisces	5 March
Aries	4 April
Taurus	4 May
Gemini	3 June
Cancer	2 July
Leo	1 August
Virgo	30 August
Libra	28 September
Scorpio	28 October
Sagittarius	26 November
Capricorn	26 December

2039 NEW MOON IN:

Aquarius	24 January
Pisces	23 February
Aries	24 March
Taurus	23 April
Gemini	23 May
Cancer	21 June and 21 July
Leo	19 August
Virgo	18 September
Libra	17 October
Scorpio	16 November
Sagittarius	15 December

2040 NEW MOON IN:

Capricorn	14 January
Aquarius	12 February
Pisces	13 March
Aries	11 April
Taurus	11 May
Gemini	9 June
Cancer	9 July
Leo	8 August
Virgo	6 September
Libra	6 October
Scorpio	4 November
Sagittarius	4 December

2041 NEW MOON IN:

Capricorn	2 January
Aquarius	1 February
Pisces	2 March
Aries	1 April
Taurus	30 April
Gemini	29 May
Cancer	28 June
Leo	28 July
Virgo	26 August
Libra	25 September
Scorpio	25 October
Sagittarius	23 November
Capricorn	23 December

2042 NEW MOON IN:

Aquarius	21 January
Pisces	20 February
Aries	21 March
Taurus	20 April and 19 May
Gemini	17 June
Cancer	17 July
Leo	15 August
Virgo	14 September
Libra	14 October
Scorpio	12 November
Sagittarius	12 December

2043 NEW MOON IN:

Capricorn	11 January
Aquarius	9 February
Pisces	11 March
Aries	9 April
Taurus	9 May
Gemini	7 June
Cancer	6 July
Leo	5 August
Virgo	3 September
Libra	3 October
Scorpio	1 November
Sagittarius	1 December
Capricorn	31 December

2044 NEW MOON IN:

Aquarius	30 January
Pisces	28 February
Aries	29 March
Taurus	27 April
Gemini	27 May
Cancer	25 June
Leo	24 July
Virgo	23 August and 21 September
Libra	20 October
Scorpio	19 November
Sagittarius	19 December

2045 NEW MOON IN:

Capricorn	18 January
Aquarius	16 February
Pisces	18 March
Aries	17 April
Taurus	16 May
Gemini	15 June
Cancer	14 July
Leo	12 August
Virgo	11 September
Libra	10 October
Scorpio	8 November
Sagittarius	8 December

2046 NEW MOON IN:

Capricorn	7 January
Aquarius	5 February
Pisces	7 March
Aries	6 April
Taurus	6 May
Gemini	4 June
Cancer	4 July
Leo	2 August
Virgo	31 August
Libra	30 September
Scorpio	29 October
Sagittarius	27 November
Capricorn	27 December

2047 NEW MOON IN:

Aquarius	26 January
Pisces	24 February
Aries	26 March
Taurus	25 April
Gemini	24 May
Cancer	23 June
Leo	22 July and 21 August
Virgo	19 September
Libra	19 October
Scorpio	17 November
Sagittarius	16 December

2048 NEW MOON IN:

Capricorn	15 January
Aquarius	14 February
Pisces	14 March
Aries	13 April
Taurus	12 May
Gemini	11 June
Cancer	11 July
Leo	9 August
Virgo	8 September
Libra	7 October
Scorpio	6 November
Sagittarius	5 December

2049 NEW MOON IN:

Capricorn	4 January
Aquarius	2 February
Pisces	4 March
Aries	2 April
Taurus	2 May
Gemini	31 May
Cancer	30 June
Leo	29 July
Virgo	28 August
Libra	27 September
Scorpio	26 October
Sagittarius	25 November
Capricorn	24 December

2050 NEW MOON IN:

Aquarius	23 January
Pisces	21 February
Aries	23 March
Taurus	21 April
Gemini	20 May and 19 June
Cancer	18 July
Leo	17 August
Virgo	16 September
Libra	15 October
Scorpio	14 November
Sagittarius	14 December

FULL MOONS

2021 FULL MOON IN:	
Pisces	20 September
Aries	20 October
Taurus	19 November
Gemini	19 December

2022 FULL MOON IN:	
Cancer	17 January
Leo	16 February
Virgo	18 March
Libra	16 April
Scorpio	16 May
Sagittarius	14 June
Capricorn	13 July
Aquarius	12 August
Pisces	10 September
Aries	9 October
Taurus	8 November
Gemini	8 December

2023 FULL MOON IN:	
Cancer	6 January
Leo	5 February
Virgo	7 March
Libra	6 April
Scorpio	5 May
Sagittarius	4 June
Capricorn	3 July
Aquarius	1 August
Pisces	31 August
Aries	29 September
Taurus	28 October
Gemini	27 November
Cancer	27 December

2024 FULL MOON IN:

Leo	25 January
Virgo	24 February
Libra	25 March
Scorpio	23 April
Sagittarius	23 May
Capricorn	22 June and 21 July
Aquarius	19 August
Pisces	18 September
Aries	17 October
Taurus	15 November
Gemini	15 December

2025 FULL MOON IN:

Cancer	13 January
Leo	12 February
Virgo	14 March
Libra	13 April
Scorpio	12 May
Sagittarius	11 June
Capricorn	10 July
Aquarius	9 August
Pisces	7 September
Aries	7 October
Taurus	5 November
Gemini	4 December

2026 FULL MOON IN:

Cancer	3 January
Leo	1 February
Virgo	3 March
Libra	2 April
Scorpio	1 May
Sagittarius	31 May
Capricorn	29 June
Aquarius	29 July
Pisces	28 August
Aries	26 September
Taurus	26 October
Gemini	24 November
Cancer	24 December

2027 FULL MOON IN:

Leo	22 January
Virgo	20 February
Libra	22 March
Scorpio	20 April and 20 May
Sagittarius	19 June
Capricorn	18 July
Aquarius	17 August
Pisces	15 September
Aries	15 October
Taurus	14 November
Gemini	13 December

2028 FULL MOON IN:

Cancer	12 January
Leo	10 February
Virgo	11 March
Libra	9 April
Scorpio	8 May
Sagittarius	7 June
Capricorn	6 July
Aquarius	5 August
Pisces	3 September
Aries	3 October
Taurus	2 November
Gemini	2 December
Cancer	31 December

2029 FULL MOON IN:

Leo	30 January
Virgo	28 February
Libra	30 March
Scorpio	28 April
Sagittarius	27 May
Capricorn	26 June
Aquarius	25 July
Pisces	24 August and 22 September
Aries	22 October
Taurus	21 November
Gemini	20 December

2030 FULL MOON IN:

Cancer	19 January
Leo	18 February
Virgo	19 March
Libra	18 April
Scorpio	17 May
Sagittarius	15 June
Capricorn	15 July
Aquarius	13 August
Pisces	11 September
Aries	11 October
Taurus	10 November
Gemini	9 December

2031 FULL MOON IN:

Cancer	8 January
Leo	7 February
Virgo	9 March
Libra	7 April
Scorpio	7 May
Sagittarius	5 June
Capricorn	4 July
Aquarius	3 August
Pisces	1 September
Aries	30 September
Taurus	30 October
Gemini	28 November
Cancer	28 December

2032 FULL MOON IN:

Leo	27 January
Virgo	26 February
Libra	27 March
Scorpio	25 April
Sagittarius	25 May
Capricorn	23 June
Aquarius	22 July and 21 August
Pisces	19 September
Aries	18 October
Taurus	17 November
Gemini	16 December

2033 FULL MOON IN:

Cancer	15 January
Leo	14 February
Virgo	16 March
Libra	14 April
Scorpio	14 May
Sagittarius	12 June
Capricorn	12 July
Aquarius	10 August
Pisces	9 September
Aries	8 October
Taurus	6 November
Gemini	6 December

2034 FULL MOON IN:

Cancer	4 January
Leo	3 February
Virgo	5 March
Libra	3 April
Scorpio	3 May
Sagittarius	2 June
Capricorn	1 July
Aquarius	31 July
Pisces	29 August
Aries	28 September
Taurus	27 October
Gemini	25 November
Cancer	25 December

2035 FULL MOON IN:

Leo	23 January
Virgo	22 February
Libra	23 March
Scorpio	22 April
Sagittarius	22 May and 20 June
Capricorn	20 July
Aquarius	19 August
Pisces	17 September
Aries	17 October
Taurus	15 November
Gemini	15 December

2036 FULL MOON IN:

Cancer	13 January
Leo	11 February
Virgo	12 March
Libra	10 April
Scorpio	10 May
Sagittarius	8 June
Capricorn	8 July
Aquarius	7 August
Pisces	5 September
Aries	5 October
Taurus	4 November
Gemini	3 December

2037 FULL MOON IN:

Cancer	2 January
Leo	31 January
Virgo	2 March
Libra	31 March
Scorpio	29 April
Sagittarius	29 May
Capricorn	27 June
Aquarius	27 July
Pisces	25 August
Aries	24 September
Taurus	24 October
Gemini	22 November
Cancer	22 December

2038 FULL MOON IN:

Leo	21 January
Virgo	19 February
Libra	21 March and 19 April
Scorpio	18 May
Sagittarius	17 June
Capricorn	16 July
Aquarius	14 August
Pisces	13 September
Aries	13 October
Taurus	11 November
Gemini	11 December

2039 FULL MOON IN:

Cancer	10 January
Leo	9 February
Virgo	10 March
Libra	9 April
Scorpio	8 May
Sagittarius	6 June
Capricorn	6 July
Aquarius	4 August
Pisces	2 September
Aries	2 October
Taurus	31 October
Gemini	30 November
Cancer	30 December

2040 FULL MOON IN:

Leo	29 January
Virgo	28 February
Libra	28 March
Scorpio	27 April
Sagittarius	26 May
Capricorn	24 June
Aquarius	24 July and 22 August
Pisces	20 September
Aries	20 October
Taurus	18 November
Gemini	18 December

2041 FULL MOON IN:

Cancer	17 January
Leo	16 February
Virgo	17 March
Libra	16 April
Scorpio	16 May
Sagittarius	14 June
Capricorn	13 July
Aquarius	12 August
Pisces	10 September
Aries	9 October
Taurus	8 November
Gemini	7 December

2042 FULL MOON IN:

Cancer	6 January
Leo	5 February
Virgo	6 March
Libra	5 April
Scorpio	5 May
Sagittarius	3 June
Capricorn	3 July
Aquarius	1 August
Pisces	31 August
Aries	29 September
Taurus	28 October
Gemini	27 November
Cancer	26 December

2043 FULL MOON IN:

Leo	25 January
Virgo	23 February
Libra	25 March
Scorpio	24 April
Sagittarius	23 May
Capricorn	22 June and 22 July
Aquarius	20 August
Pisces	19 September
Aries	18 October
Taurus	16 November
Gemini	16 December

2044 FULL MOON IN:

Cancer	14 January
Leo	13 February
Virgo	13 March
Libra	12 April
Scorpio	12 May
Sagittarius	10 June
Capricorn	10 July
Aquarius	8 August
Pisces	7 September
Aries	7 October
Taurus	5 November
Gemini	4 December

2045 FULL MOON IN:

Cancer	3 January
Leo	1 February
Virgo	3 March
Libra	1 April
Scorpio	1 May
Sagittarius	30 May
Capricorn	29 June
Aquarius	28 July
Pisces	27 August
Aries	26 September
Taurus	25 October
Gemini	24 November
Cancer	24 December

2046 FULL MOON IN:

Leo	22 January
Virgo	20 February
Libra	22 March
Scorpio	20 April and 20 May
Sagittarius	18 June
Capricorn	18 July
Aquarius	16 August
Pisces	15 September
Aries	14 October
Taurus	13 November
Gemini	13 December

2047 FULL MOON IN:

Cancer	12 January
Leo	10 February
Virgo	12 March
Libra	10 April
Scorpio	9 May
Sagittarius	8 June
Capricorn	7 July
Aquarius	5 August
Pisces	4 September
Aries	3 October
Taurus	2 November
Gemini	2 December

2048 FULL MOON IN:	
Cancer	1 January
Leo	31 January
Virgo	29 February
Libra	30 March
Scorpio	28 April
Sagittarius	27 May
Capricorn	26 June
Aquarius	25 July
Pisces	23 August and 22 September
Aries	21 October
Taurus	20 November
Gemini	20 December

2050 FULL MOON IN:	
Cancer	8 January
Leo	6 February
Virgo	8 March
Libra	7 April
Scorpio	6 May
Sagittarius	5 June
Capricorn	4 July
Aquarius	3 August
Pisces	1 September
Aries	30 September
Taurus	30 October
Gemini	28 November
Cancer	28 December

2049 FULL MOON IN:	
Cancer	19 January
Leo	17 February
Virgo	19 March
Libra	18 April
Scorpio	17 May
Sagittarius	15 June
Capricorn	15 July
Aquarius	13 August
Pisces	11 September
Aries	11 October
Taurus	9 November
Gemini	9 December

SOLAR ECLIPSES

2021 SOLAR ECLIPSE IN:

Sagittarius	4 December

2022 SOLAR ECLIPSE IN:

Taurus	30 April
Scorpio	25 October

2023 SOLAR ECLIPSE IN:

Aries	20 April
Libra	14 October

2024 SOLAR ECLIPSE IN:

Aries	8 April
Libra	2 October

2025 SOLAR ECLIPSE IN:

Aries	29 March
Virgo	21 September

2026 SOLAR ECLIPSE IN:

Aquarius	17 February
Leo	12 August

2027 SOLAR ECLIPSE IN:

Aquarius	6 February
Leo	2 August

2028 SOLAR ECLIPSE IN:

Aquarius	26 January
Cancer	22 July

2029 SOLAR ECLIPSE IN:

Capricorn	14 January
Gemini	12 June
Cancer	11 July
Sagittarius	5 December

2030 SOLAR ECLIPSE IN:

Gemini	1 June
Sagittarius	25 November

2031 SOLAR ECLIPSE IN:

Gemini	21 May
Scorpio	14 November

2032 SOLAR ECLIPSE IN:

Taurus	9 May
Scorpio	3 November

2033 SOLAR ECLIPSE IN:

Aries	30 March
Libra	23 September

2034 SOLAR ECLIPSE IN:

| Pisces | 20 March |
| Virgo | 12 September |

2035 SOLAR ECLIPSE IN:

| Pisces | 9 March |
| Virgo | 2 September |

2036 SOLAR ECLIPSE IN:

Pisces	27 February
Leo	23 July
Leo	21 August

2037 SOLAR ECLIPSE IN:

| Capricorn | 16 January |
| Cancer | 13 July |

2038 SOLAR ECLIPSE IN:

Capricorn	5 January
Cancer	2 July
Capricorn	26 December

2039 SOLAR ECLIPSE IN:

| Cancer | 21 June |
| Sagittarius | 15 December |

2040 SOLAR ECLIPSE IN:

| Taurus | 11 May |
| Scorpio | 4 November |

2041 SOLAR ECLIPSE IN:

| Taurus | 30 April |
| Scorpio | 25 October |

2042 SOLAR ECLIPSE IN:

| Taurus | 20 April |
| Libra | 14 October |

2043 SOLAR ECLIPSE IN:

| Aries | 9 April |
| Libra | 3 October |

2044 SOLAR ECLIPSE IN:

| Pisces | 28 February |
| Virgo | 23 August |

2045 SOLAR ECLIPSE IN:

| Aquarius | 16 February |
| Leo | 12 August |

2046 SOLAR ECLIPSE IN:

| Aquarius | 5 February |
| Leo | 2 August |

2047 SOLAR ECLIPSE IN:	
Aquarius	26 January
Cancer	23 June
Leo	22 July
Sagittarius	16 December

2048 SOLAR ECLIPSE IN:	
Gemini	11 June
Sagittarius	5 December

2049 SOLAR ECLIPSE IN:	
Gemini	31 May
Sagittarius	25 November

2050 SOLAR ECLIPSE IN:	
Gemini	20 May
Scorpio	14 November

LUNAR ECLIPSES

2021 LUNAR ECLIPSE IN:

Taurus	19 November

2022 LUNAR ECLIPSE IN:

Scorpio	16 May
Taurus	8 November

2023 LUNAR ECLIPSE IN:

Scorpio	5 May
Taurus	28 October

2024 LUNAR ECLIPSE IN:

Libra	25 March
Pisces	18 September

2025 LUNAR ECLIPSE IN:

Virgo	14 March
Pisces	7 September

2026 LUNAR ECLIPSE IN:

Virgo	3 March
Pisces	28 August

2027 LUNAR ECLIPSE IN:

Virgo	20 February
Capricorn	18 July
Aquarius	17 August

2028 LUNAR ECLIPSE IN:

Cancer	12 January
Capricorn	6 July
Cancer	31 December

2029 LUNAR ECLIPSE IN:

Capricorn	26 June
Gemini	20 December

2030 LUNAR ECLIPSE IN:

Sagittarius	15 June
Gemini	9 December

2031 LUNAR ECLIPSE IN:

Scorpio	7 May
Sagittarius	5 June
Taurus	30 October

2032 LUNAR ECLIPSE IN:

| Scorpio | 25 April |
| Aries | 18 October |

2033 LUNAR ECLIPSE IN:

| Libra | 14 April |
| Aries | 8 October |

2034 LUNAR ECLIPSE IN:

| Libra | 3 April |
| Aries | 28 September |

2035 LUNAR ECLIPSE IN:

| Virgo | 22 February |
| Aquarius | 19 August |

2036 LUNAR ECLIPSE IN:

| Leo | 11 February |
| Aquarius | 7 August |

2037 LUNAR ECLIPSE IN:

| Leo | 31 January |
| Aquarius | 27 July |

2038 LUNAR ECLIPSE IN:

Leo	21 January
Sagittarius	17 June
Capricorn	16 July
Gemini	11 December

2039 LUNAR ECLIPSE IN:

| Sagittarius | 6 June |
| Gemini | 30 November |

2040 LUNAR ECLIPSE IN:

| Sagittarius | 26 May |
| Taurus | 18 November |

2041 LUNAR ECLIPSE IN:

| Scorpio | 16 May |
| Taurus | 8 November |

2042 LUNAR ECLIPSE IN:

| Libra | 5 April |
| Aries | 29 September |

2043 LUNAR ECLIPSE IN:

| Libra | 25 March |
| Pisces | 19 September |

2044 LUNAR ECLIPSE IN:

Virgo	13 March
Pisces	7 September

2045 LUNAR ECLIPSE IN:

Virgo	3 March
Pisces	27 August

2046 LUNAR ECLIPSE IN:

Leo	22 January
Capricorn	18 July

2047 LUNAR ECLIPSE IN:

Cancer	12 January
Capricorn	7 July

2048 LUNAR ECLIPSE IN:

Cancer	1 January
Capricorn	26 June
Gemini	20 December

2049 LUNAR ECLIPSE IN:

Scorpio	17 May
Sagittarius	15 June
Taurus	9 November

2050 LUNAR ECLIPSE IN:

Scorpio	6 May
Taurus	30 October

FURTHER INFORMATION

This book is intended to be a general guide. If you would like to find out more about your own astrology chart and the specific individual meanings of all astrological aspects and transits for you personally, an astrologer in your area can draw up your chart and read it for you. If you have enjoyed this book and would like me to read your chart, feel free to contact me via the email address below.

If you would like to draw up your chart online my website www.astrocast.com.au provides a free chart calculator. I do not provide interpretations of individual charts via 'one template fits all' as the interpretation of an individual chart is something that should be done in consultation with you personally.

Astrology is a complex topic and serious long-term decisions and investigations into your own particular circumstances should be made under careful guidance in a private consultation. Feel free to contact me for further information at: patsybennettastrology@gmail.com.

ABOUT THE AUTHOR

Patsy Bennett is a rare combination of astrologer and psychic medium. She was born in New Zealand and relocated to the United Kingdom where, in the 1980s, she worked as a sub-editor and production editor for women's and fashion magazines including *Woman's Own* and *Elle* (UK). She studied astrology at the Faculty of Astrological Studies in London in the 1990s then relocated to Australia in 1998, working as a reporter for local newspapers in northern New South Wales and writing freelance for magazines while continuing her practice as an astrologer.

Patsy's horoscopes are published in newspapers and magazines in Australia and internationally, and she has written for publications including *Nature and Health* and *Practical Parenting* and has appeared on several live day-time TV and radio shows including *Studio 10* and *The Project*. Patsy's books *Astrology: Secrets of the Moon*, *Your Horoscope for 2022*, the *Astrology Diaries* and *Zodiac Moon Reading Cards* are published by Rockpool Publishing.

Patsy has worked as a professional astrologer and medium for over 24 years, experiencing mediumistic insights as young as the age of 12 and reading palms and tarot at age 14. She is a natural medium who has perfected her skills by studying with some of the world's foremost mediums. She is a member of the Queensland Federation of Astrologers and the Spiritualists' National Union.

Patsy provides astrology and psychic intuitive consultations and facilitates astrology and psychic development workshops in northern New South Wales and the Gold Coast. She runs www.astrocast.com.au, www.patsybennett.com, facebook@patsybennettpsychicastrology and insta @patsybennettastrology.

ALSO BY PATSY

ZODIAC MOON READING CARDS
Celestial guidance at your fingertips

ISBN: 9781925924268

Zodiac Moon Reading Cards is the first ever 36-card set depicting the sun, moon and eclipses through the zodiac signs. Drawing on predictive astrology, this insightful oracle card deck will help you to understand more about yourself and friends, family and loved ones.

Each card highlights turning points and the best way to move forward in life. Included is a booklet explaining the deep significance of each card with beautiful photographic illustrations of the sun, moon, eclipses, nature and space. A powerful deck to assist you to navigate your direction in life.

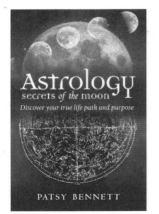

ASTROLOGY: SECRETS OF THE MOON
Discover your true life path and purpose

ISBN: 9781925017762

Astrology: Secrets of the Moon is for anyone who wants to know how to fulfil their potential, why they're here and what their unique, wonderful contribution to this extraordinary world is. It is for everyone who wants to discover their hidden talents and true gifts and make these gifts and talents work for them.

We are all familiar with our sun signs, but in *Secrets of the Moon* Patsy Bennett focuses on the new astrology and, in particular, the fascinating study of the moon's north nodes that when used in conjunction with your sun sign can provide a detailed picture of your soul's true path and your spiritual quest in life.